River Road

ST. ANDREW'S CHURCH.

RIVER ROAD

Essays on Manitoba and Prairie History

Gerald Friesen

THE UNIVERSITY OF MANITOBA PRESS

The University of Manitoba Press
Winnipeg, Manitoba
Canada R3T 5V6

Printed in Canada

Printed on acid-free paper

Cover design: Steven Rosenberg/Doowah Design

Frontispiece: St. Andrew's Church, 1860. Sketch by Manton Marble, showing York boats and canoes along bank of the Red River Settlement (see "River Road"). Courtesy of Public Archives of Manitoba.

This book has been published with the assistance of the Manitoba Arts Council.

Excerpts from Studs Terkel's *Working* are reprinted by permission of Donadio & Ashworth, Inc. Copyright 1974.

Canadian Cataloguing in Publication Data

Friesen, Gerald, 1943-

   River road : essays on Manitoba and prairie history

   Includes bibliographical references and index.
   ISBN 0-88755-639-6

1. Manitoba - History. 2. Prairie Provinces - History.
I. Title.

FC3361.F74 1996   971.27   C96-920118-4
F1063.F74 1996

Contents

Part Two: Historical Articles on Dominant and Alternative Cultures

Part Three: Toward New Historical Syntheses

Acknowledgements

I WOULD LIKE TO THANK David Carr of the University of Manitoba Press for his perceptive reading of these papers, as well as his patience in shepherding manuscript and author during the months that are required in this business. I would also like to thank Carol Dahlstrom, whose editing was exemplary, as well as Allison Campbell and Renée Fossett. Tamara Miller and John Grover provided research assistance for which I am grateful.

Several readers of this collection deserve special thanks, including Royden Loewen, Tom Nesmith, Doug Smith, David Williams, and Robert Young.

Four of the articles are co-authored, and I would like to thank my colleagues for permission to publish these papers here.

Such collections are inevitably family productions, in the sense that they are around the house and underfoot for a very long time. I would like to thank Jean, Joe, Alex, Fiona, and Max for their patience as well as their invaluable contributions.

*This book is dedicated to the University of Manitoba,
its students and staff, and to the citizens of Manitoba
who have supported this institution for 120 years.*

Introduction

BOTH MANITOBA and the Canadian prairies, two important communities in my life, are under siege in the 1990s. This state of affairs exists because popular understanding of the communities themselves – their boundaries, their histories, their place in the wider world – has diminished. Prairie Canada's popular amnesia has its origin in the sudden and apparently complete ascendancy of global electronic communications in our daily lives. An illustration might be taken from the Los Angeles murder trial of O.J. Simpson in 1995, an event that preoccupied many people in North America and around the world. During the many months that the trial unfolded, one heard in prairie people's chats over tea and coffee and beer considerable detail about the trial. However, during these same months, the federal government introduced policy changes that, in the longer term, will revolutionize the grain economy, the health system, post-secondary education, unemployment insurance, the Canadian Broadcasting Corporation, country-wide transportation systems, and perhaps even the national pension plan. About these matters I heard relatively little. One must conclude that local awareness of local realities is under siege. What does the phrase *local culture* mean when worldwide television and Hollywood movies shape the daily information intake of so many people in so many places?

Our awareness of current events is not the only casualty of this new cultural moment. In his recent survey of twentieth-century history, English historian Eric Hobsbawm contends that consciousness of *past public events*, as opposed to private or individual experience, has never been more feeble:

The destruction of the past, or rather of the social mechanisms that link one's contemporary experience to that of earlier generations, is one of the most characteristic and eerie phenomena of the late twentieth century. Most young men and women at the century's end grow up in a sort of permanent present lacking any organic relation to the public past of the times they live in. This makes historians, whose business it is to remember what others forget, more essential at the end of the second millennium than ever before.[1]

Simultaneously, there has been a remarkable outpouring of prairie historical writing. No previous generation has written so much about this history – community commemorative volumes, family genealogies, studies of historic sites, scholarly and popular books and articles – and, it seems certain, local bookshelves have never been so laden with locally published material. The problem for the ordinary reader has not been a shortage of prairie literature; rather, it has been to understand how it adds up and how to relate trends in this place to trends in the larger world.

Hobsbawm defined the problem confronting historians as one not of telling a story but of explaining the relation between past and present:

They must be more than simply chroniclers, remembrancers and compilers, though this is also the historians' necessary function. . . . No one who has been asked by an intelligent American student whether the phrase "Second World War" meant that there had been a "First World War" is unaware that knowledge of even the basic facts of the century cannot be taken for granted. My object is to understand and explain *why* things turned out the way they did, and how they hang together.[2]

The essays in this volume have been assembled in 1995-96, more than a decade after *The Canadian Prairies: A History* was published, in which I attempted to sketch a broad historical narrative for the region.[3] Most of the papers – all but one – were written after that book was completed. Where has the study of the prairies "gone" in the intervening years? Some subjects have received a great deal of attention. The history of Aboriginal people, including the history of the Métis (partly because of the centennial of the events of 1885) has attracted many writers. So has the history of women. The history of working people and ethnic groups has been chronicled in a steady stream of publications. Other topics, such as the history of religion and of communications, have been neglected. Nevertheless, the historical pattern set out a decade ago probably remains intact. It is time to reconsider this synthesis.

I suggested in *The Canadian Prairies* that a long era of Aboriginal hegemony came to a close in the seventeenth century with the development of the trade in furs with Europeans. The phase of Aboriginal-European co-operation lasted for several centuries. Then, during the second half of the nineteenth century, the industrial capitalist economic and social transformation, which commenced in England and subsequently spread around the globe, remade the northwestern interior of the continent. A phase of cultural conflict and consolidation, involving class, ethnic, gender, and occupational tensions distinguished the first half of the twentieth century. The story of the prairies since the 1940s is sketched only briefly in the 1984 book, but the differences between this and earlier eras seem unmistakable. I know that there are disagreements about the choices of subject and interpretation in this narrative but I suspect that the broad periodization retains a certain credibility.

Inevitably, the historical perceptions that help us find our bearings change with the times. One can already see in the emergence of new theoretical approaches and in the development of quite different subjects for research that prairie society has experienced considerable dislocation in the last ten years. Historian R.H. Tawney offered some advice on the consequences of such shifts for the writing of history: "Each generation must write its history for itself, and draw its own deductions from that already written; not because the conclusions of its predecessors are untrue, but for a practical reason. Different answers are required, because different questions are asked. Standing at a new point on the road, it finds that fresh ranges of the landscape come into view, whose unfamiliar intricacies demand an amplification of traditional charts."[4] This steady, rapid change has already begun to require revisions in our perception of the prairie past.

The essays in this volume are addressed to two audiences: first, to those citizens, lay rather than professional readers of history, who wish to supplement their understanding of prairie society and to become acquainted with some of the recent discussions about these prairie places and people; and, second, to students and teachers in schools and universities who wish to review specific incidents or to follow historiographical debates. One of the subjects that arises several times in these pages is the place of Aboriginal people, both the First Nations and the Métis, in prairie society. Another is the growing contest over the depiction or "construction" of the dominant culture: in the prairies, as will be apparent in these pages, debates have taken place between supporters of the French and English language, between workers and elites, and between British Canadians and ethnic groups of other cultural backgrounds.

The studies that constitute detailed inquiries into local stories occupy the first two-thirds of the book. Their division into two sections, distinguished by the code words *essays* and *articles*, is based on their original audience. The six articles in the first section were written for lay readers; here I attempt to avoid jargon and make arguments about matters that have recently been in the public eye. The five articles in the second section were written more for academic reasons and for an academic readership. They tackle such sub-disciplines as cultural history, labour history, and Aboriginal history and are designed to argue for and against certain prevailing interpretations in the field.

This book is designed partly to introduce new material and to restate old facts; it also has the broader purpose of furthering a conversation about what should be included in new syntheses of prairie history or, as Hobsbawm put it, what should be said about "how things hang together." A satisfactory synthesis (literally, "building up of separate elements especially of conceptions or propositions or facts, into a connected whole, especially a theory or system")[5] attempts to crystallize a cultural perspective. Ideally, it will constitute either a potentially authoritative version of the dominant culture's historical vision, or a more-or-less consistent alternative to that vision. In practice, the debate about such syntheses will never end, just as debate about a community's purpose and direction will never end. Moreover, such historical projects offer considerable latitude to readers who are constantly reconstructing their own versions of reality. I hope the essays in the section on new syntheses will contribute to prairie readers' reflections and discussions.

If the local community is to continue to have meaning of the sort that we have known in the past, and if such phrases as *local culture, prairie society*, or *Manitoba society* are to express identities of importance, students of the prairie experience must first find a public to listen to and participate in their conversations. Moreover, we must establish the relations between this story and stories written in and about other parts of the world. Finally, we must tell the local story in terms and concepts that make plain its intrinsic interest and worth. In this volume of essays I seek to fulfill these obligations.

NOTES

1. Eric Hobsbawm, *Age of Extremes: The Short Twentieth Century, 1914-1991* (London: Michael Joseph, 1994), 3.
2. Ibid., 3.
3. Gerald Friesen, *The Canadian Prairies: A History* (Toronto: University of Toronto Press, 1984).
4. R.H. Tawney, cited in L.S. Stavrianos, *Lifelines from Our Past: A New World History* (Armonk, NY: M.E. Sharpe, 1989), 3.
5. H.G. Fowler and F.G. Fowler, eds., *The Concise Oxford Dictionary of Current English* (Oxford: Clarendon Press, 1964).

Mary L. Kennedy as a young girl, undated tintype portrait (see "River Road").
Courtesy Provincial Archives of Manitoba (N16708).

Métis traders, 1872-1874 (see "Labour History and the Métis"). Courtesy
Provincial Archives of Manitoba (N11932).

Premier John Norquay and son, undated (see "River
Road"). Courtesy Bannatyne family collection,
Provincial Archives of Manitoba (N14680).

Margaret McWilliams, 1948 (see "The Manitoba Historical Society"). Courtesy Department of Archives and Special Collections, University of Manitoba.

William L. Morton, 1965 (see "The Manitoba Historical Society"). Courtesy Department of Archives and Special Collections, University of Manitoba.

Constituency of Assiniboia
St. James, Tuxedo, Sturgeon Creek and Brooklands

Independent Labor Party

Committee Rooms: 1731 Portage Ave., St. James
Committee Rooms: 5 Eric St., Brooklands

VOTE AND WORK FOR THE LABOR CANDIDATE

R. B. RUSSELL

Published by I.L.P. Campaign Committee

R.B. Russell's election card, about 1920 (see "Bob Russell's Political Thought"). Courtesy Ken Osborne.

Bob Russell presenting trophy at a summer camp at Gimli established by the One Big Union, undated (see "Bob Russell's Political Thought"). Courtesy Ken Osborne.

CNR shops, about 1915 (see "Bob Russell's Political Thought").
Courtesy of Western Canadian Pictorial Index (A0756-22789).

Wesley College, undated (see "Principal J. H. Riddell and Wesley
College"). Courtesy Department of Archives and Special Collections,
University of Manitoba.

Eric Nesterenko in his Winnipeg Warriors jersey, 1957
(see "Hockey and Prairie Cultural History"). Courtesy
Department of Archives and Special Collections,
University of Manitoba.

Part One:
Historical Essays
on Language and Culture

River Road

Co-written with Jean Friesen

THERE IS A RIVER STREET in Prince Albert, a River Street in Moose Jaw, a Riverside Drive in Saskatoon, and many more thoroughfares of similar name throughout the Canadian prairies. The label is common because the road beside the river was *the* path in the community when the Europeans – and their urge to label places – arrived. This is the story of the first River Road in prairie Canada, the main artery of St. Andrew's Parish near Lower Fort Garry, Manitoba.

The Red River was once a highway and a treasure house of resources. Along its banks travellers camped, particularly near meeting places such as the Forks, where the Red and Assiniboine converge. Its waters teemed with fish. In spring and autumn, migrating ducks and geese filled the air above its course. Near the river grew groves of maple trees, the sap of which was a prized food item. At one favoured point, the maple grove near "the rapids" (where St. Andrew's Church now stands), Aboriginal encampments would have been occupied every year for at least thirty centuries. When Europeans and Canadians settled in this land in the early nineteenth century, they, too, travelled the river and harvested its riches. As their settlement became more densely populated, and particularly as traffic increased between the two posts of the Hudson's Bay Company (HBC), Lower Fort Garry and Upper Fort Garry, a straight highway was built some distance inland from the river, leaving the path along its western bank as a parish road.

The modern evolution of River Road and of its more prominent accompaniment, the King's Road, can be traced in the maps of the Red River Settlement and the province of Manitoba. The Inner Road, as the River Road was called, appears as early as 1836, and is unmistakable in 1858 and 1875 maps of the district. When the provincial road system developed in the 1870s and 1880s, the riverside trail seems to have been ignored. After the advent of the automobile and the modern highway in the first three decades of the twentieth century, when the King's Road, by now a commercial route between Selkirk and Winnipeg, became a "first class trunk road," the Inner Road did not appear on some highway maps and, on others, was a "third class local road [of four possible classes], well travelled."

For a century and a half, River Road has served as the thoroughfare for an extended village, a kind of back street for a parish that had no proper main street because it possessed too little commerce to require anything so grand. It was a ten-kilometre trail that meandered from river lot to river lot with no larger purpose in view than to reach the next neighbour and, eventually, the church. It was the path along which neighbours strolled and gossiped, children played, and animals moved to work or to market. It was always dusty in high summer, frozen and windswept in deep winter, and a muddy, impassable quagmire during the brief prairie spring.

The pace of River Road was once the pace of oxen and school children. News travelled along the road by word of mouth or, occasionally, by printed decree from the Council of Assiniboia. The passage of time was measured by the sun, the seasons, and the task at hand. The community that developed along this road between the 1830s and the 1880s is not immediately evident today, but its ambience can be discerned in the hedges of the old river lots, in the bluffs of trees and the circling pelicans and the slow movement of the river, in a marsh that has developed in a disused limestone quarry, and in the remaining buildings, Scott House, Kennedy House, Hay House, Twin Oaks, and St. Andrew's Church and Rectory.

To recover the atmosphere of the nineteenth-century pathway, one must reconstruct one's sense of land transport in an age before automobiles. Road traffic was notoriously difficult in North Atlantic countries until the Industrial Revolution. In England, for example, roads in 1760 were probably worse than they had been in Roman times. The King's Highway, which had a special legal standing, merely offered a right of passage to the king and his subjects. It did not promise comfort or safety. When the road was blocked by mud or obstructions, its royal designation entitled travellers to break through fences and to detour through fields or the grounds of houses in their quest for a firm track. The maintenance of parish roads depended upon statute labour, a legal obligation imposed upon landholders that involved a certain amount of work, or its equivalent in tax payment, each year.

River Road belonged in the category of informal thoroughfare, and, despite a number of disputes between landholders over its precise path, it never attained legal standing in the years of the Red River Settlement. If it was maintained at all, the work was undertaken by those who lived along its length, often as a result of the urgings of the Council of Assiniboia. Each male householder was supposed to give three days' labour or three shillings to mend roads, fill in washouts, and build wooden bridges.

In its early years, the road always took second place to the river. The Red River Settlement, like the pioneer communities in New France and along the Great Lakes, was based upon river lot (or lakefront) agriculture. The pattern of landholding was determined by the central role of water transport in these communities and by the importance of the river in winter, both as highway and as source of ice for food preservation. The river lot also provided equitable distribution of wood and hay resources, both of which were abundant in the river valleys and could be allocated easily by the creation of long narrow lots stretching back from the river itself. The path that inevitably developed on the bank might be used when canoe or sleigh were unavailable, or when floating ice made river travel dangerous, but it was an inferior alternative to the waterway.

The legal foundation of landholding in European terms was established when Lord Selkirk negotiated a treaty with Chief Peguis in 1817. This pact enabled Europeans to assume control of territory along the Red River to the distance at which daylight could be seen under a horse's belly – about two miles, it was said. The arrangement was formalized, in European eyes, by a HBC survey. In St. Andrew's Parish, the survey fixed the width of most river lots at three to six chains, the depth at two miles.[1] On these lots, fur traders and their wives settled in the 1830s and 1840s to create the various parishes of the Red River Settlement.

One of those families was founded by Alexander Kennedy and Aggathas Bear. Alexander left his native Orkney Islands at the age of seventeen to become a clerk in the HBC. He married Aggathas in 1804, when he was living near The Pas on the Saskatchewan River. They had nine children. Around 1831, Alexander arranged to buy a lot in St. Andrew's Parish, at a prime site near the rapids and the Anglican mission, and then returned on a furlough to Scotland. He wrote Aggathas: "I intend to take Roderick and Alexander home [to Orkney] with myself and if I am alive, please God, I shall see you again next summer. In the meantime do not want for anything that I can afford to supply you with either for yourself, your mother, or the little ones, and be assured that as long as I live I shall never forsake you nor forget you, and if I die I shall not forget you."

Alexander did die during this furlough, in England in 1832, but Aggathas took up the land in St. Andrew's Parish with the three children still at home. The census reported that the "widow Kennedy" presided over a house, a stable, a barn, and seven cultivated acres. She possessed a horse, oxen, cows, calves, and pigs; in the yard lay harrows, plough, cart, and two canoes. And her children? A doctor, a schoolteacher, two wives of distinguished fur traders, a storekeeper, a farmer, and one, William, who returned to the parish lot in St. Andrew's to build a fine stone residence for his English wife and to lead the life of a gentleman. Until her death, Aggathas resided in the original log dwelling situated a few steps from the imposing new home of her son.

The farms of St. Andrew's, like the Kennedy farm, grew rapidly and in helter-skelter fashion. A typical river lot might contain one or two dwelling houses, a barn, a stable, a storage house, a summer kitchen, and several other outbuildings, as well as ten or twenty acres of cultivated land. Behind the lot would be a second lot of equal width and depth known as the "hay privilege." In many cases, the household would also possess another lot directly across the river where wood and hay could be gathered. Because few farms could have survived on the production of wheat and barley and vegetables, members of most households participated in trade, wage labour, or the annual buffalo hunts. The latter, which included 100 to 300 hunters, were essential to the survival of the settlement and have been likened to roundups in a ranch economy.

William and Ann Scott, the shell of whose house remains on River Road, might be seen as typical small farmers in St. Andrew's. When they filed a declaration concerning landholdings in 1874, they claimed three lots, numbered forty-six (west bank), 245 and 246 (east bank), containing fifty-six, thirty-four, and thirty-three acres respectively, or a total of 123 acres (49.77 hectares). On the main farm, Lot 46, which was three chains wide and 181 chains deep, there sat "1 Dwelling stone House 35 x 25 feet, Stone Kitchen 19 x 17 feet, Store 25 x 19 feet, Granary 20 x 18 feet, Stables 60 x 20 feet. Barn 45 x 20 feet. Out House 35 x 18 feet, Farm House 16 x 15 feet and about 16 acres of Land under cultivation." In an official survey in the same year, Scott was reported to possess two houses and six barns or stables. We know from various parish records that Ann was married to William when she was thirteen years old and that they had six children.

The changing seasons dictated the activities of the Scott household and of every other home in the district. Summer brought fishing, a pastime loved by many settlers: "Mrs. Sargeant came to tea. We scooped [for fish] just after," Mary Kennedy, then a teenager, wrote in her diary on 9 May 1882. The next day, she reported plans for a return trip to the Sargeant house: "Mama & I intended going up there to scoop with her"; when it seemed too late, the expedition was cancelled, but Mary and Mr. Hart, who had just arrived on the steamboat, "scooped by the river down here," and repeated their labours after breakfast the next morning. Later in the afternoon, several women gathered "to scoop" once again. "Mr. & Mrs. Sinclair came down to scoop too. We sat in the boat while they scooped – I took up my scoop. Mr. Hart & Smalley passed down. Did not bow to them nor look round."[2]

Some settlers followed Aboriginal practice by constructing fish weirs (a kind of dam often woven from saplings), but by the 1860s this was a source of controversy because the river fishery seemed to be depleted. River traffic was steady throughout the summer. HBC York boats made the run between the Upper and Lower forts en route to Lake Winnipeg and Hudson Bay, and dozens of canoes and smaller craft plied the waters daily. From 1859, steamboats became a common sight as well. Aboriginal visitors often camped under the maple trees that lined the river bank just below the Kennedy family farm, hauling their canoes onto the bank, erecting tents, and lighting fires as their ancestors had done before them.

Bare fields and falling leaves signalled autumn's return, but so, too, did the visits of Métis salt makers from Lake Winnipegosis, and of Ojibwa purveyors of fish oil (for winter lamps) from the Winnipeg River settlement near Fort Alexander. Each autumn, numbers of parish men joined the "green" hunt, which provided fresh buffalo meat for winter use as well as the pemmican that could be stored against future shortages.

Snow and ice brought colder, quieter times. The men took horses and sleighs great distances to cut the wood that burned in clay fireplaces and, later, in cast-iron stoves to keep winter at bay. They also cut great blocks of river ice in anticipation of the following summer's food-storage needs. One law in the settlement stated that if ice were cut through to the water, a six-foot pole must be erected to warn travellers of the danger. Winter's work was supplemented by dog team and horse-and-carriole races on the river, and by the festive dances, with fiddle and organ providing the accompaniment for jigs and eight-hand reels and cotillions.

The regular rhythm of the annual calendar was punctuated by the unexpected. This might be a spring flood of the Red River, as in 1852, when St. Andrew's residents fled to Bird's Hill to escape the rising waters. Or it might be the death of a parish resident, as in 1865, when news of the death of parish founder Reverend William Cockran prompted the tolling of bells and a formal procession – relays of Settlement men – to carry his coffin shoulder-high, according to the Highland custom, the eighty kilometres from Portage la Prairie to the church he had built, St. Andrew's on the Red.

The parish was the most important community unit in Red River. Its boundaries defined the limits for church and school attendance and, because it was the focus for discussion of public affairs, also of the political constituency. From its members were drawn the road superintendent, the census takers, the petty magistrates, the postmaster, and the customs collector. St. Andrew's Parish was ten kilometres in length, extending from Park's Creek on the south (where it joins the Red River) to Lower Fort Garry on the north. It was the most populous of the English-speaking parishes and was the leader of the so-called Lower District "down" the river from the Upper Fort and St. John's Parish, two alternative candidates for the title of centre of the Protestant community. Its French-speaking and Roman Catholic counterparts included St. Boniface, St. Norbert, and St. François Xavier. Perhaps because St. Andrew's contained a large number of retired HBC servants and their country-born wives, it seemed a prosperous community; the cultivated acreage per farmstead was greater, on the average, than in other parishes, and the number of small trading establishments was higher.

St. Andrew's Parish, like the Prairie West in general, experienced decisive changes in the half-century after 1840. New ideas concerning "race," "respectability," and "progress" became common currency. New attitudes associated with church marriages and private property hardened into legislated commandments. In this changed environment, the children of relationships between European and Aboriginal residents found themselves at a disadvantage. In their resistance to the social presumptions of the new order, they were not victorious, but, at the least, they were able to win a grudging acceptance from the newcomers. In their struggle to earn a living, moreover, they challenged the HBC monopoly on trade and won a degree of commercial freedom.

European and Canadian interest in northwestern North America acquired a focus and intensity from the mid-1850s. This expansionism provoked a political crisis after the creation of the Canadian Confederation in 1867 and Canada's subsequent attempts to annex the Rupert's Land territories. The English-speaking residents of St. Andrew's did not generally oppose the Métis resistance movements of 1869-70, though several anti-Riel protests were launched from households in the parish. After all, the households of St. Andrew's Parish – indeed, those of the entire Settlement – were linked by ties of "blood," marriage, and trade. As Mr. Tait of St. Andrew's said in 1869, when refusing to fight against Louis Riel and the Métis resistance: "[They] were born and brought up among us, ate with us, slept with us, hunted with us, traded with us, and are our own flesh and blood. . . . Gentlemen, I for one cannot fight them. I will not imbrue my hands in their blood."

Before another decade had passed, and, indeed, while a child of St. Andrew's, John Norquay, was Premier of the new province of Manitoba, the English-speaking Protestants of the parish had been made to feel subordinate to the incoming settlers from Ontario. They were treated as survivors from a by-gone age, interesting remnants of a fur-trade civilization that no longer represented the new majority in the district. During the next generation, their children were integrated into the larger community as if a distinctive English-speaking community of mixed European and Aboriginal heritage had never existed.

One who experienced this transition was Mary Kennedy, daughter of William and granddaughter of Aggathas and Alexander. Mary attended the local school and then was sent to England and France for "finishing" in such "womanly" arts as singing, lace making, and painting. She returned to the family home in the early 1880s, where she resumed the round of work, tea, church meetings, and chat that were the staples of a young unmarried woman's life in a community that now seemed, not the centre of historic developments, but an increasingly isolated backwater. Mary occasionally kept a diary, from which these excerpts are taken:

[Sunday, 12 March 1882] Had a good class at Sunday School [in the morning] – Missionary Sunday – . . . Taught youngsters the parable of the 10 Virgins Matt xxv. . . . Good congregation in the evening. Text: Eph[esians] v 8: For ye were sometime darkness, but now are ye light in the Lord [walk as children of light.] Thought of the last time I had heard a sermon preached from that text – Frances Ballendine went home.

[Monday, 13 March] Mama, Edgar & I drove down to the Fort . . . Mama & Mrs. Flett drove down to Selkirk – & called on the Vaughans and Colcleughs, Janie and I talked all day – We remained to tea – then drove home. It grew dark – & we had a few experiences – Mama tried to make herself believe she had had a spill out. Poor wee Edgar was very tired. . . . Mrs. Sinclair's baby is dead.

[Tuesday, 14 March] . . . Washing day – Had very big wash. I did up the muslins of my room. . . . We 3 girls went up for the mail; J. Clare was there & he told us about the big fire on Main Street. He saw it. I practised [music] after tea. Finished painting white satin mat for Mrs. Leask –

[Wednesday, 15 March] Did blk velveteen skirt – Ironed. . . . I went over to the Church & had a good time with the organ. It is a lovely day.

[Thursday, 20 April] A lovely day as usual. The river rose two or three times but at noon the general flow of ice came & with it the water rose about 4 feet & was level with the bridge at the mill. We stood out on the lawn a great deal watching it. Hundreds thousands almost of logs (beauties) floated down all afternoon. . . . I had the pleasure & gratification of killing a 1st formidable mosquito today – I committed the deed with very great satisfaction. Carrie & I went up for the mail at 12. . . . We afterwards went up to the Parsonage & Carrie went on to meet William while I stood & talked with Mrs. Young at the window she asked me to help her with her music class on Thursdays. I am going to do so. . . . Bella Ross was here to tea – we had some jam (rare occurrence) in her honour. That poor old cake is turning like flint in the cupboard. We will soon be able to have cake – and point (when visitors come) – [our] teeth will be useless. I got 2 lamp wicks from Uncle George – finished my green alpaca dress trimmed with black and old gold fancy trimming. I am writing this in bed – Roads getting good for foot, worse for wheels. Good night old book, I'm sleepy. Reading *Kenilworth* [by Walter Scott].

[Friday, 23 June] School treat [at Miss Davis's Academy]. I gardened a great deal before going – took over 15 buns, a cake and a bottle of lime juice. We cut up any amount of sweet loaves and bannock. Had a great time handing it round. . . . Minnie and I went with Mr. Smalley up into the church steeple. Mr. S walked over the belfry frame to the opposite window. . . . Miss Lewis came over in the afternoon She & I went to watch the youngsters playing cricket. We were almost the last to leave.

[Saturday, 1 July] We were up early & I made a cornstarch shape. . . . Mama packed up the provisions to go out to the Park. Several townspeople were there. . . played, & won, the match of cricket by one innings & one man. Mr. Smalley played beautifully & made more runs than anyone. I drove Leslie & Nellie Somerville about in their phaeton & we looked for berries. I had dinner with Mr. Pierce at the cricketers' table. It was jolly. Miss Young & all of our party sat round the roller & watched the game. I had tea with our party. . . . I was the last to leave the grounds – Mr. Smalley came up just as I was going away. Willie and I just said "Good gaming" – and a few civilities – Poor Mr. Smalley he looked tired. . . . I told Willie to ask Smalley, Hamber, Jephson down but he would not. Miss Lewis came over to spend the evening. It was rather stupid – I had a good cry after I went to my room. What good am I to anyone, I wonder?[3]

This diary chronicles the life of a Victorian family in St. Andrew's from the perspective of a young woman of mixed Aboriginal and European ancestry. For a girl who had been to England and France for finishing school, life along the River Road must have seemed limited in the 1880s. Nonetheless, Mama's word was law. Mary may have yearned to travel to Winnipeg, but her mother refused to let her catch the steamboat. A few months earlier, in March, when winter was still deep, she wrote:

A soft dullish sort of day. Snow soft and thick. . . . I am getting more & more into the blues. . . . Whatever was St. Andrew's discovered for? It might just as well have been left for little primal gnomes and wizards to occupy. Even they would have put a little life into it. . . . What a goose I am! We 3 girls walked up to Omands to see if he could take Mama & us up to town on Monday – Very ponderously he scratched his head & "well don't know, one horse is pretty weak & I'm not sure even if he'll reach to the town!" . . . Mr. Ross left this morning about 11:30. I wished he had been staying. He cheers one up – & is a gentleman & can talk; more than most town dandies can do. We talked at breakfast about "conver-

sational powers." I only wished I possessed more of them. I am afraid my ideas
are too deep for utterance – quite too, too, Miss K; so I need not talk about town
gentlemen, (case of sour grapes perhaps). Well I am awfully sleepy, me. I also feel
like writing a novel. I must put my book away in case I begin. I do want a letter so
from – or someone. She has quite deserted me but what can a sinner do with a
young baby forsooth. Moral, never marry – MLK take the good advice & let it
smite deep down into thy soul. I'll try dreaming on Frances Linklater's wedding
cake of which she sent us three girls a piece today. Good night old diary – I wish
I were an angel gone home.[4]

After her father's death in 1890, Mary and her mother moved to Virden,
where Mary became a court reporter. She painted and wrote a little, and,
when she retired, she moved to Winnipeg.[5] She died there in 1945 at the
age of eighty-four.

By the 1940s, the racial stereotypes of the "white" Commonwealth
prompted a different reaction among the grandchildren of old Red River.
Thus, at the very time that Mary's long life was coming to a close, some
St. Andrew's descendants were denying that their families had ever had
any contact with Aboriginal people, let alone were descended from marriages between European fur traders and Aboriginal or partly Aboriginal
women. One illustration of the difference occurred in 1947-48, when a
plaque commemorating the career of John Norquay, to that time the only
"Manitoba"-born citizen to hold the position of premier, was unveiled in
the Legislature. Though there had never before been any question about
Norquay's mixed-race family background, and though he had declared in
the Legislature in the 1870s that he was proud of every drop of Aboriginal
blood that flowed in his veins, his descendants refused to accept the word-
ing of the plaque that described him as "Halfbreed" and provoked a minor scene, and then a continuing agitation, despite the drafting of a genealogical report that demonstrated fairly clearly the identity of Norquay's
partly Aboriginal foremothers.[6]

The River Road Parkway project of the early 1980s was designed to
commemorate this partly Aboriginal, partly European story and, by linking aspects of historical interpretation to this particular site and these historic buildings, to offer testimony concerning its character. River Road is
the physical expression of a history encompassing many centuries and
not a little conflict.[7]

NOTES

This essay is based on research carried out as part of the Canada-Manitoba Agreement on
Recreation and Conservation (ARC) projects associated with River Road and Kennedy
House between 1982 and 1985.

1. Approximately 60.35 to 120.7 metres wide and 3,200 metres deep.
2. Provincial Archives of Manitoba (PAM), Mary Kennedy Diary, entries for 9, 10, and 11 May 1882.
3. Ibid., 12 March to 1 July 1882.
4. Ibid., 25 March 1882.
5. According to a *Winnipeg Free Press* obituary, her painting *Manitoba Crocuses* was then on display in the Manitoba Legislative Building, and two more studies of Lower Fort Garry were hanging in the Fort Garry Hotel (*Winnipeg Free Press,* 13 October 1945).
6. Gerald Friesen, "John Norquay," *Dictionary of Canadian Biography,* vol. xi, *1881-1890* (Toronto: University of Toronto Press, 1982), 642-47. Also, PAM, Manitoba Historical Society Papers, "Programme, 28 October 1947 . . . John Norquay," and Legislative Library of Manitoba, Norquay File.
7. A campaign to preserve River Road commenced in the 1940s, when erosion first threatened to carry the river bank, road and all, into the Red River. This discussion became more intense in the 1960s and 1970s, especially after the new Provincial Heritage Branch and the Historic Sites and Monuments Board of Canada focussed public attention on the resources of Lower Fort Garry and the historic houses along the road. The establishment of the federal-provincial Agreement on Recreation and Conservation (ARC) in 1978 marked a turning point in the campaign to preserve and restore selected portions of this community treasure. As a result of the federal-provincial initiative, Scott House, a modest nineteenth-century cottage, has become an interpretive site, and there are historic markers in the marsh, at Hay House (a larger nineteenth-century stone building) and at each end of River Road itself. Parks Canada has arranged for the restoration and interpretation of the St. Andrew's Rectory. St. Andrew's Church has also been restored. The gardens of Kennedy House have recovered the formal splendour they possessed in the 1920s, and the house itself has been rebuilt as a museum and tea room in the fashion it would have known when its first occupants, William and Eleanor Kennedy, lived there in the 1860s and 1870s. River Road continues to thrive, though the absence of design controls and the seemingly inevitable suburbanization of its former farm and market-garden character have extended the distance between the present traveller and the nineteenth-century parish.

La Vérendrye and the French Empire in Western North America

Co-written with Kathryn Young

This was a British colony from 1670, when that [Hudson's Bay Company] charter was granted, to the present time.
            – Manitoba Attorney-General A.B. Hudson (29 February 1916)

I saw this morning your note . . . to the effect that "Western Canada . . . had been British territory long anterior to" 1763. For anyone who has studied the early history of this country, this is somewhat startling, nay incomprehensible. . . . Will you then kindly tell your readers who was sent by the British government to explore and take possession by means of forts of what is today Manitoba (save the narrow strip of land along the "Bay"), Saskatchewan and Alberta, before LaVérendrye was commissioned to do so by the King of France through Governor De Beauharnois? Who before him and his did establish posts under the authority of the British monarch and so made the country British? If nobody did, how was it that said territory was British long before 1759? By answering these few questions, you will greatly oblige: [signed] A.G. Morice, O.M.I. St. Boniface, Man.

(A sufficient reply . . . is the statement that the British view – which happily is the one which governs – is that [sic] the British ownership of territory, set forth in the grant to the Hudson's Bay Company – i.e. the watershed of Hudson Bay – was not affected by the incidents to which our correspondents refer. [signed] Editor *Free Press.*)
            – An exchange in the *Winnipeg Free Press* (1 March 1916)

A STUBBORN MYTH in western Canadian history insists that the Hudson's Bay Company Charter of 1670 and the British conquest of New France constituted the two founding moments of Britain's empire in northwestern North America and, therefore, of western Canada's language policies. As the above quotation, taken from a speech by Manitoba's Attorney-General, A.B. Hudson, illustrates, the myth was alive and well in the opening decades of the twentieth century. Perhaps not surprisingly, it could still be heard in the 1980s.

The first European trading post in the northwestern interior of North America, Fort Maurepas, located near present-day Selkirk, was erected by a crew under the direction of Jean-Baptiste Gaultier, the son of Pierre Gaultier, whom we know as La Vérendrye, in June 1734. La Vérendrye reported the news of this habitation to the governor of New France: "I have established a fort at Lake Winnipeg, five leagues up the Red River, on a fine point commanding a distant view. There are many fish in this river; it is a fine spot and a pleasant place to live at; game abounds."

The rude shelter constructed by this small expedition was later replaced by a stronger outpost on the north bank of the Winnipeg River, near present-day Fort Alexander and Pine Falls. And this base was supplemented by a chain of trading forts that included Fort Rouge (forks of the Red and Assiniboine, 1738), Fort La Reine (near Portage la Prairie, 1738), Fort Dauphin (on Lake Winnipegosis, 1741), Fort Bourbon (at the mouth of the Saskatchewan River, 1741), and Fort Pasquia (The Pas, 1743). By the end of the 1740s, the French dominated the trade of this region and were undercutting the English posts on the shores of Hudson Bay.

It is fitting that Manitobans should remember the La Vérendrye expeditions. The ambition, strength, and business abilities of the various members of this family were to affect the course of prairie history for generations to come.

Pierre Gaultier de Varennes et de La Vérendrye was born in Trois Rivières, New France, in 1685, to one of the first settler families in the French colony. He was the thirteenth and last child to be raised in his parents' substantial wooden house just outside the palisade of the fort on the St. Maurice River. He went to school in Quebec City, joined the army, and fought in North America and France. In his mid-twenties, having received eight sabre cuts and been wounded by a musket shot in Flanders, he was promoted to lieutenant and then taught an unhappy truth: he was not sufficiently wealthy to maintain himself as a French officer. He returned to Canada, married at twenty-seven, and became, through his wife's property, a prosperous farmer and trader.

A new challenge arose when La Vérendrye joined one of his brothers as a supervisor of the French fur trade around Lake Superior (Commandant de la Poste du Nord) in 1729. He was then forty years old, and his six children were growing up. He was interested in Aboriginal stories of a western sea, of rich lands full of fruit trees and animals, of "a great river which flows toward the setting sun," and of distant Indians who carried "their cabins with them continually from one place to another, always camping together to form a village." For purposes of exploration as well as profit, he sought government support for an expedition to these western lands.

The French had long sought a route to the Western Sea and had supported earlier expeditions. The Governor of New France, Charles Beauharnois, offered La Vérendrye considerable support. The Governor was interested in the military and economic advantages that might accrue to the French global empire, and, in any case, he knew that French posts in the West would harass the English traders on Hudson Bay.

Such expeditions were miracles of organization. Fifty men had to be recruited, given some advance pay, rounded up on the appointed day (some always tried to take the money and run), and licensed to carry muskets and depart the colony. The barrels of drink, the ninety-pound packs of guns, powder, blankets, trade goods, and food (and even chickens and pigs) had to be stowed in the canoes. Once under way, a routine of eighteen-hour days was established. At dusk, the canoes were beached, shelters prepared, and the evening meal and next day's purée (peas and corn meal for breakfast and lunch) cooked.

Once in the Northwest, the men began to erect trading posts. Fort St. Charles, established on the North-West Angle of Lake of the Woods in 1732, was described by the expedition leader as a 100-foot square enclosed by a double row of fifteen-foot palisades. It had four bastions and contained eight or nine log buildings, including a chapel, a powder magazine, a storehouse and several cabins. In such posts dwelt the leading traders, their clerks, and the voyageur-labourers. They soon adjusted to the rhythms of the winter trade. Their hooded cloaks, fur hats, deer-skin shoes, and *ceintures flêchées* (always tied on the left), along with the inevitable pipe, became features of European life in the western parkland and forest.

From 1730 to 1749, La Vérendrye was the driving force in the western expansion of the French fur trade. The work was extremely taxing. He had to maintain close ties with Quebec to ensure that his licence was renewed and that his investors continued to support the enterprise. Many times he travelled east – a long and difficult journey – to mend his political fences and reorganize his finances. And, always, he was under pressure from his investors to earn more money. At the same time, he was being pushed by importunate government officials to produce tangible results, such as the discovery of a river to the Pacific. The demands of shareholders and governments were contradictory, but he had to reconcile them and still retain the loyalty of his own men.

Aboriginal diplomacy presented a different challenge. La Vérendrye could secure access to the trade and to the knowledge of the prairie Aboriginal people only by establishing an alliance with them. He was given a substantial grant by the government of New France for this purpose. In 1734, he set powder, ball, knives, axes, needles, and clothing before six Lake Winnipeg chiefs – two Cree and four Assiniboine – as an inducement to conclude an alliance. The gifts would "smooth all the roads to the fort," he told them, so they should declare themselves henceforth allies of the French and not the English.

La Vérendrye was competing against the bayside forts of the English Hudson's Bay Company, but he was also enmeshed in the Native diplomatic world. He understood that trade in this western territory was associated with a struggle between the Dakota, on the one hand, and a Cree-Assiniboine-Ojibwa alliance, on the other, to control access to European technology. La Vérendrye chose to work with the Cree alliance. Though this brought great rewards in trade and aided his men when they built posts further west, it ensured conflict with the Dakota. It also led directly to the death of his son, Jean-Baptiste, and the Jesuit, Father Aulneau, at Lake of the Woods in 1736. But this was the risk of such military alliances and an inevitable accompaniment of European attempts to profit from the Aboriginal trade.

La Vérendrye's explorations represented a substantial achievement. His men set up trading posts that cut across Indian trade routes to Hudson Bay. His expeditions travelled throughout the Missouri and Saskatchewan River country and thereby supplemented Europe's geographical understanding of the continent. His profits from the western fur trade were considerable. The alliances he negotiated with the Native peoples helped to ensure relative peace in the western interior for most of the eighteenth century. Most important, the French-Aboriginal co-operation provided the western foundation for a separate country on the northern half of the North American continent. Pierre La Vérendrye was a French founder of Manitoba. In his own right and as an example of the eighteenth-century French fur trade in North America, La Vérendrye represents the establishment of the French language and the French-speaking community – *Métis* and *Canadien* – in Manitoba and western North America.

NOTES

This essay is a slightly revised version of the article that appeared in the *Winnipeg Free Press* on 6 October 1984; it is reprinted with the permission of the *Winnipeg Free Press*. Our aim was to outline the historical significance of the unveiling that day by Queen Elizabeth II of a plaque on Promenade Taché in St. Boniface. At the ceremony, canoes of the "Voyageurs of the Red River Brigade" commemorated the 250th anniversary of the founding of La Vérendrye's Fort Maurepas. That the article's publication coincided with the "French language services debate" of 1983-84 (see "Bilingualism in Manitoba: The Historical Context" in this volume) was not coincidental. We would like to thank David Williams for pointing out the quotations from the *Winnipeg Free Press* that open this essay.

The Collected Writings of Louis Riel

AT 2:00 A.M. ON 16 NOVEMBER 1885, only hours before his execution, Louis Riel wrote a brief note: "I, the undersigned, nominate by this document the Reverend Father Alexis André to be the legal executor for my papers. My wish is that all my papers be sent to him and that he look after them and that their publication be in his care."[1] The document must be seen as unusual. As far as is known, nothing was done to undertake such an archival and publishing project at the time. Yet it testifies to the direction of Riel's thoughts about his entire career. What is more unusual is that Riel's wish found a response among scholars a century later. In 1986, *The Collected Writings of Louis Riel / Les écrits complets de Louis Riel,* under the general editorship of George F.G. Stanley, was published by the University of Alberta Press. What does this remarkable collection, five volumes and 2,500 pages, contribute to our understanding of one of the most enigmatic and important figures in prairie history?

Two brief quotations drawn from his writings in 1885 illustrate something of Riel's perspective in the tumultuous months that culminated in the North-West uprising and his eventual execution: "My God! . . . be with me personally as I choose my arguments: help me place them in relief and drive them home with a sure stroke as one drives home a lance with one's hand." "My God! Give . . . to all my speeches and all my writings an immense impact."[2] This is a man of the written word, the linear argument, the legal text, and the printed contract. He would have appreciated profoundly this edition of his writings.

The survival of so much of Riel's writing is the first surprise delivered by this remarkable collection. The second is the force and ingenuity of the prose. Despite the many fine works on Riel, the reader is not fully prepared for the man who appears in these pages. This is not the venal and vainglorious character depicted by Donald Creighton and Thomas Flanagan.[3] Nor is it the tragic innocent of recent dramatic presentations. Rather, Riel appears as a powerful political essayist, a serious writer who adopted that vocation after 1878 as a means of furthering the cause of his people when circumstances and his own limitations prevented a return to political leadership. The numerous drafts of articles, letters, and poems demonstrate that Riel polished his ideas and the expression of them as carefully as any Victorian essayist would have. An essay he prepared in the autumn of 1885, for example, probably destined for the American journal *North American Review*, constitutes one of the finest statements of Aboriginal claims in Canadian history and should receive attention in today's classrooms and meeting halls, and in constitutional debates.[4]

Riel's political thinking in the 1880s was clear and innovative. As Thomas Flanagan has suggested, and the many drafts of various aspects of Riel's theories make plain, Riel devoted his life to the development of arguments that would secure an economic buffer for the Métis and provide them with a political voice during the difficult decades of adaptation to the new order. Flanagan, especially in *Riel and the Rebellion: 1885 Reconsidered*, was not kind to Riel's crusade. Gilles Martel, in *Le messianisme de Louis Riel*, and Maggie Siggins, in *Riel: A Life of Revolution*,[5] were more sympathetic. When one reviews the documents and has the opportunity, rare in Canadian scholarship, to examine crucial drafts, often just fragments and notes, drawn from several dozen archives and dated with care, one begins to appreciate the unity and strength of Riel's outlook. The prayers and religious visions, which have received prominence in recent years, no longer overshadow the larger volume of personal correspondence and petitions that represent an equally important part of his thought. Rather, like the unusual elements in Mackenzie King's diaries, the dreams seem the expressions of another consciousness, of a darker and less certain *alter ego*.

Leaving to psychologists and philosophers his discussion of monads, his perception of his place in God's plans, and other metaphysical notes that at least help to explain his faith in his mission, students of history will be struck by the racial definition of Riel's *peuple métis canadien-français*. Riel argued that the Métis constituted a new nationality and, as such, had the right under the law of nations to a portion of the earth's surface. Be-

cause they lacked the "intellectual endowment" of the European newcomers, the Métis could expect to exact some compensation from Canada
to sustain them during the era of transition. As members of a "new world"
community, like the African-Americans, they had the right to be respected
as full citizens.[6] Riel believed that the amount of compensation to be paid
to Aboriginal people by the Canadian government should be based on
the value of Northwest land. For Métis, whose use of the land was "pass-
ably civilized" (his words), the value could be set at twenty-five cents per
acre; for Indians, whom he did not treat generously, Riel proposed vari-
ously twelve and a half or fifteen cents per acre.[7] If the Canadian government failed to meet the Métis demands for a sum that was reasonable,
then Riel would be forced to consider alternatives: perhaps forming alliances with other national groups in need of land; perhaps campaigning in
a Montana Métis newspaper for Native rights; perhaps even proposing
American annexation of the Northwest.

    Having had considerable experience in constitutional debates, Riel
devoted much effort to the preparation of statements defending the rights
of the Métis. The resistance of 1869 was defensible in law, he said many
times, and the negotiations leading to the Manitoba Act constituted official Canadian recognition of his provisional government. When Canada
broke the promises of the Manitoba Act, Riel believed, it forfeited its claim
to control the Northwest, which reverted to Native possession. Because
Ottawa owed him land and compensation for services rendered in the
1870s, he had the right to campaign for Native claims on Canadian soil in
1884-85. And the North-West Mounted Police harassment of Batoche-area
residents justified the measures taken by the Métis soldiers at Duck Lake.
Canada was the aggressor in 1885; the Métis fought only in self-defence.
There is a degree of casuistry in this last thesis, the claim of self-defence,
but there is merit in Riel's larger criticism of Canadian administration in
the West. Moreover, in the very process of debate, in the insistence that
he had a legal interest in the case despite his American citizenship and
residence, Riel provided the most plausible explanation for his requests
for personal compensation in 1885. The allegation that he was a weak,
self-seeking character, on which Creighton and Flanagan built their condemnation of the Métis uprising, is unfair. One is dealing with a political
thinker who dedicated himself to the discovery of legal defences for the
Métis, not a venal and duplicitous crook who misled his people in the
hope of personal gain.

    The question of Riel's mental state will also receive new attention with
the appearance of this collection. One recent paper on the issue is Thomas
Flanagan's "Louis Riel: Was He Really Crazy?"[8] Following Thomas Szasz,[9]
Flanagan contended that, in the absence of persuasive evidence of physical causation, "crazy behaviour should be understood in the same terms –

emotional, purposive, interpersonal, and moral – as behaviour in general." Thus, Flanagan argued that Riel was morally responsible for his behaviour and, though "certainly mad from a common sense point of view," should have been held accountable for his actions. Presented with a much more complete record of Riel's mental state, what will trained observers make of his condition? It seems evident that Riel was unable to control his emotional outbursts in the years 1875 to 1877, but, that period aside, his accounts of torment and ecstasy are balanced by letters of clarity and maturity. One can only sympathize with his furious complaint in the Beauport asylum when he was told that, despite his objections to a daily glass of milk fouled with straw and animal excrement, the drink would be good for him. However, the balance to be struck by historians must await a proper psychiatric review.

The creation of a corpus of writing from the hundreds of documents and fragments scattered in dozens of repositories is the great contribution of the University of Alberta's Riel project. This is especially important if one is to re-create his thinking during the Montana years. The re-dating of a crucial portion of the Riel diary from 1885 to the spring of 1884, and the reconstruction of a draft of Riel's book *The Massinihican* – for that reconstruction appears to have been accomplished – opens for scrutiny not only the Métis leader's cosmology but also his role in the Aboriginal political campaign of 1880 to 1884.[10] On this topic, readers will want to reconsider the evidence of Riel's writings from January to June 1884 – before the Saskatchewan delegation arrived in Montana to invite him to lead their protest movement – and to ask whether Riel's own campaign had not begun earlier than previously suggested and whether it was associated with Big Bear's activities.

The publication of this remarkable collection has sustained another round of Riel scholarship. Most of all, it has encouraged the revision of an interpretation set out by Donald Creighton in the early 1950s and reinforced by Thomas Flanagan in his analysis of the 1885 uprising published in 1983. Like Creighton, Flanagan believes that the federal government's land policy in the North-West Territories was reasonable, if a little slow in implementation, and that the Métis were unco-operative, even stubborn, in their approach to the new order. Like Creighton, Flanagan argues that Riel himself was motivated by self-interest in provoking the crisis and, therefore, that his role did not arise "solely, or even chiefly, from disinterested idealism." Rather, Flanagan suggests, Riel used the Métis as "pawns in his own game," and thereby misled them and their protest movement. Like Creighton, Flanagan judges the legal proceedings in Riel's treason trial to have been fair and Prime Minister Macdonald's decision not to commute the death sentence to have been appropriate.

Though a number of recent volumes have challenged aspects of this interpretation, a sound alternative has yet to be established. One misses in all of this work a sense of the political dimensions of the era. For example, Riel, the millenarian leader, required followers; what were Gabriel Dumont and the 100-odd Métis thinking when they chose to collaborate with Riel? Violence was not the rule in the North-West Territories in 1885; did the Métis choose the path of armed rebellion without giving thought to the consequences? Was Riel in any shape to exert continuous effective leadership over the Métis community in the spring of 1885? Did he abandon that responsibility as he succumbed to visions of another world, or did alternative leaders – Dumont and some of the buffalo hunters – shoulder him aside? Flanagan dismisses the issue of Riel's mental instability as a "fruitless non-question" but, surely, if the Métis relied on his written arguments and petitions, they were reposing a degree of confidence in him that was unwarranted after the struggle moved from textual debates to military calculations. Did Riel play a crucial role in the military decisions? Was the intransigence of Sir John A. Macdonald, the country's Prime Minister, an appropriate response to the Métis challenge of 1885, or was Macdonald driven by a vindictiveness greater than Riel's?

The events of Riel's life and times have not yet been explored to the point that Canadians can learn nothing further from them. They remain central to the history of the Canadian prairies. The publication of Riel's collected writings, however, will permit the next generation of students to see these events from Riel's perspective. This is an extraordinarily valuable set of documents and a remarkable feat of editing. It will stand the test of time and will influence Canadians' perception of this country, particularly their appreciation of the Aboriginal role in Canadian life. It has taken 100 years, but, in the completion of this enterprise, one of the last requests of a great Aboriginal Canadian has been fulfilled.

NOTES

This essay is based on three book reviews: The review of *The Collected Writings of Louis Riel* (1986) appeared in the *Canadian Historical Review* 69, no. 1 (1988) (reprinted with permission); that on Thomas Flanagan's *Riel and the Rebellion: 1885 Reconsidered* (1983) in *Saskatchewan History* 37, no. 3 (1984) (reprinted with permission); and that on Maggie Siggins's *Riel: A Life of Revolution* (1994) in the *Canadian Historical Review* 76, no. 4 (1995) (reprinted with permission).

1. The original reads: "Je, sous-signé, constitue par les présentes le Révérend Père Alexis André pour mon exécuteur testamentaire au sujet de mes papiers. Ma volonté est, que tous mes papiers lui soient remis et qu'il en ait le soin et que la publication lui en appartienne" (*The Collected Writings of Louis Riel / Les écrits complets de Louis Riel*, vol. 3, ed. Thomas Flanagan [Edmonton: University of Alberta Press, 1985], 256).
2. Ibid., 462; 423.
3. Donald Creighton, *John A. Macdonald*, II, *The Old Chieftain* (Toronto: Macmillan, 1955); and, Thomas Flanagan, *Louis "David" Riel: "Prophet of the New World"* (Toronto: University of Toronto Press, 1979).

4. *Collected Writings*, vol. 3, 278-94. Indeed, this and a number of other documents, including two September 1884 statements of Métis claims (vol. 3, 25-29, 33-39), two analyses of the 1870 Red River Resistance written in 1874 (vol. 1, ed. Raymond Huel), and some of his letters to his family (especially the sensitive and mature notes dispatched from the jail cell), some of his pun-filled poetry (Mair/mer), and the apparent drafts of his Montana book, *Le Massinahican*, are worthy of wider circulation. They might be translated into English in a cheaper format for use in Native studies classes.

5. Gilles Martel, *Le messianisme de Louis Riel* (Waterloo: Wilfrid Laurier University Press, 1984); Thomas Flanagan, *Riel and the Rebellion: 1885 Reconsidered* (Saskatoon: Western Producer Prairie Books, 1983); Maggie Siggins, *Riel: A Life of Revolution* (Toronto: Harper Collins, 1994).

6. This American aspect of Riel's thought, and the effect of Lincoln's presidency in particular, deserve greater attention than they have received.

7. *Collected Writings*, vol. 3, 27-29.

8. Thomas Flanagan, "Louis Riel: Was He Really Crazy?" in *1885 and After: Native Society in Transition*, ed. F. Laurie Barron and James B. Waldram (Regina: Canadian Plains Research Center, 1986).

9. Flanagan cites: Thomas Szasz, *The Myth of Psychotherapy* (Garden City, NY: Doubleday, 1978); Szasz, *The Therapeutic State: Psychiatry in the Mirror of Current Events* (Buffalo: Prometheus Books, 1984); and, Szasz, *Law, Liberty, and Psychiatry: An Inquiry into the Uses of Mental Health Practices* (New York: Collier Books, 1963).

10. Thomas Flanagan, in *The Diaries of Louis Riel* (Edmonton: Hurtig Publishers, 1976) places this text in 1885; the document is re-dated to the spring of 1884 and reprinted in *Collected Writings*, vol. 2, ed. Gilles Martel.

Bilingualism in Manitoba: The Historical Context

IN THIS ESSAY I address a question that agitated Manitobans in the early 1980s: What are the traditions and laws that govern the official use of the French language in Manitoba? To establish appropriate answers, one must delve deep into Manitoba's past.

European settlement in the western interior of Canada has two origins. The English-owned Hudson's Bay Company (HBC) established posts on the shores of the Bay, notably at Churchill and York Factory, in the century after 1670, and sent annual infusions of labour to those forts in order to maintain a complement of about 200 servants. And the French, from their towns and seigneuries on the St. Lawrence, dispatched dozens of brigades into the interior in the same era. It was the French, through the La Vérendrye expeditions of the 1730s and 1740s, who established European trading communities in present-day southern Manitoba.

More extensive settlements of English-, Gaelic-, and French-speaking immigrants clustered at the junction of the Red and Assiniboine Rivers between 1812 and the 1850s, though their numbers seemed small in comparison to the several thousands of French- and English-speaking people of mixed Aboriginal and European parentage who constituted the vast majority in the Red River Settlement.

The administration of Red River after 1835 was supervised by the HBC and was called the Council of Assiniboia. It contained representatives of the Company and the community, and it published its laws in both French and English.

When pressure from Canada and the United States forced British and HBC authorities to consider new political arrangements for Red River in the late 1860s, the citizens of the community resisted the "sale" of Rupert's Land and Assiniboia. Led by Louis Riel and supported by a majority of local residents, both French- and English-speaking, a representative assembly passed a list of "rights," which formed the basis of Manitoba's case in its negotiations to enter Confederation. The list included this clause: "That the English and French language be common in the legislature and in the courts, and that all public documents . . . [and] Acts of the legislature be published in both languages." The list also specified that the judge of the Manitoba "Supreme Court" should speak both French and English. Later, the Third List of Rights, probably written by Riel, added that the lieutenant-governor should also be "familiar" with both languages.

The Manitoba Act, passed by the House of Commons in May 1870, established in Section 23 that French and English would be the languages in Manitoba's official record and journals, in the legislative debates, and in the courts. It also specified that the acts of the legislature be "printed and published" in the two languages. In addition, the Manitoba Act contained provisions for an Upper House, a kind of provincial senate as existed in Quebec, on the grounds that minority rights and a sober second thought on other legislation would be better ensured by such a chamber.

The Manitoba Act was passed first by the Canadian Parliament and then re-enacted by the British Parliament in 1871, thus endowing it with a status greater than ordinary legislation.[1] The federal authorities made certain, in selecting the first lieutenant-governors, Adams Archibald, Alexander Morris, and Joseph Cauchon, that their nominees were bilingual. Insofar as legislation and administration at the time guaranteed language "rights," French and English were to be regarded as the only "legal" languages – languages of law and record and official discourse – in Manitoba.

The province was governed and administered in the two languages from 1870 to 1889. The debates were not recorded in an official "Hansard," but a nearly verbatim account of the legislative sessions appeared in French and English in two local newspapers. The Journals of the Legislative Assembly, the official records of its business, were published in two versions, one French and one English, from 1871 to 1889. So were the statutes. The cabinet, usually a five-person group, always contained French-speaking representatives in this period. And the boundaries of the constituencies were drawn to ensure linguistic and religious as well as regional representation.

All was not sweetness and light in early Manitoba politics. Many of the English-speaking newcomers, led by the soldiers who made up Canada's military expedition under Colonel Garnet Wolseley, were determined to claim the new land as the child of Ontario. They harassed and intimidated the old Red River settlers, especially the French Métis, and eventually purchased much of the land of the "old settlers." In many cases, the methods employed appear to have been unfair, even illegal. Today, the issue of land claims has been sent to the courts for redress after a century of Métis protest.

The land issue was only one illustration of English-French discord in the 1870s. The original electoral law created twelve "French" and twelve "English" constituencies. As English-speaking newcomers arrived, mainly from Ontario, they demanded changes. In 1874, eight "French," eight "English (old settlers)," and eight "English (new settlers)" seats replaced the ridings of the first map. In 1876, as an economy measure, the federal Liberal government of Alexander Mackenzie persuaded the province to abolish its Upper House in exchange for a larger grant from Ottawa. One protector of minority rights was thus eliminated. In 1879, during a cabinet crisis, Premier John Norquay united the English-speaking MLAs by agreeing to abolish all French rights in the province. He passed this bill reluctantly in order to save his own position, but the lieutenant-governor reserved his assent, and there it died, to Norquay's evident relief. Norquay then appointed a new French deputy leader in his caucus and ruled with his coalition of about six French and ten to fifteen English representatives for almost a decade.

A new party developed in opposition to Norquay in the 1880s to represent some of the thousands of English-speaking newcomers who had inundated the "old settlers" and the French.[2] This party was an offspring of a southern Ontario political movement that was led in the House of Commons by George Brown, Alexander Mackenzie, and Edward Blake, and that can be described as the forerunner of the Liberal Party. These Manitoba Liberals, led by Thomas Greenway and Joseph Martin, defeated Norquay after accusing him of financial impropriety in 1887. Norquay's departure and sudden death then took the strongest defender of Manitoba's "old order" from the public stage.

Premier Greenway and his new Liberal government ran into financial and railway problems of their own in 1889. Perhaps coincidentally, the Greenway cabinet resolved to abolish the dual school system (Roman Catholic and Protestant), and to replace it with a single non-denominational "national" school system. Due in part to the influence of a notorious anti-French campaigner from Ontario, D'Alton McCarthy, the Manitoba government also decided to abolish the official use of French in legislative documents and the courts. The school and language acts, passed in 1890, were devastating blows to the French-speaking Catholic community.

Neither Prime Minister Macdonald nor Opposition Leader Wilfrid Laurier supported federal disallowance of the Manitoba statutes, an intervention that was well within the federal power and was supported by numerous precedents. A federal election was only months away, and Ontario voters were growing increasingly agitated about French-English issues, so the Conservative and Liberal leaders temporized by urging that the questions be taken to the courts.

What did Manitoba's French Catholics do? Because their children's religious instruction was so important to them, because French might remain a language of instruction in the schools, and because they could establish a powerful political alliance with the English-speaking Catholics of Winnipeg, they chose to fight the school law rather than the language law. After seven years and three long legal cases, they won a compromise in 1897 that permitted religious instruction at the end of the school day. The compromise also guaranteed bilingualism – English and another language – in the schools.

This arrangement lasted twenty years. However, as thousands of Europeans flooded into Manitoba, the 1897 compromise raised unforeseen problems. German-, Polish-, and Ukrainian-language schools (including teachers' colleges) were just the thin edge of the wedge, some Manitobans feared. It was a provincial Liberal government, led by Premier T.C. Norris, that abolished the bilingual school guarantee in 1916. The French had lost again, though this time their bitter disappointment was shared by Germans, Ukrainians, Poles, and other linguistic minorities.

In the next half century, the French raised the issue of public tax support for Roman Catholic schools on several occasions. The federal Liberal government of Mackenzie King intervened on their behalf secretly and informally in the late 1930s but made no headway with Manitoba's Bracken government. Another secret initiative was launched around 1960, apparently with the sanction of Premier Duff Roblin, but it, too, failed to find support. In these many years, the French language was taught and used as a language of instruction, but it was done without public notice and with the tacit approval of provincial school inspectors. The issue of its legal standing was pursued once in the courts but in a half-hearted effort and without success. Franco-Manitobans evidently believed that education, not the use of French in the legislature, was the key to language and community survival.

Finally, in 1976, a Franco-Manitoban, Georges Forest, challenged the legality of an English-only parking ticket and eventually won a Supreme

Court of Canada judgement declaring the 1890 language act unconstitutional (that is, beyond the competence of the provincial legislature), thereby restoring the official use of French in Manitoba.

What can one learn from the history of Manitoba's language troubles?

First: Assiniboia was a bilingual community for many years before 1870.

Second: French and English representatives both in Manitoba and in Ottawa endorsed the use of the two languages in the courts and the legislature of Canada's first new province during the negotiations of 1870.

Third: The 1890 legislation abolishing the official use of the French language was not within the competence of the Manitoba legislature – was illegal, in short – as the Supreme Court ruled in the 1979 Forest decision.

Fourth: Both Prime Minister Macdonald and Opposition Leader Laurier, facing the prospect of a federal election, preferred the easier course of a court challenge to the politically dangerous option of federal disallowance of the Manitoba statute.

Fifth: Franco-Manitobans, given two distasteful choices in 1890, placed a higher priority upon the restoration of public support for confessional schools and upon the use of French as a language of instruction in those schools than upon its use in courts and legislature.

Sixth: Manitoba is not a province "just like the others," because it has a bilingual compact entrenched in its founding statutes. This legal provision, it should be emphasized, was not an imposition from outside, whether Ottawa or Québec, but rather had its origins in *local* circumstances.[3]

NOTES

In 1983-84, Manitoba public life was convulsed by a proposed expansion of French-language government services. Inevitably, one focus of discussion concerned the historical status of the French language. This essay was part of the debate. It is a revised version of the paper that appeared in the *Winnipeg Free Press* on 19 March 1984; it is reprinted with the permission of the *Winnipeg Free Press*. Though I wrote the article, nine other members of the Department of History at the University of Manitoba reviewed it and endorsed it as reflecting their views. They included: W.H. Brooks, L.C. Clark, J.M. Friesen, V.J. Jensen, J.E. Kendle, M.K. Mott, J.E. Rea, W.D. Smith, and D.N. Sprague. The late professors Vincent Jensen and Lovell Clark contributed substantially to these discussions, and I would like to pay tribute to their counsel.

1. An Act Respecting the Establishment of Provinces in the Dominion of Canada, 1871, 34-35 Vict., c. 28 (U.K.).

2. French was the principal language of seven percent of Manitoba's 152,000 residents in 1891.

3. Cornelius J. Jaenen reaches this conclusion in "The History of French in Manitoba: Local Initiative or External Imposition?" *Language and Society / Langue et Société* 13 (spring 1984). An interesting survey of an important part of the historiography is in D.J. Hall, "The Spirit of Confederation: Ralph Heintzman, Professor Creighton, and the Bicultural Compact Theory," *Journal of Canadian Studies* 9, no. 4 (1974). A recent survey of some of these issues is Nelson Wiseman, "The Questionable Relevance of the Constitution in Advancing Minority Cultural Rights in Manitoba," *Canadian Journal of Political Science* 25, no. 4 (1992). A comment on the situation in the 1980s is Andy Anstett and Paul Thomas, "Manitoba: The Role of the Legislature in a Polarized Political System," in *Provincial and Territorial Legislatures in Canada*, ed. Gary Levy and Graham White (Toronto: University of Toronto Press, 1989).

Manitoba and the Meech Lake Accord

MANITOBA HAS BEEN A FORUM for several political debates of national importance. Premier John Norquay opposed Sir John A. Macdonald in the struggle over the federal power to disallow provincial legislation and fell from office in 1887 as a result. The Manitoba school law of 1890 provoked a national crisis, the implications of which are still being worked out. The federal amendments to the Criminal Code definition of seditious intent, Section 98, which were designed to suppress the revolutionary socialism of the 1919 Winnipeg General Strike, were repealed only in 1936 after repeated criticism by civil-rights and labour representatives. The 1983-84 debate over French-language services in Manitoba received national attention because the participants were addressing the changed circumstances of bilingualism in modern Canada. Finally, in 1987-88, the commencement of a Manitoba debate over the Meech Lake Accord, a proposed amendment to the Canadian Constitution, received national attention. Once again, the Province of Manitoba seemed to be in a position to clarify a national issue. Why did the Meech Lake Accord run into such stiff resistance in Manitoba? What role did Manitoba play in the eventual demise of the Meech Lake constitutional amendments?

An obvious explanation of Manitoba's resistance lies in the composition of the provincial population. Indeed, the prominence of natives and ethnic groups and French-speaking citizens in Manitoba's public affairs offers reason enough for the province's careful scrutiny of the Accord. Another plausible explanation is the relative ease of debate in a small, centralized province. Manitoba has just over one million citizens, two-thirds of whom live in Winnipeg or in its shadow; its public discussions are dominated by a small number of media outlets and by well-organized party networks that can generate interest remarkably quickly. A third explanation is the intense partisanship of recent politics. The competitiveness of the Conservative and New Democratic parties after twenty years of increasingly heated debate, and the complications introduced by a revitalized Liberal Party ensure that most issues receive attention as the parties jockey for position. None of these answers is sufficient. The crucial factor in the emergence of a Manitoba debate lies in the nature of the constitutional amendment process itself and the response to that process by former Manitoba Premier Howard Pawley. Pawley's insistence that Manitobans have an opportunity to consider the amendments at public hearings provided the occasion for the debate. And the apparent haste with which other parties to the agreement attempted to entrench the changes, including both the federal Conservative government and its provincial allies in the governments of Alberta and Saskatchewan, provoked the suspicion of Manitobans.

Howard Pawley's role in the Meech Lake process reflected his position as Canada's only New Democratic Party (NDP) premier between 1986 and 1988. Pawley attended the first bargaining session at Meech Lake expecting that the talks would end in failure. He had no idea that the federal government preparations included considerable discussion of Quebec's aspirations with other western premiers. Closeted in an upstairs room in the conference cottage and without the benefit of advice from his three Manitoba colleagues, who were in another part of the building, Pawley felt isolated, not for the first time at such federal-provincial meetings. Though interpretations of the Meech Lake agreement differ, Pawley left the meeting with the assumption that the constitutional proposals were flexible and would almost certainly be revised at the next conference. Other leaders did not share this impression. As the "odd man out" in party terms, Pawley had no one to defend his perspective.

Pawley's commitments as a social democrat also underlie his role in the next stage of amendments to the Accord, now known as the Langevin Block Amendments (named after the building in Ottawa where these negotiations took place). Pawley had returned to Winnipeg after the Meech Lake meetings to a mixed but generally favourable reaction. However, a few critical comments had reached his office, particularly as a result of disquiet among Aboriginal leaders, and he had immediately prepared a list of specific amendments to be presented at the next round. This list included a clearer clause on the federal spending power, a defence of northern Canadian participation in national institutions, a clause on Aboriginal government, a clause on multicultural rights, and a statement guaranteeing that Canadians would be able to participate in public hearings before the constitutional revisions came into effect. Once again, when the nation's leaders convened at the Langevin Block to consider the Meech Lake document, Pawley apparently found himself in the minority. He won sufficient support on some parts of his list to make several changes, but on a matter dear to his heart, Aboriginal rights, he was flatly rejected. In the wee hours of the morning, he sat on the back stairs with Premier David Peterson of Ontario debating whether to jettison the entire Accord. The two men returned to the conference room, Peterson endorsed the Accord, and Pawley, too, gave his assent. He then returned to the unstable political situation in Manitoba knowing that he was committed to hold provincial hearings before a final decision was made on the entire Meech Lake package.

The NDP government was situated precariously. In the 1986 provincial election, the NDP had won thirty seats to the twenty-six held by Gary Filmon's Conservatives and the one seat occupied by the Liberal leader, Sharon Carstairs. Then, in the autumn of 1987, a veteran NDP minister, Larry Desjardins, whose health was uncertain, decided to leave the government, his resignation to take effect on the opening of the 1988 session. A second crucial NDP vote was also in question. James Walding, NDP backbencher and former Speaker of the Assembly, was no longer attending caucus meetings and was rumoured to be hostile to the government. If one vote was lost and the other switched sides, the Pawley administration would collapse.

The Meech Lake Accord was not one of the pressing issues on the NDP government's agenda during its final six months. Plans for the legislative hearings into the Accord were slowly taking shape, and a paragraph on the hearings was drafted for the Throne Speech. Premier Pawley had not wavered in his support. Then, between October 1987 and January 1988, members of his party, including, it was said, a sizable proportion of his caucus, began to question the "seamless" web woven by Canada's other First Ministers. This dissenting movement was drawn from almost every region and interest group in the provincial party. Moreover, despite the conventional wisdom that constitutions are not the stuff of popular debate, the Accord's Manitoba opponents discovered a remarkable degree of interest in and concern about the proposed changes. In January 1988, at least fifteen NDP constituency associations passed resolutions critical of the Meech Lake Accord that were forwarded in turn to the provincial executive for consideration at the annual party convention in early March. At this point, Pawley recognized that he could no longer assume endorsement of the Meech Lake principles in the Manitoba Legislature.

Pawley had commenced discussions with representatives of the party dissenters in December, but, at that early stage, his main concern was to ensure that they were not motivated by anti-French sentiments and that they appreciated the difficult situation of the national party leader, Ed Broadbent, who had to acknowledge Quebec views. As the convention approached, however, Pawley acted to avert a contest over the Accord. This was a wise move because the dissenters were certain that a motion rejecting the Accord would easily win party approval. A composite statement, drafted and redrafted to meet the views of the various groups on both sides, was presented to delegates at the provincial convention. It called on the government to hold hearings before it decided whether to support the Accord in the Legislature. Pawley was able to speak in favour of the resolution, Broadbent avoided embarrassment, and the opponents of the Accord were encouraged to launch a campaign at the forthcoming public hearings in the expectation that the party could be persuaded to reject the constitutional resolution in the Legislature.

Three days later, Walding deserted his party on the budget vote and the government fell. Pawley resigned, the New Democrats commenced a leadership campaign, and the province entered a general election. Given the disastrous state of the New Democrats – February was the month of large increases in Autopac rates (the government-controlled car insurance program), April the month to calculate increased income tax payments – all signs pointed to the demise of the NDP government. The sudden turn of events implied rapid passage of the Accord under a new Conservative government.

The people of Winnipeg chose to confound the electoral experts. A cautious and uninspired Conservative campaign actually lost votes for the party's candidates in Manitoba's capital city. The New Democrats, clearly out of favour with the people despite its new leader, Gary Doer, lost even more votes. These losses and an unusually large turnout favoured the Liberals. Final standings in the election were twenty-five Conservatives (a minority government), twenty Liberals (all but one from Winnipeg), and twelve New Democrats. Suddenly the fate of the Meech Lake Accord was in doubt.

The Liberal leader, Sharon Carstairs, an emphatic opponent of the Accord, had made it a secondary issue in the election. Now that she led the Official Opposition, she could happily declare to the media that Meech Lake was "dead." It was hyperbole, but one might judge her exaggeration understandable in the first flush of success, though unwise. Because the sudden rise in her party's fortunes could be attributed to her forceful leadership, no one in her caucus of neophytes would want to challenge her conclusion. Certainly, Premier Filmon was not about to test her resolve. He assured questioners that the Accord was not a legislative priority of his government. He would take no action to precipitate an unnecessary crisis – even the hearings seemed to be in doubt – and would await the unfolding of national political events. The leader of the New Democrats, Gary Doer, continued to advocate that hearings take place and, like his predecessor, seemed determined to introduce amendments on such matters as Aboriginal, northern, and women's rights.

Why was the Accord stalled in Manitoba? On the surface, the Pawley government's sudden fall and the unexpected rise of a third party seemed to account for the pause. But this was not the full story. In addition to Pawley's determination to proceed slowly and with due attention to public consultation, many Manitobans were now suspicious of the proposal. The very absence of public debate in English-speaking Canada and the failure of national political representatives to articulate the strengths and weaknesses of the measure may have roused doubts. The concerns of Manitobans probably reflected those of many other western and English-speaking Canadians. Those concerned may be placed in five categories: social democrats; the Charter of Rights coalition; native and northern citizens; constitutional critics; and the anti-French.

Members of unions, mostly affiliated with the Canadian Labour Congress, may be taken as representative of the social democratic strain. Several union leaders concluded that the Accord, by decentralizing Confederation, was part of a neo-conservative agenda that included the proposed Canadian-American trade deal, the de-regulation of some industries, and the privatization of certain government-controlled companies and services. In this view, the Accord was striking at the country's social democratic foundation and the community consensus favouring the labour movement. The Accord, instead, reflected the drift to a market-based, American-style social system. Those in service-sector occupations, including members of civil-service unions and day-care and teachers' and nurses' associations, were particularly interested in these discussions. The fact that the Canadian work force was much more unionized than the American (about thirty-seven percent of non-agricultural workers compared to about sixteen percent) lent strength to the arguments as well as to the numbers of those sympathetic to the cause.

Affiliated with the unions in these social democratic concerns were members of the left-wing farm movement, the National Farmers' Union, and numerous members of the NDP. The farmers believed that several crucial principles for which they had fought throughout the twentieth century, including supply management and freight-rate controls, were challenged by the Conservative agenda. Though the Meech Lake Accord was less pressing than were several other federal initiatives (such as the free-trade deal and the dismantling of the Crow's Nest Pass freight-rate agreement), it seemed to these farm families, as it did to the union members, part of a larger perspective with which they disagreed. The New Democrats added to this list their concern that the federal spending power, which had created and maintained national standards for the medical care system, could not in a post–Meech Lake era play the same role in the establishment of, for example, a national non-profit day-care system of the type that Manitoba's NDP government had been pioneering. Such concerns motivated social democrats to question the Meech Lake Accord rather than to reject it outright. However, given the absence of a public forum for this debate, questions often became criticism and then hardened into opposition.

The "Charter" concerns with the Accord crossed all party lines, but the term is appropriate because it reflects the concentration on particular rights that is evident in Canada's Charter of Rights. These concerns included women's rights and the place of multiculturalism in the national fabric. Representatives of the women's movement and of multicultural groups were divided in their analysis of the Accord; in each case, some regarded it as benign, and others believed that it contained potential problems that should be addressed before it became law. When the Accord's supporters rejected amendments, however, increasing numbers in these groups moved into the opposition camp.

The single clearest flaw in the Accord was its failure to acknowledge the rights and aspirations of northern Canadians. Tony Penikett, NDP leader of the Yukon territorial government, won sympathy across the country when he challenged the proposed rules for the nomination of senators and Supreme Court judges and for the creation of new provinces. His case was made stronger by another crucial omission from this round of constitutional talks – Aboriginal rights. Having failed to win agreement on Aboriginal self-government in the preceding five years, as had been mandated by the constitutional settlement of 1982, the premiers and prime minister had simply left the issue out of their discussions in this "Quebec round," or "provinces' round." Native leaders resented this silence on a pressing issue, but, more important, they regarded the rule for the creation of new provinces as a serious setback to the Aboriginal cause. If ever a Native-controlled territory were to have a test, it would probably be in some portion of the North and under some version of provincial status. The new Meech Lake rules would ensure that the ten "southern" provinces, some of which would inevitably be closely aligned with international resource corporations, could forever block the establishment of a predominantly Native province in northern Canada. Once again, Aboriginal leaders felt betrayed.

The concerns of constitutional analysts would never generate a campaign in the streets or even stir up a flurry of calls to a radio open-line show (the modern Canadian equivalent), but these legal specialists also played a role in the Meech Lake debate. Conducted in newspaper columns and public speeches as well as in private correspondence, the Manitoba discussions reflected national concerns. Bryan Schwartz, a law professor, lamented the rigidity of the Accord in a book, *Fathoming Meech Lake*.[1] Israel Asper, former provincial Liberal leader, and Jack London, law professor, debated Senator Nathan Nurgitz and Member of Parliament Leo Duguay, both Conservatives, in a televised battle of celebrities that offered more misinformation than one might have expected but also a good deal of popular entertainment. Behind the public talks, which were at best sporadic and inconclusive, an informal private circulation of briefs, drafts of scholarly articles, and copies of letters kept the issue to the fore. This was not a clandestine activity, by any means, but the academic network did add fuel to the debate. Thus, a speech to the Alberta NDP task force on Meech Lake by retired Senator Eugene Forsey, to take one example, was distributed privately in Manitoba because it was a forceful criticism of the Accord and because there was insufficient room or interest in the popular media for such extended discussions of these matters. The academic analysis of the Accord was conducted in parallel with the public political campaign. Inevitably, criticisms spilled over into the partisan arena and fuelled further controversy.

The debate provoked in the NDP was the largest popular movement against the Accord in 1987, but another important expression of public opposition came from the Union of Manitoba Municipalities (UMM). Based in the local governments of small-town and rural Manitoba, the UMM had fought the extension of French-language services in the province in 1983-84 and perceived the Meech Lake proposals as another concession to French-language interests. The distinct-societies clause, in particular, was anathema to citizens who insisted on a one-nation rather than two-nation definition of Canadianism. These rural political leaders also believed that the Accord would undercut their campaign for a new senate, a chamber that might be based on equal regional or provincial representation. Though the UMM was close to the Conservative party on many issues, the Meech Lake Accord threatened to divide the rural electorate and to fuel a renewed round of western separatist activity. The founding of a new western Canadian party under the leadership of Alberta's Preston Manning in the autumn of 1987 even gave brief public prominence to this sentiment, but rural Manitobans did not rally to the Reform Party of Canada in succeeding months. Disquiet and uncertainty remained in rural Manitoba, but they had not found political expression.

It might be argued that the Liberals and New Democrats mobilized opinion against the Meech Lake Accord in the 1988 provincial election campaign. It is true that both parties criticized the Accord and emphasized the importance of public hearings. Nonetheless, the Accord was never a significant issue in the campaign, though it probably enabled Carstairs to establish herself as a force to be reckoned with. The real story of the Manitoba response to the Accord lay in the problems associated with establishing an informed public debate during 1987-88. The refusal of the federal Opposition parties to oppose, an obligation of Her Majesty's Loyal Opposition, placed significant constraints on provincial wings of the national Liberal and New Democratic parties. The federal government's insistence that the Accord was a seamless web, not open to amendment or to complementary clauses, frustrated provincial Conservatives. Movements of dissent arose in all three parties, however, and in extra-political circles.

The Manitoba public hearings before an all-party task force took place in 1989. An important report was issued, and the province's proposed revisions to the Meech Lake Accord were placed in the national debate. Those suggested revisions included a "Canada clause," which named the "fundamental characteristics" of the country. To a list that had formerly included only French-speaking and English-speaking Canadians as well as Quebec, the Manitoba amendments added "a federal state with a distinct national identity," "aboriginal peoples," and "Canada's multicultural heritage."[2]

The Mulroney government was unmoved by Manitoba's proposed amendments. Instead, the prime minister believed that an unravelling of the Accord would commence the moment any portion was made subject to revision. As the four-year deadline (established in June 1986) came ever closer, Mulroney convened an extraordinary First Ministers' conference in Ottawa. A bizarre drama was renewed day after day in front of the television cameras as Canadian unity seemed to hang in the balance. Drama descended into farce when, at the last possible moment, the prime minister and premiers agreed once again to pass the Accord. They then engaged in an unseemly round of self-congratulation on live, late-night television, one premier going as far as to thank "the big guy in the sky" for this national deliverance.

The deal unravelled in the next two weeks. All three party leaders in Manitoba – Filmon, Carstairs, and Doer – had embraced the Accord during the Ottawa negotiations and returned to the province knowing that a constitutional resolution must proceed through the Legislature immediately.

Elijah Harper, NDP Member of the Legislature for the vast northern riding of Rupertsland, then became the individual embodiment of rule by parliamentary tradition as well as of Aboriginal resistance to this particular constitutional accord. While Aboriginal protesters gathered in crowds around the Legislature, and just before an Aboriginal land dispute at Oka, near Montreal, exploded into international prominence with the shooting of a police officer (the standoff between Canadian Army and Aboriginal resisters lasted all summer), Harper refused the suspension of House rules that alone would enable the Assembly to deal with the constitutional agreement. The Meech Lake Accord died on the floor of the Manitoba Legislature because Elijah Harper said no.

Manitoba had once again provided a forum for a national debate. Moreover, the decisive blow that killed the Meech Lake constitutional amendments had been delivered in Manitoba's provincial Legislature. The province's centrality to these events can easily be overestimated, but it should not be forgotten. Of course, the debate flared up in every province, and, of course, partisan loyalties played a large role in the resistance of Newfoundland and New Brunswick as well as Manitoba. However, one should also recognize that the government of Howard Pawley prolonged the debate and enabled its opponents to accumulate intellectual "authority" within the provincial community. The three-party balance in the Legislature from 1988 to 1990 lent the Manitoba Constitutional Committee's proposed amendments further credibility and, in particular, heartened the Aboriginal leadership in the province. The rules of the Legislature, which required unanimous consent for the consideration of the Meech resolution, and the resolute opposition of an Aboriginal New Democrat represented the final elements in the mix. Elijah Harper's actions determined the outcome; Manitoba provided the setting and shaped the events.

NOTES

This is a revised version of an article that appeared in Roger Gibbins et al., eds., *Meech Lake and Canada: Perspectives from the West* (Edmonton: Academic Printing and Publishing, 1988); it is reprinted with the permission of Academic Printing and Publishing. A broader survey of the constitutional question is contained in Nelson Wiseman, "In Search of Manitoba's Constitutional Position," *Journal of Canadian Studies* 29, no. 3 (1994).

1. Bryan Schwartz, *Fathoming Meech Lake* (Winnipeg: University of Manitoba Legal Research Institute, 1987).
2. Manitoba Constitutional Task Force on the Meech Lake Accord, *Report on the 1987 Constitutional Accord* (Winnipeg: Queen's Printer, 1989), 18-19.

Constitutional Politics:
Cardinal Points on a Prairie Compass

CANADIAN POLITICAL JOURNALISM is encumbered with directional metaphors – the West, the North, the East. I would like to argue that Canadians hear too much about that monolithic entity, the West, and not enough about the crucial division within the Prairies, that between "conservatives" and "social democrats." This distinction, which could be described as the difference between right and left, constitutes a very important aspect of the prairie compass. It derives even greater importance from the current state of Canadian politics because the discussions of constitutional reform and Quebec sovereignty often refer to the attitudes of "western Canadians" – as if we all could be described by one sweeping generalization.

Prairie people are not monolithic in political outlook. It is an oversimplification to say there are only two sides in prairie debates. Nevertheless, one can say confidently that there are two important directional tendencies in prairie discussions of public policy. Prairie residents do debate the merits of Klein and Romanow, Filmon and Doer, as a duel between opposites. When talk turns to national politics, the pattern remains left-right. If the speakers are conservatives, their favourite themes are deficits, interest rates, and grain policies. If they are social democrats, they add privatization, the GST (goods and services tax), and free trade to the list.

This pattern will sound familiar; it is the dominant pattern in Canadian politics.

A casualty in the growing influence of left versus right, or social democracy versus conservatism, is the old assumption about a homogeneous prairie society. The idea of "West" belongs to another age. It had resonance in the days of the *pays d'en haut,* the fabulous fur country beyond the Great Lakes. It meant a great deal to "easterners" when their children headed "out there," or "up there," to farm. In those long-lost days, every eastern Canadian family had, as Stephen Leacock wrote, its "western odyssey."[1] This western myth mattered even in politics, when Ottawa governed the land and resource policy for the entire western interior (1880 to 1930), and when Aboriginal people resisted the Canadian government's race-based policies. And it had some economic meaning when agriculture dominated the economies of the prairie provinces. But times have changed, and we live in a different age.

The prairie provinces are urban. Very few prairie people farm. About two-thirds of all jobs are in the service or tertiary sector. Though national journalists, when they turn to the Prairies, talk about farm-income programs and the Canadian Wheat Board, they would be justified in devoting equal space to health care and education. Media workers, by virtue of their numbers, if not their historic wealth-creation roles, are just as important in the local economy as are farmers.

A key question in this modern prairie world, as in other developed economies, is to identify one's employer. Are you paid out of tax dollars and thus sustained by the entire community? Or do you depend on a consumer who pays you directly for your wares? And does the distinction between state and private sector employment influence your political perceptions?

The market dominates prairie political debates. If you choose to concentrate on the collapse of the centrally run command economies of eastern Europe, the greater economic efficiency of Japan, the alleged featherbedding in government bureaucracies, and the "lean, aggressive" approach to production and sales in private enterprise corporations, you belong on the right. If you prefer to discuss social issues in terms of safety nets, goods production in terms of use values and environmental impact, marketing in terms of consumer education and personal control, you belong on the left. Of course, the overlaps may be infinite in number. But the pattern is clear in the Prairies, as it is in many other parts of the world.

Prairie people choose one side or the other of the great left-right divide in national politics, too. Free trade and privatization are, of course, the recent code words for our national political discussions. Most prairie New Democrats opposed both. Most prairie Conservatives supported both. The difference of opinion was left-right; for example, social democrats preferred some regulation of the market, some crown corporations, some nationally established standards in health care and day care. The Tories preferred a more decentralized, privatized, de-regulated, open trading environment.

There are, of course, issues on which prairie perspectives seem to reflect a distinctive prairie political and cultural experience. The Senate leaps to mind. So do multicultural and Aboriginal policies. But they do not add up to a "western" vision for the nation. Rather, in each case, one can discern differences of opinion and particular western interests at work.

The "triple-E senate" is often described as a "western" demand in constitutional discussions. Behind the policy proposal – to *elect* an *effective* and *equal* senate (equal to the power of the House of Commons? or equal representation from each province?) – lies the argument that western interests are not taken into account in national policy making. This is nonsense.[2] The problem will not be corrected by electing senators. Recent western complaints arise from the ruling parties' policy choices. In the 1980s, CF-18 was the code name that best illustrated the problem in Manitoba; a Montreal firm won the fighter jet maintenance contract, even though a Winnipeg firm made a lower and stronger bid. Another illustration, this one from Alberta in the early 1980s, was code-named NEP (National Energy Policy); Ottawa wanted all Canada to "share" Alberta's petroleum riches. And, a decade before that, in Saskatchewan, under the code name LIFT (Lower Inventories for Tomorrow), we saw a wheat-acreage reduction scheme that flew in the face of a century of farm history by paying farmers not to grow grain. The details of these ill-fated programs matter to the leaders of Manitoba's aerospace industry, Alberta's petroleum industry, and Saskatchewan's grain industry, respectively, but they need not be rehearsed again. From today's perspective, instead, these policy choices are important because, though simply that – policy choices – they were interpreted in the Prairies as regional affronts. The explanation of that leap in logic, from necessary policy choice to regional crisis, lies first in the history of prairie protest (the "regional bias" of prairie politics from Riel to Lougheed), and second in the structure of a national electoral system that reinforces territory-based dissent.

An elected, or "triple-E," senate would not end the need for difficult policy choices, nor would it ensure that mistakes never occurred. On the other hand, a *reformed* and *respected* senate would offer a forum in which to air grievances and present alternatives. Perhaps we should launch a "double-R," rather than a "triple-E," campaign. Other societies, among which the Aboriginal and Asian come immediately to mind, find important roles for elders in their social, family, and political deliberations. Our task is to create a better vehicle for the voices of experienced government leaders and for province-based perspectives to be heard in an appropriate national forum. The campaign led by the Canada West Foundation, a conservative publicity and research organization, to create a triple-E senate is not a "western" demand in constitutional talks. Instead, it is one western contribution to a debate – *driven by advocates of a decentralizing, market-based approach* – that requires much more attention before the country chooses a revised constitution.

Another "western" perspective on the Constitution, or so it is often treated, concerns linguistic and cultural policies in Canada. Indeed, popular disturbances about bilingualism and multiculturalism are often given a western colouring in the so-called national media. French-language services in Manitoba, the use of French as an "official" language in Saskatchewan and Alberta, petitions concerning the integration of Sikh turbans and Indian braids into RCMP uniform and dress codes, distribution of racist pamphlets, and the teachings of an anti-Semite who wishes to rewrite the history of the European Holocaust have all received media attention. They offer easy and spectacular targets. Treated in isolation, they can blacken unfairly the reputation of entire communities. They do not, however, represent "the West."

The creation and maintenance of a plural society is a difficult task. If any community has grappled seriously with the assignment and achieved a modest degree of success, it is prairie Canada. Let us look, for a moment, at the past century, when we have experienced suppression of Aboriginal religion and culture; exclusion policies and riots over Asian immigration; Mennonite exodus; Doukhobor marches; Ukrainian internments; "enemy alien" disfranchisement; ethnic quotas in universities targeting especially, but not exclusively, Jews; eviction, property confiscation, and resettlement of Japanese Canadians; and the unsubtle daily racism of majoritarian public schools. The list is long and painful, and yet it represents, in retrospect, small victories. No item on it should be defended as appropriate policy today. Every episode has invoked group resistance at some point. Still, the persecuted groups remain in this community, having adapted and yet having retained a vivid recollection of the injustices. The consequence, one hopes, is greater collective sensitivity (however slight) to such issues.

Multiculturalism is today's term associated with prairie Canadian attempts to continue and improve upon our inherited pluralism. It reflects a desire to seek a less-uniform, less-fervent identity than that created in another great, but different, model of multinational readjustment, the United States. The concept finds its political expression in the wish of long-established ethnic groups such as the Ukrainians and Italians and Germans to see the plural ideal enshrined in the Constitution as one of Canada's fundamental characteristics. This may or may not be wise – like the Senate issue, it requires careful review – but it is worthy of serious discussion. Having left its "British century" behind, Canada may yet be embarking upon what Laurier prematurely labelled the "Canadian century." In an ideal world, this new age would be plural without being plagued by racism, on the one hand, or insistently majoritarian and conformist, on the other. Given that such utopias are unlikely to lie just around the next corner, one can only urge that all citizens of good will conduct an unending campaign for pluralism and tolerance.

Aboriginal issues must occupy a special place in western Canadian contributions to constitutional discussions. The hearings of the Manitoba Legislature's Constitutional Task Force in 1991 encountered strong popular support for immediate action on the concerns of Canada's Aboriginal people. Left-right or East-West politics played little part in this debate. The citizens who presented briefs were urging the completion of the unfinished business of the 1982 Constitution. The urgency has faded in the intervening years, but the issues remain important – and unresolved.

In the aftermath of the Aboriginal crisis at Oka, of the British Columbia court decision in the Gitksan and Wet'suwet'en lands case, the Ontario court ruling in the Temagami land case, and the Nova Scotia hunting rights trials, prairie Canadians cannot claim a unique interest in Aboriginal issues. However, they can claim to be acutely aware of Aboriginal concerns and to be in daily contact with Aboriginal people. Moreover, Aboriginal representatives have won a public hearing in the Prairies. To use the Manitoba example, Murray Sinclair, Tina Keeper, Tom Jackson, Phil Fontaine, Elijah Harper, and Ovide Mercredi are celebrities not only in the facile sense that they are media stars, but also because they have earned a degree of respect by their words and behaviour in difficult situations. Aboriginal issues have acquired a special resonance in prairie society; one might hope that prairie Canadians, particularly those who meet daily with Aboriginal people, can offer a degree of sensitivity and a helpful perspective when these very difficult cultural and political questions again secure national attention.

Canadians face important decisions. The economic restructuring that confronts the entire globe demands Canadian responses. The Pacific Rim nations at once command the attention of British Columbians and dispatch immigrants who have changed the character of that province. The American northwest, as rich and diverse as the two adjoining Canadian provinces, British Columbia and Alberta, raises the prospect of a transnational entity of a different kind; already a committee of civil servants has met to discuss the potential of this cross-border zone that they call Cascadia. Saskatchewan turns increasingly toward Alberta for support. Manitoba looks to Ottawa and Toronto for political understanding but also to the United States as an export market. The pressures on Confederation, in short, are as real in this part of the country as they are elsewhere.

There is no natural law that decrees the continued existence of a trans-continental country on the northern half of North America. Rather, political will alone sustains Canada. This will must be rallied every day. One can only hope that our compatriots in Quebec will see, as we in the Prairies do, convincing reasons to renew the homeland that has endured for so long.

As they reflect on such matters, let the Quebecois be assured about the attitudes of prairie residents who disputed the Meech Lake Accord and bilingualism in terms that seemed to disregard or even to deny the place of French-speaking citizens in this country. Too often, this impression was conveyed by media generalizations about "the West" and the "western attitude." Instead, Quebeckers should understand that many prairie residents (though not all, one hastens to add) were driven by concerns about a different political compass, one measured by left and right, not by hoary old notions concerning "the West" and "Quebec."

Many prairie social democrats have no wish to revisit the French-English, Roman Catholic–Protestant quarrels of an earlier day. Rather, they are determined to resist an international corporate agenda that serves the interests of great metropolises while dooming small countries and regions on the periphery to the status of ciphers. They saw the decentralizing contained in the Meech Lake Accord as an attempt to entrench a continental perspective in Canada's Constitution. Because these prairie social democrats place a high priority on the country's distinctiveness, they embrace a seemingly anti-American and leftist policy approach. This does not entail opposition to Quebec in Confederation.

Prairie "conservatives," that is, those who supported the Free Trade Agreement and the Meech Lake Accord, are not less-fervent nationalists or less-perceptive citizens than their social democratic compatriots. The difference between such conservatives and the social democrats, or between right and left, lies in their views of changing global economic circumstances. Those on the right believe that nothing should be permitted to stand in the way of Canadian adaptation to the "global economy." Far from dominating "the West," however, these advocates of the multinational corporate strategy probably constitute a minority of prairie citizens.

The "West," as a generalization about the contemporary prairie provinces, is simply misleading. As in the rest of Canada and, indeed, much of the developed world, the crucial litmus test involves immersion in a solution that combines global economic forces, market de-regulation, and privatization. Our political litmus paper establishes two possible responses: those who embrace, and those who resist, global market forces.

In Quebec, too, these divisions are pivotal. However, the strategies for approaching such questions differ in Quebec. There, the party system has established alternatives that focus on globalism and Quebec sovereignty. In the longer term, however, this choice may seem less than wise. An historic, and different, position has been to insist that the larger country – Canada (including Quebec and all the other prominent political communities, whether one imagines them as "nations," "provinces" or "regions," or in more limited terms) – gives greater clout in international cultural negotiations and produces a more tolerant and flexible social climate. If Quebec is to continue within Canada, and if Canada is to continue as a separate entity in North America, patriots in both (so this argument went) would do well to make common cause. Thus, left and north, like Quebec and north, appear to be similar directions on the new compass; the alternative is right and south, an ever-closer integration into one of the handful of remaining world empires.

NOTES

This is a revised version of an essay that was published in J.L. Granatstein and Kenneth McNaught, eds., *"English Canada" Speaks Out* (Toronto: Doubleday Canada, 1991).

1. Stephen Leacock, *My Discovery of the West: A Discussion of East and West in Canada* (Toronto: T. Allen, 1937), preface.
2. A Maritimer might well reply that westerners dominated the Mulroney Conservative government and, between 1988 and 1993, branches of the same party held power in the three prairie provinces. If they couldn't get their way during that conjuncture, what difference would a senate make?

Part Two:
Historical Articles on Dominant and Alternative Cultures

"Justice Systems" and Manitoba's Aboriginal People: An Historical Survey

Co-written with Associate Chief Justice A.C. Hamilton and Associate Chief Judge C.M. Sinclair

ABORIGINAL PEOPLE are playing an increasingly important role in every aspect of Canadian society. Moreover, their right to participate in decisions affecting their own communities seems now to be generally recognized. Nevertheless, their relations with the justice system have reached a point of crisis. To ensure that today's policies are grounded in a sound understanding of Aboriginal culture and, even more important, to ensure that Canadians come to terms with this crisis, one must review Aboriginal experience with legal authority and with systems of justice.

Until very recently, high-school and university textbooks treated Aboriginal history inappropriately or not at all. Thus, a 1971 study of eighty-eight books that most frequently appeared on Canadian history courses concluded that Aboriginal people were treated as part of the background to a European story.[1] Sometimes, this study noted, Aboriginal people were discussed in an introductory chapter on the environment and then relegated to a minor role. They might be enemies of Europe, as in the case of the Iroquois in New France, or allies, including Joseph Brant in the American Revolution and Tecumseh in the War of 1812, but rarely were they treated as political strategists or significant historical figures. This circumstance is now being corrected.

Manitoba's Aboriginal people have known three different justice regimes. The first, a product of custom and negotiation and experience, developed before the arrival of Europeans during the centuries when Aboriginal people inhabited this part of the Americas. The second, which commenced with the arrival of Europeans in the seventeenth century, did not end Aboriginal law but merely introduced English, Scottish, and French complements. The third began with Manitoba's entry into Confederation in 1870. Though it has remained essentially unchanged to the present, this third regime has had a devastating impact on Manitoba's Aboriginal people during the last four decades.

I. LAW IN THE PRE-CONTACT ABORIGINAL COMMUNITY

Aboriginal people have resided in this part of the globe for thousands of years, or hundreds of generations. Aboriginal legends speak of the original peoples being on this land from the time of its creation, from "time immemorial." Archaeological evidence of hearths at the forks of the Red and Assiniboine Rivers, of garden plots at Lockport near Selkirk on the Red River, of rock paintings in the Whiteshell, and of bison jumps in the Assiniboine River Valley near Brandon are merely the best-known physical evidence of this long occupation. As this evidence accumulates, scholars have sketched a picture of hunting and agriculture-based societies, of trade, and of effective environmental adaptations. The politics, diplomacy, and family relations of these communities are less evident, however, and require some elaboration.

Law in a traditional Aboriginal community was founded in unwritten conventions. It could be discerned in the treatment of such matters as relations with other nations, family problems, and disputes about behaviour and property. The rules became part of Aboriginal oral tradition and were passed from generation to generation. One can easily speak about these patterns in terms of "law" and "justice."

A brief description of customary law, drawn from oral histories and the few extant written histories, will underline that a distinct legal system existed in pre-contact Aboriginal history.[2] Ojibwa and Cree decision making involved the participation and consent of the community at large. Behaviour was regulated by ostracism, shame, and compensation for the victim's loss, even if only symbolic compensation was possible. Elders undertook the regular teaching of community values and warned offenders on behalf of the community. They publicly banished individuals who persisted in disturbing the peace. Elders might undertake to mediate dangerous disputes and to reconcile offenders with victims. In cases of grave threats or offences such as murder, physical punishment and even execution of the offender might be undertaken either by the community or by those who had been wronged. But in all instances the sanction of tribal elders was necessary.

A murder in the Eagle Hills in 1775-76 illustrates the practice. According to Matthew Cocking, the Hudson's Bay Company (HBC) trader at Cumberland House, who had heard the story from "Pedlar Henry," a quarrel had occurred among the Beaver Indians of the Eagle Hills (probably Cree in the area northwest of present-day Saskatoon). Cocking's report is worth close attention: "That no account has been recieved [sic] from the Beaver Indians, only from the reports of others they are not expected to come down even in the Summer, on account of a Quarrel having happened between them and some others last Winter. That an Indian was shot by another the first of this Winter at the upper Settlement, the Indian killed having murdered his Wife last Summer was the reason of the other's taking the same revenge, the Woman being his Sister: Tis supposed that the affair will stop here."[3]

Cocking's choice of words is significant. A man had "murdered" his wife. As a matter of "revenge," that man was "shot" by the woman's brother. Note that the latter's act of retaliation is not described as murder and that the traders assumed the "quarrel" had been settled.[4]

The role of elders and their regular use of shame and expulsion in Ojibwa, Assiniboine, and Cree society illustrate how "force," defined broadly to include mild sanctions, was used in these cultures. Roman Catholic missionary Father de Smet described how Assiniboine Indians in Manitoba and adjoining lands disciplined offenders in the hunt: "Their guns, their bows and arrows are broken, their lodges cut in pieces, their dogs killed, all their provisions and their hides are taken from them. If they are bold enough to resist the penalty, they are beaten with bows, sticks, and clubs."[5]

The Métis of Manitoba conducted their buffalo hunts in a fashion that reinforces de Smet's observations. Alexander Ross, a leading citizen of Red River, recorded the rules of a hunt in the 1840s:

1. No buffalo to be run on the Sabbath-day.
2. No party to fork off, lag behind, or go before, without permission.
3. No person or party to run buffalo before the general order.
4. Every captain with his men, in turn, to patrol the camp, and keep guard.
5. For the first trespass against these laws, the offender to have his saddle and bridle cut up.
6. For the second offence, the coat to be taken off the offender's back, and be cut up.
7. For the third offence, the offender to be flogged.
8. Any person convicted of theft, even to the value of a sinew, to be brought to the middle of the camp, and the crier to call out his or her name three times, adding the word "Thief," at each time.[6]

Crime and punishment became part of each Aboriginal group's oral

record, preserved by elders in story and legend. A British Columbia illustration will clarify the process. When the Gitksan-Wet'suwet'en Tribal
Council began its project to record traditional laws, the elders had trouble
understanding what was sought by the researchers under the title of "law."
Eventually, the word was translated as *ada'awk*, which means "history" in
literal translation. In those societies, each of the major social units, called
a "house," has its own history, which is passed down from one chief to the
next. This history establishes continuity from past to present, asserts a
claim to resources and territory, and recounts the story of its relations
with other houses. Each member of the house must act in conformity with
the principles of the *ada'awk*; thus, for the Gitksan and Wet'suwet'en, principles of historical record are principles of behaviour and can be translated as "law."[7] This perspective was expressed by Delgam Uukw, a Gitksan
chief, to the British Columbia Supreme Court:

> By following the law, the power flows from the land to the people through the
> Chief; by using the wealth of the territory, the House feasts its Chief so he can
> properly fulfil the law. This cycle has been repeated on my land for thousands of
> years. The histories of my House are always being added to. My presence in this
> courtroom today will add to my House's power, as it adds to the power of the
> other Gitksan and Wet'suwet'en Chiefs who will appear here or who will witness
> the proceedings. All of our roles, including yours, will be remembered in the
> histories that will be told by my grandchildren. Through the witnessing of all the
> histories, century after century, we have exercised our jurisdiction.[8]

As in British Columbia, so in Manitoba, each Aboriginal group had its
history and its codes of behaviour.

The existence of social norms, the use of force and ostracism to enforce
them, and the existence of a group – the elders – accustomed to asserting
the integrity of such rules underlay the Aboriginal approach to justice
before Europeans arrived in this part of the world.

II. ABORIGINAL AND EUROPEAN LEGAL REGIMES DURING THE ERA
OF PEACEFUL CO-EXISTENCE, 1600 TO 1870

The arrival of Europeans in the northern half of North America in the
seventeenth century set events in motion that changed the context of
Aboriginal law, though not the customs and laws themselves. This can be
described as a second "justice regime" in Manitoba.

Aboriginal people and European newcomers lived in peace in Manitoba for more than 200 years, from the early seventeenth to the mid-
nineteenth century. They established mutually satisfactory economic relations while dwelling in essentially separate worlds. In the view of the
Aboriginal people themselves, the Europeans dwelt on the rim of an

Aboriginal universe. As the English missionary John West discovered to his surprise, the Aboriginal people in the area around the forks of the Red and Assiniboine Rivers "consider themselves the standard of excellence. In their fancied superior knowledge they are often heard to remark, when conversing with a European, 'You are almost as clever as an Indian.'"[9]

Seen from the European perspective, from within the palisades of a trading post or from the middle of a trading canoe, Aboriginal people were crucial to all activities in the region, at least until the early decades of the nineteenth century. Food supply, trade patterns, diplomacy, even marriage and family matters, were often controlled by the Aboriginal inhabitants of this land. Europeans, far from dictating the course of events, negotiated to secure their own means of existence. This balance shifted as the decades passed, however, and by the early nineteenth century Europeans in eastern North America were sufficiently numerous to have established rules that favoured their interests. In the western interior, it was slightly different. From the early 1600s to 1870, the Aboriginal people of prairie Canada lived within a society defined by traditional Aboriginal laws, while Europeans in the region increasingly demanded a justice system for themselves akin to those in Britain and Europe.

The customary seasonal cycle of resource harvesting continued among Aboriginal people after the introduction of the European fur trade into northwest North America. Small family-based bands dispersed during the depths of winter to hunt game (and gather furs) and congregated on the edge of lakes or on the plains in the spring and summer when food was plentiful to attend to ceremonial and religious affairs. European traders simply fit into the accustomed annual cycle when they exchanged European goods for furs and food.

Trade did not result in Aboriginal dependence on Europeans. One Mandan chief, commenting on the members of the Lewis and Clark expedition who travelled through his land (south of present-day Winnipeg) in the early nineteenth century, said that there were "only two sensible men among them, the Worker of Iron and the Maker of Guns," and concluded that there was so little strength among the rest that his "young men on horseback would do for them as they would do for so many wolves."[10]

The arrival of increasing numbers of traders after France ceded its interest in Canada to British rule in 1763 was part of a significant change in Aboriginal circumstances in the western interior. Increasingly, trading posts were erected near Indian hunting territories. Europeans assumed direct control of the fur and goods exchange, thus eliminating Aboriginal middlemen, and took Aboriginal women as partners, thereby establishing mixed-race families. The Europeans also contributed to the growing trade in guns and horses that altered the Aboriginal diplomatic and military balance in the interior of the continent. European diseases, too, devastated a number of Aboriginal communities during the next century. Despite great changes, however, Aboriginal cultures continued as they had for centuries. As Archbishop Taché commented in 1868 about the Aboriginal peoples of this land, "all of them . . . retain their original social customs."[11]

Aboriginal Status and International Law
If Aboriginal customary law remained unaltered in this era, the European legal context of North American society was revised in two important respects. First, the application of principles of international law and sovereignty affected Aboriginal tenure. Second, local legal arrangements made by fur-trading companies and by the settlement at Red River also had an effect upon the justice system.

"Discovery," that is, the planting of flags and the declaration of territorial claims, did not establish European ownership of Canada.[12] Instead, early European writers on international law acknowledged that Aboriginal nations had status in international society. This status could be subverted by negotiation or conquest. This is not to suggest that, in all cases, Aboriginal nations retained internationally acknowledged sovereignty after their territory had been "acquired" or claimed by imperial powers. Rather, it implies that Aboriginal nations had the right to be treated under the domestic law of the colonizing nation in a way that respected either their status in international law *or* the treaty or cession commitments that they had negotiated, or both.[13]

The crucial agreements shaping British-Aboriginal arrangements after the fall of New France to British control were the Royal Proclamation of 1763 and the various treaties signed in the next few decades. The Proclamation was part of Britain's assumption of control over New France. It was precipitated by a political crisis, an Aboriginal siege at Detroit led by Chief Pontiac. The Proclamation forbade white settlement beyond a "proclamation line" and it confirmed principles by which Aboriginal-European relations should be conducted. Britain declared that the Crown *must* formally extinguish Indian rights, that the Crown *alone* could undertake such obligations, that *private* interests could not extinguish Aboriginal claims to land, and that negotiations for the surrender of Aboriginal title must occur at an *open* assembly with the full consent of all the people. It should be underlined that, in legal terms, the Royal Proclamation did not establish Aboriginal rights in North America. Rather, as James Crawford has written and the Supreme Court of Canada has stated, it *assumed* their existence.[14] Moreover, the Proclamation did not create a treaty tradition but merely confirmed a practice that had begun in the eastern colonies in previous generations. It was logical and natural that the British government would extend this practice to another North American colony.

The Application of European Law
The second "justice regime" in Manitoba was also evident in the daily give and take of trade, marriage, property claims, disputes over personal goods, and relations between employer and employee. At times, European and Aboriginal people accepted the need for adaptation of inherited legal practices. On other occasions they employed legal principles unique to one culture or the other.

The emergence of marriage and family conventions in the eighteenth and early nineteenth centuries demonstrates the extraordinary nature of the Manitoba legal "frontier." As historian Sylvia Van Kirk has explained, inter-marriage between fur traders and Indian or Métis women was fundamental to the growth of a distinct society:

The norm for sexual relationships in fur-trade society was not casual, promiscuous encounters but the development of marital unions which gave rise to distinct family units. . . . Fur-trade society developed its own marriage rite, marriage *à la façon du pays*, which combined both Indian and European marriage customs. In this, the fur-trade society of Western Canada appears to have been exceptional. In most other areas of the world, sexual contact between European men and native women had usually been illicit in nature and essentially peripheral to the white man's trading or colonizing ventures. In the Canadian West, however, alliances with Indian women were the central social aspect of the fur traders' progress across the country.[15]

These aspects of the second justice regime represented a merger of two cultures, not the dominance of one over another. Fur traders offered substantial presents to the parents of their brides; Aboriginal families, in turn, accepted political and economic responsibility for their new allies. When, near the end of this era, some fur traders raised problems by threatening to abandon their families, the HBC even instituted a law requiring that they "make such provision for their [families'] future maintenance, more particularly for that of the children, as circumstances may reasonably warrant and the means of the individual permit."[16]

Both Europeans and Aboriginal people believed that serious crimes such as murder demanded immediate and equivalent retaliation. We have already noted Matthew Cocking's report on the retaliatory shooting among Aboriginal people at the Eagle Hills in 1775-76. A striking example of a comparable European murder occurred at Cumberland House in 1796. The North West Company employees at that post suspected two recently arrived Swampy Cree men of having killed a Company employee at Isle à la Crosse. The Nor'Westers shot one of the two Cree as he attempted to evade their "arrest" and, having bound the other, threw him beside the corpse in an attempt to win a confession. Though this failed, "they then made him confess everything with the rope about his Neck, which he did, and informed him of every one who was accomplices with him – he said that he was the Sole cause of the Death of the Canadian, and seemed perfectly satisfied that he deserved this ignominious Death." He was hanged immediately. The two bodies were dragged outside the stockade and left as a lesson to others. Men at the nearby HBC post interred the bodies on the following day. According to a trader, the local Indians appeared "very much terrified and shocked, never seeing a [sic] hearing of the like before." This is an unlikely assertion. Rather, the fact that there is no record of Indian retaliation for the Cumberland House "executions" of 1796 may illustrate that the deaths had been seen as balancing an account. As historian Paul Thistle comments, swift retaliation by the victims' relatives would have been the rule just a few years earlier.[17]

The deaths at Cumberland House in 1796 illustrated the sense of insecurity that prevailed among European traders in Manitoba. The Europeans clearly understood the limits of their own authority in an essentially Aboriginal land. The deaths also demonstrated that, though they were prepared to delay briefly in order to secure a confession, the Europeans did not shrink from murder in order to intimidate Aboriginal people in the vicinity.[18] One might conclude from Paul Thistle's detailed study of the Cumberland House district that the Indians lived according to their own rules, the fur traders accepted Company discipline, and moments of disagreement in Indian-European relations were sometimes resolved by force, sometimes not.

Under the HBC Charter of 1670, the Company itself could enact laws for the "good government" of its territory and could judge Company personnel "in all causes whether civil or criminal, according to the laws of this Kingdom." Thus, at least for the HBC and its employees, the law of the western interior was the English law of 1670 and its subsequent development. The fall of New France caused some confusion because the new administration of Canada, according to Britain's Royal Proclamation of 1763, specifically excluded the "Indian Territory" west of the province of Quebec. Within two years, a law was passed (the first of several in the next few decades) to provide for the arrest of offenders in Indian Territory and their conveyance to the nearest British colony for trial.[19] Whether the HBC Charter or the laws of Canada prevailed in the West during the next century is unclear. Recognizing the problem, the British Parliament passed the Canada Jurisdiction Act in 1803, but that statute provided no better direction.[20]

The death in 1816 of twenty of Selkirk's colonists and of the colony governor, Robert Semple, at the hands of Cuthbert Grant and his Métis soldiers, who were allegedly under orders from the North-West Company, raised a public outcry in Britain and Canada for settlement of the jurisdictional question. The HBC introduced laws and courts that applied to the European inhabitants of these territories, and especially to the growing settlement at the Red River (under the title of Assiniboia), while the rest of the western interior was left in a kind of legal limbo until 1870.[21] Within this "vacuum," it need hardly be added, Aboriginal law prevailed as it had done for centuries.

The HBC-sponsored legal authority inaugurated an interesting and unusual era of experimentation in European-Aboriginal judicial relations. The courts in the district known as Assiniboia (approximately southern Manitoba) developed slowly. At first, Indians in the district were not subject to this jurisdiction. Thus, the murder of one Indian by another in 1824 produced a trial, a reprimand from the governor, but no punishment. After the reorganization of local government in 1835, however, a regular police and judicial system was set in place and all residents of the community, including Indians, became subject to this jurisdiction. A resolution of the Council declared in 1837 that "the evidence of an Indian be considered valid and be admitted as such in all Courts of this settlement," implying that Indian testimony had not been accepted before.[22] Local magistrates, several of whom were Métis, presided over the district courts. A higher court, the General Quarterly Court of Assiniboia, was instituted as well, and it, too, had a number of Métis magistrates. In short, a distinctively Manitoban mix of European and Aboriginal legal cultures was evolving in Red River.

Inevitably, enforcement was a problem in a world where armed Métis horsemen constituted the single most powerful military force. As long as the HBC could count on Imperial troops for support, as in 1846 to 1848 and 1857 to 1861, its rule was secure. But when left to its own devices, the Company could not control the Settlement, let alone the entire western interior. The first casualty of this weakness was the Company's very monopoly over trade, the crucial gift of the Charter of 1670, which fell by default after the trial of Guillaume Sayer in 1849. Sayer was prosecuted in a Company court and found guilty of trading illegally for furs. The Company did not have the strength that would have enabled the court to impose a punishment. Its weakness permitted the armed Métis on the courthouse steps to exult that trade was free, "Le commerce est libre."

Laws concerning bounties for wolves and the placing of flags over holes cut in the river ice (to warn horse and rider) could be enforced without much difficulty in the Red River Settlement. However, the big legal and political issues – sovereignty, property rights, language, and religion – became increasingly difficult as the pace of economic development quickened. News that the territory would cease to be ruled by the HBC began to circulate in the 1860s, but neither the British nor Canadian governments discussed the matter with the residents of the Northwest. Then, in 1869, "Canadians" arrived from the East and the rumours increased.

When Louis Riel and his Métis allies challenged the Canadian government's survey and barred the entry of the Canadian Governor, William McDougall, in the autumn of 1869, they were merely demonstrating what had become evident in the preceding generation: without the presence of troops in Red River, HBC law depended on the consent of Rupert's Land residents. That consent was no longer forthcoming.

Historian W.L. Morton described the Métis action of 1869-70 as a "resistance," not a rebellion. His interpretation declared that a power vacuum existed in the Red River Settlement. British, Canadian, and Company claims to sovereignty over this territory had ceased to have any force. Riel had stepped into the void and established a legitimate "provisional government."[23] It cannot be denied that the Riel government negotiated the terms by which Manitoba entered the Canadian confederation. Its delegates secured some important gains and sustained reverses. Louis Riel described the legislation that sealed the bargain, the Manitoba Act, as a "treaty," in order to convey his view that the deal had the character of an arrangement between "nations."

Prime Minister John A. Macdonald, by contrast, regarded the Manitoba Act as a domestic rearrangement, a transfer of responsibility within the British household. The existence of Manitoba was a political necessity, in his view, part of the price paid to acquire once and for all an extraordinary land and an ocean-to-ocean future for the new nation. The views of the two men were never reconciled.

In the legislation arranging for its assumption of control over the Northwest, Canada made several promises concerning Aboriginal people. First, it agreed to accept responsibility for compensation offered to Indians for land lost to incoming settlers. Second, it accepted the obligation of protectir*g* Indian interests in the new order. Third, it promised 1.4 million acres to be divided among "the children of the half-breed heads of families" as a step "towards the extinguishment of the Indian Title." Fourth, it accepted a number of clauses that were sought by the Métis or their representatives as the means of their community's survival, including provincial status itself, the use of French in courts and Legislature, an Upper House (that is, a bicameral Legislature) based on the Quebec model, and a guarantee concerning denominational schools.[24] In each case, the promises were of considerable importance to the Aboriginal people. Moreover, the fact that the Manitoba Act was passed by the Canadian Parliament and then re-enacted by the Imperial Parliament in 1871 ensured it a status greater than that of ordinary legislation.[25]

Two hundred years of relative peace and co-operation between Aboriginal and European peoples had been distinguished by continuity within each community and two sets of legal assumptions. Manitoba's justice system between 1600 and 1870 consisted of two distinct bodies of rules, penalties, and enforcement mechanisms. This flexibility ended with the creation of the Canadian province of Manitoba on 15 July 1870.

III. THE JUSTICE REGIME UNDER CANADIAN RULES, 1870 TO 1990

The third justice regime differed drastically in official character from its predecessor. Indeed, all the rules changed for Manitoba's Aboriginal inhabitants. After Canada assumed responsibility for the West, its administrators actually attempted to take control of the lives of Aboriginal people. Their approach relied on three key steps: first, the signing of treaties which transferred legal control of vast tracts of land to the federal government; second, passage of an "Indian Act" which granted absolute power over Indian people to the federal government and its agents; third, the separation, in administration and legal status, of Métis from Indians. The Métis were then pushed aside by incoming settlers, neglected both by Ottawa and by the province.

The Canadian prairies entered a global economy in the last half of the nineteenth century. Within one generation, the world price of grain and the international forces that affected the local economy had become crucial matters for prairie dwellers. Canadian immigrants to the western interior now set the rules in local politics. Aboriginal people were governed by legislation originating in Ottawa and by exceptionally powerful local bureaucrats. The two communities, Aboriginal and white, reserve and town, had few points of political intersection.

How had this revolution happened? The virtual extinction of the buffalo was pivotal. Suddenly, between 1870 and 1882, the foundation of the plains economy for millennia – a foundation of greater relative importance than oil or electricity today – was no more. Moreover, the context of Aboriginal society had always been established by the land itself. Now, private property and cultivation and cattle grazing and railways changed forever the place of the land in Aboriginal culture. In earlier days, Aboriginal people understood that government and its laws flowed from daily life itself; henceforth, however, an alien and distant institution would determine the rules of Aboriginal existence.

Both Aboriginal and non-Aboriginal people recognized the importance of establishing an understanding between the two societies. Treaties were the foundation of the new order. The key documents for Manitoba, Treaties One through Six, were signed between 1871 and 1876. Treaty Ten followed, as did adhesions of individuals and groups. Though they were based upon the principles elaborated in the Royal Proclamation of 1763, the prairie treaties also reflected the concern of the new Canadian government to control the pace of development and to ensure peaceful occupation. The treaties guaranteed reserves where Indian people would be free from European incursion. They also guaranteed the payment of annuities, the right to hunt and fish in traditional use areas, and transitional economic assistance, including schools and equipment. In exchange, Canada would assume absolute sovereignty over other land. There is much debate about the character and purpose of these treaties. Were they real estate transactions, once-and-for-all purchases that had no further implications beyond the words on the page and the transfer of "ownership"? Or were they alliances, ongoing relationships that would have to be renewed and reviewed as circumstances changed?

Earlier treaties had assumed Aboriginal self-government. After 1874, however, when federal Indian legislation was declared to be in force in Manitoba, Canadian authorities argued that Aboriginal people in the West bargained away not only their lands but also their powers over local affairs when they signed the treaties. Thus, the treaties were not what they seemed nor, indeed, what the Indians had accepted in the 1871 and 1873 negotiations. By an act of the federal Parliament, unilaterally and without Indian knowledge, Ottawa had drastically altered the circumstances of Aboriginal life.[26]

The new justice system, as represented by the Indian Act and supplementary legislation, soon was being employed to prevent Aboriginal people from expressing their traditional beliefs, from pursuing their traditional economy, and from asserting their political rights as individuals or as members of Canadian society. In every aspect of life, from criminal law to education and religious expression, from hunting to agriculture, from voting to the use of lawyers, Aboriginal people ran into regulations that restricted their freedom. Far from simply "civilizing" Indians, as had been the apparent purpose of government policy in the first half of the nineteenth century, the new system actually utilized aggressive, coercive methods to bring about Aboriginal assimilation.

The use of Canadian law to control Aboriginal education and religion illustrates the depth of the cultural divide between the two communities. European and Aboriginal Canadians recognized that schools were influential cultural institutions. In the treaty discussions of the 1870s, Indian negotiators had sought and obtained promises from the government that schools would be provided on their reserves. By choosing to ask for schools and to send their children to them, these leaders were acknowledging that their people must adapt to the European Canadian cultural milieu. They were not agreeing to become European Canadians or to cease to be Aboriginal peoples. Instead, they were accepting an economic transition and agreeing to learn the arts of communication associated with writing, print, and the telegraph.

The fact that Aboriginal people voluntarily made this choice is important. Government records contain numerous Aboriginal requests for schools. As Dan Kennedy, later an Assiniboine chief, recalled, he was told at the age of twelve that he must learn "the whiteman's magic art of writing, 'the talking paper.'"[27] Despite their wish to learn these communication skills, many Aboriginal people did not want lessons in the Christian religion. As soon as possible, they believed, their own people would become teachers. As they had done in the past, they wished to control the values that were being communicated to their children.

Even those Aboriginal parents who chose to send their children to schools would not have expected that the curriculum included a great deal more than reading, writing, and arithmetic; or that the children might be taught to hate their former culture and to reject their families. However, the Annual Report of the Department of Indian Affairs in 1889 explained the government's purpose in just such terms: "The boarding school dissociates the Indian child from the deleterious home influences to which he would otherwise be subjected. It reclaims him from the uncivilized state in which he has been brought up. It brings him into contact from day to day with all that tends to effect a change in his views and habits of life. By precept and example he is taught to endeavour to excel in what will be most useful to him."[28] In 1894, the federal government passed legislation that provided for the arrest and conveyance to school of truant children and for fines or jail terms for parents who resisted.

Indian agents (civil servants who supervised Indian reserves) were given the power to commit children under sixteen to such schools and to keep them there until they were eighteen. The province of Manitoba did not introduce compulsory schooling for non-Indians until 1916, twenty-two years later. As a way of ensuring that the most compelling cultural messages were delivered to the children, and of keeping government costs to a minimum, the government increasingly relied on missionary societies, particularly of the Methodist, Presbyterian, Anglican, and Roman Catholic churches, to operate residential schools. The harshness of this cultural experiment is only now beginning to be comprehended in the larger Canadian society.

The economic crisis associated with the near-extinction of buffalo, the political struggles caused by the Indian Act, and the conflicts over educational policy all caused tension and conflict in Aboriginal communities. These anxieties were made worse, in the view of Aboriginal elders, by the growing struggle between government and Indian over Aboriginal religious expression. For many elders, the freedom to worship in traditional ways was crucial to Aboriginal cultural survival. However, the Canadian government made it a crime to practise traditional prairie and British Columbia Aboriginal religious ceremonies, including the Thirst Dance, the Sun Dance, and the Potlatch. The law that introduced the religious prohibition was an 1884 amendment to the Indian Act banning "give-away ceremonies." Another amendment in 1895 prohibited "wounding or mutilation" ceremonies (associated with plains Indian rituals by uncomprehending non-Aboriginal observers). Yet another amendment, in 1906, revised slightly in 1914, forbade dancing of every description. The rules were eliminated only in the Indian Act amendments of 1951.[29]

The history of government and church opposition to the religious ceremonies, and of Aboriginal resistance, has been documented with precision.[30] Aboriginal leaders showed consistency and patience as they fought to retain the right to worship in their own way. Their letters to the Department of Indian Affairs deplored the moral dilemma in which they had been placed: obey either the secular law of Canada or the law of God. Thus, in 1908, Joe Ma-ma-gway-see wrote in defence of the Aboriginal right to hold a Sun Dance: "The law you make is of this world and we follow the law of God. If you stop everything we do we may as well go without the law of God. . . . I have never seen him but it is in his command to us and you are trying to stop it."[31]

Aboriginal leaders understood full well the legal implications of the government ban. One of the great traditional chiefs of that generation of negotiators, Thunderchild of the Plains Cree, explained his case in his own language to Reverend Edward Ahenakew, also a Cree, who then translated it:

Can things go well in a land where freedom of worship is a lie, a hollow boast? To each nation is given the light by which it knows God, and each finds its own way to express the longing to serve Him. It is astounding to me that a man should be stopped from trying in his own way to express his need or his thankfulness to God. If a nation does not do what is right according to its own understanding, its power is worthless.

I have listened to the talk of the white men's clergy, and it is the same in principle as the talk of our Old Men, whose wisdom came not from books but from life and from God's earth. Why has the white man no respect for the religion that was given to us, when we respect the faith of other nations? . . . The white men have offered us two forms of their religion – the Roman Catholic and the Protestant – but we in our Indian lands had our own religion. Why is that not accepted too? It is the worship of one God, and it was the strength of our people for centuries.

I do not want to fight the white man's religion. I believe in freedom of worship, and though I am not a Christian, I have never forgotten God. What is it that has helped me and will help my grandchildren but belief in God?[32]

Other laws and regulations also had an effect on religious expression. The government imposed a "pass system," which disrupted religious ceremonies by preventing extended families dispersed on different reserves from meeting together. The pass system had been discussed by government officials in 1884-85 in response to the diplomatic campaigns for Aboriginal solidarity led by Big Bear and other Saskatchewan chiefs. It was imposed by a local agent without senior government approval in 1885. As well as a means of restricting dancing, the pass system was used to control or prevent parent-child meetings at residential schools and to undercut political activities. Though the pass system was enforced fairly strictly by the North West Mounted Police in the 1880s, neither Indians nor police accepted the legality of the prohibition for long. It was a makeshift policy, intended to control and monitor people's movements, and it would have been thrown out of any court. No less an authority than Sir John A. Macdonald recognized its illegality, and yet he thought that the introduction of the system was "in the highest degree desirable." The prime minister made the damning admission that "no punishment for breaking bounds can be inflicted and in case of resistance on the grounds of Treaty rights should not be insisted on."[33] Despite attempts by the Indian Affairs staff to enforce the restrictions, the pass system fell into disuse by the opening decades of the twentieth century.

Destruction of Aboriginal culture was associated, in the government's view, with the image of a new type of Aboriginal citizen, one who worked and thought and spoke in the country's common cultural "language," including its economic assumptions. Yet, Aboriginal culture was not hostile to field crops and animal raising. Indeed, Aboriginal people in northern Ontario and the prairie provinces had earlier seized the opportunity to become farmers for the obvious reason that they faced an economic crisis. Unfortunately, a combination of climatic reverses, inconsistent government financial support, and disastrous policy decisions destroyed the hope of Aboriginal agriculture.[34]

The legal system itself played a large part in this episode. The law was used to forbid Indian sales of produce off the reserve without the approval of the Indian agent. It later prevented Indians from mortgaging reserve lands in order to purchase farm implements. Such controls undermined the very initiative that the government claimed it wished to inculcate. Aboriginal people, according to the expressed intent of Indian Affairs officials, could not be permitted to develop their agricultural operations beyond "peasant farming." As one policy declaration put it, the government should "restrict the area cultivated by each Indian to within such limits as will enable him to carry on his operations by the application of his own personal labour and the employment of such simple implements as he would likely be able to command if entirely thrown upon his own resources, rather than to encourage farming on a scale to necessitate the employment of expensive labour-saving machinery."[35]

Indians would have to walk their fields with hoe and scythe before they could purchase binders and reapers. By the end of the nineteenth century, Aboriginal hopes for agriculture had been dashed. Residents on the reserves had been reduced to garden plot and subsistence farming. The relative weakness of reserve agriculture created a new crisis when prairie settlement began to boom in the late 1890s. The demand for farmlands, when combined with European Canadian cultural values concerning the "proper" use of land, posed new threats to the Aboriginal reserves. As local pressure on the prairies increased, laws were revised to permit, first, rental of reserve lands to white farmers and, second, sale of these lands by the Department of Indian Affairs to local farmers. Though this story will take years to unravel, one scholar estimates that half of the land allocated to reserves in southern Saskatchewan – 270,000 of 520,000 acres – was sold between 1896 and 1928.[36]

Every Manitoban should be told at least one chapter in the provincial story of Aboriginal land surrenders. This case concerns the Aboriginal community situated along the Red River between Lower Fort Garry and Lake Winnipeg. The Indian settlement in this area had been recognized in the Selkirk treaty of 1817 and was led for nearly half a century by one of the signatories of that treaty, Chief Peguis. Under the title of the St. Peter's "Indian Settlement," a large tract of this land was set aside as the home of nearly 2,000 Aboriginal people in the Stone Fort Treaty, known as Treaty One, in 1871. However, the pressure for "development" of this prime agricultural land and the uncertain status of many river-bank lots that had been granted years before by Peguis and later sold to non-Indians produced legal disputes in the late nineteenth century. In 1906, the federal government appointed a Royal Commission headed by the Chief Justice of the Manitoba Court of Appeal, Hector Howell, to investigate the disputes. Rather than investigate, Howell suggested that the solution to the problem was simply to move the Indians. A series of rigged meetings of questionable legality followed. The campaign for surrender of the reserve, led by men who wished to speculate in forthcoming land sales, was abetted by insider trading in lands by government officials, bribe payments to Indians, and a rigged vote among St. Peter's residents.

Having been cheated out of the land that had been theirs for more than a century, the St. Peter's Indians waged a campaign for its restoration. A provincial Royal Commission reviewed the circumstances of the surrender and concluded in 1912 that "the Surrender was not only voidable but void, could not be ratified and was not so ratified."[37] Nonetheless, the federal government chose not to intervene. Instead, it confirmed the allocation of a distant tract on the Fisher River (the present Peguis Reserve) and enacted the St. Peter's Reserve Act in 1916 to validate legal titles possessed by the purchasers of land on the old reserve.[38] Despite the protests of the St. Peter's band, the case was closed, at least as far as the government was concerned.

The St. Peter's case was not unique. Manitoba chiefs contended in 1978 that no fewer than twenty-five bands in the province had not received their full land allotment under the terms of their treaties.[39] Many of these surrenders seem to have been marked by "moralistic, self-righteous, and dictatorial" actions by government officials and the wrongful extinguishment of Aboriginal land claims, as one historian concluded after investigating the disappearance of the Turtle Mountain Dakota reserve.[40]

Aboriginal people spoke out many times against such injustices. However, just as law could be used to forbid a religious ceremony or an economic initiative, so it could crush a movement of political resistance. The Canadian government effectively weakened Aboriginal advocates throughout the period of the "third justice system."

The government also used the treaties to undermine Aboriginal sovereignty. Chiefs, who had been independent in the pre-1870 era, were regarded as agents of the federal administration in the new order. Alexander Morris, a lieutenant-governor of Manitoba in the 1870s, suggested to the government that the chiefs "should be strongly impressed with the belief that they are officers of the Crown, and that it is their duty to see that the Indians of their tribes obey the provisions of the treaties." He argued that it would be advantageous to the government "to possess so large a number of Indian officials, duly recognized as such, and who can be inspired with a proper sense of their responsibility to the Government."[41]

After the passage of the Indian Act, the government had much greater power over Aboriginal political activity. It controlled the decision over who could be admitted to membership in the political community: an Indian was someone designated by federal law as an Indian. It also controlled the process by which leaders were selected. Traditional chiefs could be removed. White Indian agents regulated the meetings of band councils and the elections of chiefs and councillors, and were given the powers of a stipendiary magistrate or police magistrate in respect to the Indian Act. Moreover, the agent could suspend Indians who, in his view, had conducted their family relations badly. Finally, the agent could control the band's economic planning.

The assumption of the original Indian Act was that, as they gained experience with European Canadian life, Indians would want to leave their bands and join the larger society. The formal transfer would occur when they acquired the franchise. However, very few Indians followed this path. In 1920, as a result, the Act was amended to give the federal cabinet power to take away Indian status from an Indian family head (and family) and to make enfranchisement compulsory. This clause was repealed in 1922, reinstated in 1933, and finally dropped in 1951. It illustrated that the destruction of Indian culture and the control of political decisions remained at the heart of federal government policy in the twentieth century. As the department's Deputy Minister, Duncan Campbell Scott, wrote, "Our object is to continue until there is not a single Indian in Canada that has not been absorbed into the body politic, and there is no Indian question, and no Indian Department."[42]

Manitoba Indians rejected the assimilative goals of the federal government. The Indian Association of Manitoba, led by, among others, Tommy Prince of Scanterbury, a decorated war veteran, called in 1947 for the repeal of the Indian Act and a return by both parties to the original treaties.[43] The key Aboriginal political goal was self-government. The secretary of the Fort Alexander Catholic Association told the Joint Committee reviewing the Indian Act that "much self-reliance and an urge to progress would ensue . . . if . . . more and more power was left to the council for management of the local affairs with the friendly cooperation of the Indian agent."[44]

The Métis

The Métis, despite their Aboriginal origins, were separated from Indians by the numbered treaties and the Indian Act and followed a very different course. Métis struggles over land in the Red River Valley in the decade after the Manitoba Resistance of 1869-70 produced disagreements that have been raised in the courts in the present day. Certainly, there has never been a secure settlement of outstanding differences between Métis people and the larger Manitoba society.

Definition of the term *Métis* is complicated. Though the label applied to children of mixed European and Aboriginal parentage, even this generalization is misleading. In the nineteenth century, a Métis might also be an individual who occupied a position as an economic or cultural intermediary between the two societies. Thus, mixed-race individuals who lived and hunted with Indians, or who accepted a plot of land in St. Peter's Mission on the Red River, might well be seen as Indians, but, if they served as translators or freighters and lived in a farm-based parish nearer the Forks, they might be regarded as Métis.

Language also played a role in attribution of identity. This meant not only Aboriginal and European language usage, however, but whether one employed in daily life the European-Aboriginal language combinations known as Bungi and Michif.

Religion, too, could distinguish Aboriginal from Métis identity, just as it separated English-speaking Protestant mixed-race households from French-speaking Roman Catholic "Métis" families. After the 1870s, former Indians who had lost their status under the Indian Act (which was the case for Indian women who married European Canadian or "non-status" men until the act was changed in the 1980s) also complicated the Métis category.

In the early twentieth century, family networks, political forces, and group consciousness combined to select those who wished to maintain a Métis identity. From that time, a significant number of Canadians have identified themselves as Métis. This has acquired political relevance since the 1982 revision of the Constitution of Canada that recognized "Métis" as a distinct category of Aboriginal person.[45]

It will be apparent that the history of the families themselves has been crucial in the evolution of a Métis consciousness. The Métis decided to tell their story in the early twentieth century because they believed the histories then available, mainly by English Canadians, did not do them justice. Auguste-Henri de Trémaudan's *Histoire de la nation métisse dans l'ouest canadien* was published in 1936.[46] In a foreword to the work, the Historical Committee of L'Union Nationale Métisse Saint-Joseph de Manitoba explained its purpose: "The Métis owed to themselves, and to those who have gone before, a chronicle that will inspire in the new generation of French-Canadian Métis a pride in their ancestry and their past. The knowledge of these facts will enable them to hold their heads high and say, 'This is our land. It has the right to our love, loyalty and life. For it, our fathers suffered and triumphed. By it, they marked the path of our national future.'"[47]

The history of Manitoba's Métis people began in conflict and was followed by neglect. In the 1870s, Winnipeg was likened to an armed camp that denied peaceable access to French-speaking citizens of mixed race.[48] As Lieutenant-Governor Archibald commented in 1871, the Métis were concerned "not so much, I believe by the dread about their land allotment as by the persistent ill-usage of such of them as have ventured from time to time into Winnipeg from the disbanded volunteers and newcomers who fill the town. Many of them actually have been so beaten and outraged that they feel as if they were living in a state of slavery. They say that the bitter hatred of these people is a yoke so intolerable that they would gladly escape it by any sacrifice."[49]

A 1959 government report by Jean H. Lagassé concluded that heredity (some degree of Indian ancestry) and a way of life (associated with poverty and with proximity to Indian communities) still distinguished a group of Manitobans as Métis. It argued that the Métis were an important component (nearly 24,000) of the provincial population, and that it would be "helpful to re-establish the solidarity of the Métis as an ethnic group. It would link the people of the fringe settlements with a past of which they could be proud. It would give them a group with which they could feel at home and through that group a place in modern society. Some Métis parents told the research office that they had never revealed their Métis background to their children." The main recommendations of the study were based on the conclusions that Métis, like Indians, had a lower standard of living than other Canadians and that new policies were necessary to address their problems.[50]

Aboriginal people sustained serious blows in the eighty years after Confederation. They lost not only their traditional economy but also, thanks to an extraordinary series of official interventions, their political and religious autonomy. Though some bands managed to avoid the long arm of Canadian bureaucracy, most felt the increasing pressure brought about by changes in their legal status.

The Franchise and the Constitution

The most important barrier to Aboriginal participation in the wider society was denial of the franchise. Manitoba's Aboriginal people, at least the hundreds who lived within the boundaries of the "postage stamp province" in 1870-71, including the inhabitants of the large community in St. Peter's Parish, possessed the right to vote in the provincial election of 1870. Like their fellow Manitobans, they had only to be "householders," meaning "master or chief of a household." A statute of 1871 introduced a formal property qualification (a voter must own property worth $100 one year before the election or, in the case of tenants, pay a yearly rental of at least twenty dollars), but Aboriginal people retained the franchise.[51] However, Prime Minister Macdonald's administration passed a federal franchise law in 1885 that changed the Aboriginal right to participate in elections. The Act permitted certain Indians to vote by providing that the word *person* meant "male person," including an Indian, but disqualifying "Indians in Manitoba, British Columbia, Keewatin and the North-West Territories, and any Indian on any reserve elsewhere in Canada who is not in possession and occupation of a separate and distinct tract of land in such reserve, and whose improvements on such separate tract are not of the value of at least one hundred and fifty dollars, and who is not otherwise possessed of the qualifications entitling him to be registered on the list of voters under this Act."[52] In 1886, the Manitoba government revised its Election Act to disqualify Indians or persons of Indian blood receiving an annuity from the Crown.[53] It should be understood that both exclusions were enacted in the aftermath of the 1885 uprising in Saskatchewan. Nonetheless, the removal of a fundamental right of citizenship was a profound blow to Aboriginal people. In 1931, Manitoba followed the Ontario example by amending this legislation to permit Indians who had served in the British or Canadian armed forces, or in the forces of a British possession, or the forces of a British ally during the Great War, to vote in provincial elections.[54] Finally, in 1952, Manitoba returned the franchise to Aboriginal people.[55] Only in 1960, seventy-five years after the first legislation, did the federal government return the franchise in national elections to Manitoba's (and the nation's) Indian people.[56]

Though the Indian Act was revised after extensive hearings in 1951, the revisions did not answer Aboriginal requests for greater self-government. Nevertheless, the rapidly changing context of Canadian politics and increasing pressure from Aboriginal organizations forced the government to review its Indian policies again in the 1960s. The result was the White Paper of 1969. Influenced by Prime Minister Trudeau, this statement of policy opposed continuation of a distinct Indian status and of treaties between Canada and Aboriginal people. The proposed policy would repeal the Indian Act and transform reserves into communities no different from their non-Aboriginal neighbours. The ideal being set out was equality under the law. Three centuries of legal and customary arrangements would have been abrogated in one legislative stroke.

The White Paper provoked condemnation from Aboriginal groups across the country and soon was dropped. If the policy proposals died, the Aboriginal political response did not. The national Indian campaign against the White Paper became a cause, a movement, and an organization. The rallying points included self-government and Aboriginal rights but at the centre of the discussions were land claims, treaties, and the Aboriginal relationship with the Crown.

A consequence of the federal government's disastrous failure in launching the White Paper was that, in the following years, Ottawa was much more interested in seeking the opinions of Aboriginal people. It dropped its proposal to repeal the Indian Act. It funded separate regional and national organizations for Indians, Inuit, and Métis peoples and devolved some administrative responsibility upon local chiefs and councils.

The national campaign to patriate the Constitution also drove Aboriginal politics. By promising constitutional renewal after the Quebec referendum of 1980, Prime Minister Trudeau implicitly raised the issue of treaty and Aboriginal rights. Aboriginal organizations seized upon an opportunity to entrench these rights beyond the reach of future governments. Indian, Inuit, and Métis national leaders co-operated in the presentation of a joint case and, in January 1981, the Joint Parliamentary Committee and the federal cabinet agreed to include a clause on these topics in the draft constitution. After a year of intense lobbying, a diluted version of the Aboriginal and treaty rights clause became part of the constitution that was proclaimed in April 1982.

Patriation of the Constitution was a turning point for Canadian Aboriginal people. Section 35 recognized and affirmed the "existing Aboriginal and treaty rights of the Aboriginal peoples of Canada" and defined Aboriginal peoples as "the Indian, Inuit and Métis peoples" (S. 35 [2]). Another section shielded those rights, as well as other rights and freedoms

of the Aboriginal peoples, from challenge under the Charter of Rights
and Freedoms (S. 25). A third section promised a First Ministers' conference on Aboriginal constitutional matters before 17 April 1983 (S. 37).
That conference, in turn, agreed that both Sections 25 and 35 of the Constitution Act, 1982, would be amended to protect the rights contained
within past and future land claims settlements as treaty rights. It also decided to amend Section 35 to guarantee sexual equality among Aboriginal men and women in the enjoyment of their rights. The Conference
declared, too, that none of the provisions of the Constitution Acts of 1867
and 1982 expressly referring to Aboriginal peoples could be amended
without prior consultation between legislators and Aboriginal peoples at
a First Ministers' conference. Finally, having listed issues of mutual concern but being unable to agree on a definition of Aboriginal and treaty
rights, the Conference decided to meet at least three more times.

The amendments to the Constitution were passed by all provincial legislatures except that of Quebec and by the Parliament of Canada and
were proclaimed in force in June 1984. In that year, and again in 1985
and 1987, Canadians watched the dramatic First Ministers' conferences
with Aboriginal leaders. In the full glare of the television lights and with
the advantage of national media attention, these meetings generated public awareness of Aboriginal issues and focussed debate on the constitutional recognition of an Aboriginal right to self-government.[57]

Crisis in Aboriginal Relations with the Justice System, 1950-1990
The third justice regime continued to operate after the Second World War,
but its effects were dramatically different. Though official rules did not
change, the reality of contact and enforcement, as opposed to the theory,
did supplant Aboriginal law in this period.

Manitoba was merely a tiny part of an integrated international economy
and trading community in the decades after 1950. Like citizens all over
the world, Manitobans were required to adjust to the new patterns of trade
and technology. Farms and country towns could no longer hold their children. The proportion of the population able to work in agriculture declined steadily. At the same time, Winnipeg grew in population. As global
competition increased, entrepreneurs and government turned to the northern lands of the province – to rivers and forests and mineral wealth – for
resources that might provide additional revenue and jobs. Each of these
trends had an impact on Manitoba's Aboriginal population.

Enforcement of Canadian law among Aboriginal Manitobans became
increasingly important in these decades. Though the statistics are notoriously unreliable, the superintendent (later commissioner) of penitentiaries did report annually to Parliament on the numbers of inmates in federal correctional institutions. The proportion of Aboriginal people in the

Manitoba penitentiary during the first half of the twentieth century reflected almost exactly the Aboriginal proportion of the Manitoba population.[58] The Aboriginal proportion of the Manitoba penitentiary population increased in an extraordinary fashion during the decades after 1950. By 1989, about fifty percent of the Manitoba prisoners were Aboriginal, whereas the Aboriginal proportion of the provincial population was just under twelve percent.

Policing agreements with the Royal Canadian Mounted Police play a part in this story by introducing consistent enforcement of Canadian law into communities where, until that time, Aboriginal law still operated. Construction of highways and the increased use of automobiles added an important new sphere of police activity. The wider availability of alcoholic beverages in the province accelerated the trend to greater Aboriginal involvement in the justice system. So, too, did closer supervision of and amendments to social and family legislation.

Aboriginal people also ran into more frequent conflicts with government bureaucracies after 1950. Judicial rulings on hunting and fishing rights and on land claims produced instability and more than a little anger among Manitoba Indians as they seemingly won, then lost, then regained the right to pursue a treaty-protected right. Their renewal of claims under the treaty promises of a century ago similarly provoked legal contests. Particular resources, such as wild rice, that had been part of Aboriginal life for centuries also became subject to provincial regulations and, thus, were seemingly taken out of Aboriginal control and placed in the hands of distant bureaucrats whose priorities might differ from those of the people who had once "owned" the natural product.

The Department of Indian Affairs managed its "wards" much more aggressively in the decades after the Second World War. Henceforth, it seemed, the issues of housing and economic development on the reserve, education in both reserve and urban settings, the use of friendship centres to stimulate Aboriginal migration to the cities, and family-centred matters including income support and adoption, in particular, would require an army of civil servants, on the one hand, and Aboriginal acquiescence, on the other.

Child justice and family welfare issues entered the public sphere during these decades. Family crises propelled children into courts and expanded the size of welfare-agency case files. Too often, family members were separated. Too often, as Manitobans have learned in recent years, Aboriginal children were sent out of the community and out of the country.

Northern Manitoba and central Manitoba differed from the south in recent Aboriginal history. A crucial difference concerned the effect of resource-development "megaprojects" upon these formerly "isolated" communities. The experience of the band at Tadoule Lake illustrated how law and government administration can affect an Aboriginal group in our own time. This group of about 300 Dene people hunt and fish in the territory west of Churchill. They returned there about twenty years ago. Though life is far from easy, the community members believe it is preferable to the alternatives they have seen.

The band had been living near the HBC's Duck Lake trading post in 1956, trapping furs and hunting caribou in the region as they had done for years. Fur prices declined, the Company decided to close the post, and the services that the band had received, from supplementary food to medical assistance and emergency radio transmissions, were in jeopardy. A band elder related the following sequence of events at a hearing of the Aboriginal Justice Inquiry: government officials visited the band and informed them that, in the circumstances, they should move to the nearest large community, Churchill, then a thriving defence and shipping centre and the hub of northern trade activities; the band members said they did not want to move and asked the officials to assist them to stay in their traditional area; officials cited the annual costs and declined; several months later, without further discussion, airplanes arrived and the people were all taken to Churchill where, as elder Thomas Duck told the Commission, they were "just dumped out on the beach . . . and people were living . . . in tents and then finally they were hauled to another location by boat in fall . . . [when] little shacks, 12 x 16 or 12 x 14 one room shacks" were erected for them.[59] This was in 1956.

Fifteen years of social devastation followed. In the 1970s, a substantial proportion of the community decided to return to traditional life and eventually established the Tadoule Lake settlement. Band Councillor Albert Thorassie reported that his people

bear the wounds and carry the physical and psychological scars for those tormenting years; . . . it continues to haunt us in ways unimaginable to outsiders. We lost one whole generation of people who would now be the backbone of our community . . . through violent deaths from freezing, hit and run . . . homicide, suicide and alcohol-related incidents. . . . We find it hard to this day to rebuild from the destruction and chaos of those years. . . . We find it hard to re-grasp the drum and . . . to sing and play the hand game, because during those years in Churchill . . . the only thing we knew was alcohol and violence and all the disgusting things that go with it.

In the past, a Sayisi Dene was respected and feared by all Athapaskan people and other tribes, because of our great numbers and fearlessness and our abilities to live in a beautiful but harsh environment.

Today, we are just fragments of a great tribe, beaten and down, but not out. And we are not giving up. We long to hear our drum beating again, our heart that stopped beating for so long. . . .

We have so much to tell the world regarding the injustices that . . . were imposed by society and by the federal government without our people's consent.[60]

The Tadoule Lake experience is not unique. Moose Lake, Chemawawin, Grand Rapids, South Indian Lake, and Brochet all have equally compelling stories. This northern experience has been repeated time after time from 1869 to the present. Economic opportunity is assessed; development is launched; the environment is drastically altered. European Canadians take resources and Aboriginal Canadians suffer the consequences.

Chief Esau Turner of the Swampy Cree Tribal Council described the Grand Rapids and Saskatchewan Power projects in exactly these terms when he addressed the Aboriginal Justice Inquiry:

> Huge changes have been imposed on native people. . . . Economic activity has come into our area which has changed our way of life, but has rarely given us a substitute in terms of jobs and ownership of that economic activity. Lost, too, in the changes were many traditions and values that kept our culture strong and our communities united. The taking of land, the imposition of another economic system and replacement of our social systems with systems of laws and government from outside meant the decline in local customs, local responsibility and local ways of life. The changes to the economy and the systems that have developed around native people have taught dependency rather than independence. . . . In abdicating responsibility we have fallen into many problems. Alcohol, welfare and Indian Affairs threatened to replace our culture, our independence and our strength as a people. . . . What we want to stress is that self-government means the ability to have local decision-making regarding matters which affect the lives of our people, . . . the ability to develop independence, . . . the ability to reinforce culture, customs and traditions.[61]

Manitoba's Aboriginal people have known three justice regimes. During two of them, they exercised control over their lives. In the third, this control was taken from them. By treating Aboriginal people as less than adults, by smothering their political and cultural expressions as well as extinguishing their claims to this land, Canadian governments have made serious mistakes. The loss of Aboriginal self-determination is obvious. On the other side of the ledger, we can record in a discussion of the post-1870 record that the Aboriginal people resisted injustice. This story is not one of defeat. One must acknowledge the Aboriginal people's great achievement in maintaining a collective sense of community and continuity.

If one is to appreciate fully the problems that are addressed in the *Report of the Aboriginal Justice Inquiry of Manitoba,* one must take heed of this history.

NOTES

This paper is a revised and abridged version of Chapter 3 of the *Report of the Aboriginal Justice Inquiry*, vol. 1, *The Justice System and Aboriginal People*, by A.C. Hamilton and C.M. Sinclair (Winnipeg: Queen's Printer, 1992). I would like to thank my co-authors and the Queen's Printer, Manitoba, for permission to reprint portions of the chapter.

1. For a review of the history texts, see, James W.S. Walker, "The Indian in Canadian Historical Writing," *Canadian Historical Association Historical Papers*, 1971.
2. There are problems of definition in the study of Aboriginal or "customary" or "traditional" law. In its broadest application, customary law includes three different subjects: specific rules that prescribe proper behaviour in a community; observable regularities in everyday human behaviour; and definable approaches to instances of dispute (Simon Roberts, *Order and Dispute: An Introduction to Legal Anthropology* [Harmondsworth, England: Penguin Books, 1979], 185; see also, Michael Coyle, "Traditional Indian Justice in Ontario: A Role for the Present?" *Osgoode Hall Law Journal* 24, no. 3 [1986]).
3. E.E. Rich, ed., *Cumberland House Journals and Inland Journal, 1775-1782*, First Series, 1775-1779 (London: Hudson's Bay Record Society, 1951), 36.
4. Fur trader Daniel Harmon discovered when he visited southern Manitoba in the early nineteenth century that "it is a common thing among all the Natives, for an offender to offer property in satisfaction for an injury, and when this is accepted by the injured party, contention between them entirely ceases. Even murder is, sometimes, in this way atoned for; but not commonly. In ordinary cases, nothing but the death of the murderer, or of some of his near relatives, will satisfy the desire for revenge" (W. Kaye Lamb, ed., *Sixteen Years in the Indian Country: The Journal of Daniel William Harmon, 1800-1816* [Toronto: Macmillan, 1957], 87).
5. Hiram Martin Chittenden and Alfred Talbot Richardson, eds., *Life, Letters and Travels of Father Pierre-Jean de Smet, S.J., 1801-1873* (New York: Francis P. Harper, 1905), vol. 3, 1,028. See also, H.E. Driver, *Indians of North America* (Chicago: University of Chicago Press, 1969), 312-15.
6. Alexander Ross, *The Red River Settlement: Its Rise, Progress, and Present State* (Minneapolis: Ross and Haines, 1957), 249-50. See also, Peter R. Grant, "Recognition of Traditional Laws in State Courts and the Formulation of State Legislation," in *Indigenous Law and the State*, ed. Bradford W. Morse and Gordon R. Woodman (Dordrecht, Netherlands: Foris Publications, 1988), 260.
7. Scott Clark, "Aboriginal Customary Law: Literature Review" (research paper prepared for the *Aboriginal Justice Inquiry*, 1990), 8. The papers of the *Aboriginal Justice Inquiry* are located in the E.K. Williams Law Library, University of Manitoba.
8. Gisday Wa and Delgam Uukw, *The Spirit in the Land: The Opening Statement of the Gitksan and Wet'suwet'en Hereditary Chiefs in The Supreme Court of British Columbia* (Gabriola, BC: Reflections, 1989), 8. See also, Robert Gordon and Mervyn Meggitt, "The Customary Law Option," in *Law and Order in the New Guinea Highlands*, ed. Gordon and Meggitt (Hanover, NH: University Press of New England, 1985), 202-4.
9. John West, *The Substance of a Journal during a Residence at the Red River Colony, British North America, in the Years 1820-1823* (Vancouver: Alcuin Society, 1967), 140.
10. Meriwether Lewis and William Clark, *History of the Expedition under the Command of Captains Lewis and Clark to the Sources of the Missouri*, vol. 2 (Toronto: Morang, n.d.), 108.
11. Alexandre-Antonin Taché, *Sketch of the North-West of America* (Montreal: John Lovell, 1870), 110.
12. A critic of this conclusion is L.C. Green, in L.C. Green and O.P. Dickason, *The Law of Nations and the New World* (Edmonton: University of Alberta Press, 1989). But see also, James Crawford, "The Original Status of Aboriginal Peoples in North America: A Critique of L.C. Green and O.P. Dickason, *The Law of Nations and the New World* (1989)" (research

paper prepared for the *Aboriginal Justice Inquiry*, January 1991).

13. Aboriginal communities in Canada exercised a sovereign right to govern themselves, in law as well as practice, before European colonization of this land and, to the extent that they did not surrender their right to do so, thereafter. As James Crawford has explained, "International law accepted 'tribes or peoples having a social and political organization' as entities entitled to govern their own affairs and possessing authority over their territory; where these entities exercised a degree of independent governmental authority sufficient for the general maintenance of order, they could be regarded as States in international law, and thus as sovereign. . . . It does not matter whether particular groups were fully independent, or were to some degree subject to the control or direction of another group: collectively the Indian tribes exercised the full range of governmental powers. Applying these tests, there can be no doubt that Aboriginal peoples in North America exercised a sovereign right to govern themselves before European contact, and until the acquisition of sovereignty and the assumption of control over their lands by the European colonizers." This interpretation is presented most clearly in Crawford, "Aboriginal Self-Government in Canada" (research report for the Committee on Native Justice, Canadian Bar Association, 1988), 22. Also useful are: Crawford, "The Original Status of Aboriginal Peoples in North America"; and Crawford, *The Creation of States in International Law* (Oxford: Clarendon Press, 1979). In western Canada, this sovereign right continued and was respected throughout the era of the "second justice regime."

14. *Guerin v. The Queen* [1984] 2 S.C.R., 335.

15. Sylvia Van Kirk, *"Many Tender Ties": Women in Fur-Trade Society in Western Canada, 1670-1870* (Winnipeg: Watson and Dwyer, 1980), 4.

16. Cited in J. Lagassé, "The Métis in Manitoba," in *The Other Natives: The Métis*, vol. 2, ed. A.S. Lussier and D.B. Sealey (Winnipeg: University of Manitoba Press, 1978), 110.

17. Paul C. Thistle, *Indian-European Trade Relations in the Lower Saskatchewan River Region to 1840* (Winnipeg: University of Manitoba Press, 1986), 73-74, citing the Cumberland House Journal of the HBC. In 1777, to give another example, Indians killed three Canadian traders to avenge harsh treatment.

18. When some Indians attempted to raid a trading post in 1823, they were given "a good drubbing for their trouble" by the HBC staff. The Indians then vented their frustration by cutting off part of the tail of a cow that belonged to the post employees (Thistle, *Indian-European Trade Relations,* 73-74, 67, 77, 86).

19. S.C. 1765, 6 Geo. III, c. 18.

20. When confronted by serious wrongdoing by one of their fellows, Europeans were much more likely to resort to their accustomed legal system. Thus, when one fur trader was shot by another in a quarrel over furs in 1802, the surviving actor (who claimed he fired in self-defence) and a witness travelled all the way from the Northwest to Montreal in order to secure a trial in the courts of Lower Canada (Dale Gibson and Lee Gibson, *Substantial Justice: Law and Lawyers in Manitoba, 1670-1970* [Winnipeg: Peguis Publishers, 1972], 1-5).

21. See, Desmond H. Brown, "Unpredictable and Uncertain: Criminal Law in the Canadian North West Before 1886," *Alberta Law Review* 17, no. 3 (1979):497-512, for a summary of these issues.

22. Gibson and Gibson, *Substantial Justice,* 27.

23. W.L. Morton, *Manitoba: A History,* reprint ed. (Toronto: University of Toronto Press, 1967); W.L. Morton, ed., introduction to *Alexander Begg's Red River Journal and Other Papers Relative to the Red River Resistance of 1869-70* (Toronto: Champlain Society, 1956).

24. Manitoba Act 1870, R.S.C. 1985, app. 2, no. 8.

25. The legislative record includes: Rupert's Land Act 1868, 31-32 Vict., c. 105 (U.K.), reprinted in R.S.C. 1985, app. 2, no. 6; Act for the Temporary Government of Rupert's Land and the North-Western Territory, S.C. 1869, c. 3; "Order of Her Majesty in Council Admitting Rupert's Land and the North-western Territory into the Union, 23 June 1870," and a sequence of 1868-69 documents contained in E.H. Oliver, *The Canadian North-West: Its Early Development and Legislative Records* (Ottawa: Government Printing Bureau, 1914-15),

939-63. Other documents appear in W.L. Morton, ed., *Manitoba: The Birth of a Province*, vol. 1 (Altona, MB: Manitoba Record Society Publications, 1965). The 1871 British legislation was entitled Act Respecting the Establishment of Provinces in the Dominion of Canada 1871, 34-35 Vict., c. 28 (U.K.).

26. The subject is discussed fully in: John S. Milloy, "The Era of Civilization: British Policy for the Indians of Canada, 1830-1860," D.Phil. thesis, Oxford University, 1978; and Milloy, "The Early Indian Acts: Developmental Strategy and Constitutional Change," in *As Long As The Sun Shines and Water Flows: A Reader in Canadian Native Studies*, ed. Ian A.L. Getty and A.S. Lussier (Vancouver: Nakoda Institute and University of British Columbia Press, 1983).

27. Dan Kennedy, *Recollections of an Assiniboine Chief*, ed. James R. Stephens (Toronto and Montreal: McClelland and Stewart, 1972), cited in J.R. Miller, *Skyscrapers Hide the Heavens: A History of Indian-White Relations in Canada* (Toronto: University of Toronto Press, 1989), 196.

28. Cited in Miller, *Skyscrapers Hide the Heavens*, 196. William Duncan, Church of England missionary, condemned the idea that mere "civilization" without the Gospel would convince Aboriginal people to adopt Canadian ways: "No, civilization apart from Christianity has no vitality – how then can it impart life? It is the fuel without the fire, how then can it radiate heat? Civilization appeals to the eye and to the hands, but not to the heart. It may move the muscles but it cannot reach the hidden springs of life" (Jean Usher, *William Duncan of Metlakatla: A Victorian Missionary in British Columbia* [Ottawa: National Museum of Man, 1974], 63).

The purpose of government policy was to re-make Indians into "good Canadians." In the words of a prairie newspaper, in its review of Aboriginal exhibits at an agricultural fair, it would make "the Red Man White in all but colour" (*Regina Leader*, 9 October 1888, cited in Jacqueline Kennedy Gresko, "Qu'Appelle Industrial School: White 'Rites' for the Indians of the Old North West," Master's thesis, Carleton University, 1970, 116).

29. F. Laurie Barron, "A Summary of Federal Indian Policy in the Canadian West, 1867-1984," *Native Studies Review* 1, no. 1 (1984):28-39.

30. Katherine Pettipas, *Severing the Ties that Bind: Government Repression of Indigenous Religious Ceremonies on the Prairies* (Winnipeg: University of Manitoba Press, 1994); Douglas Cole and Ira Chaikin, *An Iron Hand upon the People: The Law against the Potlatch on the Northwest Coast* (Vancouver: Douglas and McIntyre, 1990).

31. Department of Indian Affairs, J.M. to Secretary, 19 September 1908, National Archives of Canada (NAC), RG 10, v. 3825, file 60, 511-2, cited in Pettipas, *Severing the Ties that Bind*, 128.

32. Edward Ahenakew, *Voices of the Plains Cree*, ed. Ruth Buck (Toronto: McClelland and Stewart, 1973), 69, 72.

33. Vankoughnet to Macdonald, 14 August 1885, NAC, RG 10, v. 3710, file 19, 550-3, cited in F. Laurie Barron, "The Indian Pass System in the Canadian West, 1882-1935," *Prairie Forum* 13, no. 1 (1988):28.

34. Sarah Carter, *Lost Harvests: Prairie Indian Reserve Farmers and Government Policy* (Montreal and Kingston: McGill-Queen's University Press, 1990).

35. Canada, Sessional Papers, 14, 1896, *Report of the Deputy Superintendent-General of Indian Affairs*, cited in Sarah Carter, "Agriculture and Agitation on the Oak River Reserve, 1875-1895," *Manitoba History* 6 (fall 1983):5. See also, Carter, *Lost Harvests*.

36. Stuart Raby, "Indian Land Surrenders in Southern Saskatchewan," *Canadian Geographer* 17, no. 1 (1973).

37. Cited in Tyler, Wright and Daniel Ltd., "The Illegal Surrender of St. Peter's Reserve" (manuscript report prepared for the Treaty and Aboriginal Rights Research Centre of Manitoba, Winnipeg, 1983), 534.

38. S.C. 1916, 6-7 Geo. V, c. 24.

39. Treaty and Aboriginal Rights Research Program, *Treaty Land Entitlement in Manitoba, 1970-1981* (Winnipeg: Treaty and Aboriginal Rights Research, 1982).

40. Peter Douglas Elias, *The Dakota of the Canadian Northwest: Lessons for Survival* (Winnipeg:

University of Manitoba Press, 1988), 146.

41. Cited in John Milloy, "A Partnership of Races: Indian and White, Cross-Cultural Relations and Criminal Justice in Manitoba, 1670-1949" (research paper prepared for the *Aboriginal Justice Inquiry*, June 1990), 67.

42. Miller, *Skyscrapers Hide the Heavens*, 206-7.

43. Canada, Parliament, Special Joint Committee of Senate and House of Commons on Indian Act, "Minutes and Proceedings of Evidence," no. 30, 1,563-1,600, cited in Milloy, "Partnership of Races," 81-94.

44. Ibid, 1,585.

45. A wide sample of the literature on this theme is presented in: Jacqueline Peterson and Jennifer S.H. Brown, eds., *The New Peoples: Being and Becoming Métis in North America* (Winnipeg: University of Manitoba Press, 1985); and in F. Laurie Barron and James B. Waldram, eds., *1885 and After: Native Society in Transition,* proceedings of a conference held at the University of Saskatchewan, Saskatoon, May 1985 (Regina: Canadian Plains Research Center, University of Saskatchewan, 1986). A survey is presented in Jennifer S.H. Brown, "Métis," *Canadian Encyclopedia,* 2nd ed. (Edmonton: Hurtig Publishers, 1988), 1,343-46.

46. Auguste-Henri de Trémaudan, *Histoire de la nation métisse dans l'ouest canadien,* reprint ed. (St. Boniface: Les Editions du Blé, 1979), published in English as *Hold High Your Heads: History of the Métis Nation in Western Canada,* trans. E. Maguet (Winnipeg: Pemmican Publications, 1982).

47. de Trémaudan, *Hold High Your Heads,* xvi.

48. Allen Edgar Ronaghan, "The Archibald Administration in Manitoba 1870-72," Ph.D. dissertation, University of Manitoba, Winnipeg, 1987.

49. Archibald to J.A. Macdonald, 9 October 1871, in *Journals of the House of Commons of the Dominion of Canada, 1874,* 8, app. 6.

50. Jean H. Lagassé, *A Study of the Population of Indian Ancestry Living in Manitoba* (Winnipeg: Department of Agriculture and Immigration, 1959), 54-57, 78, 3.

51. M.S. Donnelly, *The Government of Manitoba* (Toronto: University of Toronto Press, 1963), 72.

52. An Act Respecting the Electoral Franchise, S.C. 1885, 47-49 Vict., c. 40, ss. 2 and 11(c).

53. Election Act, S.M. 1886, 49 Vict., c. 29, s. 130(5).

54. Ibid., S.M. 1931, c. 10, s. 16(5); also R.S.M. 1940, c. 57, ss. 15(1)(b) and 16(5); similar Ontario legislation was The Elections Act, R.S.O. 1927, c. 8, s. 18(s). In 1945 the Manitoba legislation, The Active Service Election and Representation Act, S.M. 1945 (2nd sess.), c. 1, s. 3, extended the right to Indians who had served in the Second World War.

55. An Act to Amend The Manitoba Elections Act, S.M. 1952 (1st sess.), c. 18, ss. 5 and 6.

56. 8-9 Eliz. II, c. 39 repealed R.S.C. 1952, c. 23, the relevant clauses of which were s. 14(2)(e) and 14(4).

57. One measure of the gains made by Aboriginal people in this period was the boldness of the report of the House of Commons Special Committee on Indian Self-Government (Canada, House of Commons, Special Committee on Indian Self-Government, *Indian Self-Government in Canada* [Penner Report], Ottawa, 1983).

58. Canada, Sessional Papers, *Annual Report of the Superintendent of Penitentiaries,* reporting on "Indians" and "Indian half-breeds," and equivalent designations in the reports for 1900, 1913, and 1932-33, and in the annual reports from 1934-35 to 1949-50. Figures from 1900 to 1960 can be extracted from tables published in the annual reports of the superintendent, latterly commissioner, of penitentiaries. After 1960, statistical data concerning correctional facilities are published in various Statistics Canada reports under the rubric of the "85" series. Ethnicity was not used again as a description of prisoners until 1975.

59. Thomas Duck, Tadoule Lake, vol. 3, 642, in Aboriginal Justice Inquiry Hearings.

60. Albert Thorassie, Tadoule Lake, vol. 3, 607-9, in Aboriginal Justice Inquiry Hearings.

61. Chief Esau Turner, The Pas, 151-54, in Aboriginal Justice Inquiry Hearings.

Labour History and the Métis

THE LABELS DESIGNATING cultural groups evolve with changes in society, it is said, so one should pay careful heed to the shift in terminology in recent studies of Canadian history that refer to the "Métis peoples" or "Métis Nation." Earlier designations, including "mixed-blood" and "mixed-race" and "half-breed," have been consciously rejected by today's scholars as they have, by and large, by the Aboriginal and Aboriginal-European peoples themselves. The very discussion of names, however, has made clear that Canadians are being asked to acknowledge a distinct category for people who combine Aboriginal and European ancestry. Thus, the Constitution Act, which patriated Canada's constitution in 1982, declared in Section 35 that the Aboriginal peoples of Canada, whose "existing Aboriginal and treaty rights" are "recognized and affirmed," included "the Indian, Inuit and Métis peoples of Canada." The meaning of that section, like so much else in the Constitution Act, will evolve with the generations, but it will certainly reinforce a group identity among the Métis people.

The development of "new peoples" is by now a familiar story in the Americas and in southern Africa and India. In western Canada, it has produced a growing literature on land claims in the 1980s and 1990s. This concentration has good and reasonable explanations because the Métis have launched a number of legal cases concerning economic and land issues. However, the inevitable result has been the brief eclipse of alternative approaches to the Métis story and, thus, the risk that popular understanding of Métis communities may be limited. One different approach places the western Métis experience in the context of global economic and social change in the nineteenth century. In this paper I propose that an examination of nineteenth-century Canadian Métis history be conducted from the perspective of the international literature on working people. Such an approach will establish the social and cultural continuity from past to present that undergirds the cultural category of "Métis" as an essential addition to the mental maps of all Canadians.

Contact between Europeans and Aboriginal peoples in the northern half of North America, as in the South Seas and South America, resulted in the birth of many children of mixed parentage. Under the French in the Atlantic and St. Lawrence regions of America, where official policy for a century actually endorsed cross-cultural family formation, the children sometimes became French.[1] As opposition to such marriages grew stronger in the eighteenth century, these children lost official recognition. Their numbers grew substantially, however, especially in the Great Lakes region, where perhaps fifty communities contained as many as 10,000 or 15,000 Métis by the 1820s.[2]

Simultaneously, in the lands to the north, where the Hudon's Bay Company (HBC) conducted its trade operations, another, less-populous, Métis tradition took form.[3] The two currents met in the Red River region and in several other districts, notably Montana (the Missouri basin), and the upper Saskatchewan, in the first half of the nineteenth century. In prairie Canada, a number of circumstances combined in the closing decades of the nineteenth century to unite a number of the Métis people into an identifiable political community. These circumstances included the development of a relatively stable sedentary economy in the western interior of the continent, the sudden precipitation of armed confrontations between Métis and Canadians, and the increasing racism of European Canadians. Or so the story is told.[4]

In most Canadian historical writing from the 1930s to the 1960s, the Métis were depicted as partly European and partly Aboriginal not only in parentage but in character. That is, they were perceived to be guided in part by the constraints and ideals of the "civilized" world and in part subject to the alleged child-like willfulness of the "savage" condition. It was as if the historical interpretations of a society and culture were shaped by the metaphor of "mixed blood" that informed the scholars' biological vision. Thus, describing the emergence in the eighteenth century of a Métis peoplehood, Marcel Giraud, the French historian whose *Le Métis Canadien* stands as the central volume in this literature, wrote of a Métis "collective personality . . . in which primitive elements survived alongside the civilized ones."[5]

Earlier historical interpretations were also affected by the French-English, Catholic-Protestant dichotomies that have always been prominent in Canadian life. Just as Indians were believed by some historians to occupy lower rungs on the hierarchical ladder of civilization, so the French Métis were perceived by some English Canadian writers to be more profligate, less patient, more eager to pursue the momentary thrills of the buffalo hunt than were their mixed-race compatriots of Scots Protestant paternity who allegedly buckled down to the longer-term fulfillment of families, possessions, and expanded farms.[6] French Canadian historians, needless to say, were quick to defend the Métis against alleged Protestant fanaticism and to assert the virtues of Roman Catholic clerical guidance.[7]

Another characteristic of the historical writing of this generation was its concentration on the Métis of Red River. The Métis had an eventful history in the district, including an armed confrontation at Seven Oaks in 1816 (labelled a "massacre" by some English-speaking Red River historians), and had conducted an armed resistance to Canadian annexation of the West in 1869-70 on behalf of the settlement's 12,000 residents. A consequence of this undeniably turbulent tale was that the Red River Métis became enmeshed in the story of Canada's emergence as a transcontinental nation. Moreover, because the Métis President of the Red River government, Louis Riel, returned to the Northwest from American exile fifteen years later, in 1884, to lead another armed uprising against the Canadian government (and was hanged after its collapse), Riel and Red River eclipsed the other regional traditions in Métis life.[8]

Recent scholarship has produced an unusual number of publications on the Métis and some heated controversy. One clear conclusion is that a distinctive "fur trade society," separate from Aboriginal communities but also removed from European and European Canadian ways of life, developed slowly and relatively peacefully in the Northwest interior of America between the 1640s and the 1830s.[9] Second, it is asserted (and several government investigations verify this perception) that many Métis remained in poverty on the remote fringes of settlement during at least the first half of the twentieth century.[10] Between these two periods, in the decades stretching from the 1830s to the 1890s, lies the battleground of current historical debate.

Modern scholars of the nineteenth-century Métis experience are divided by questions related to racism, then and now. Did the HBC discriminate against Métis in its hiring policies?[11] Is it true that a handful of Europeans – women and missionaries to be precise – were responsible for the introduction of racism to the Canadian Northwest?[12] Did the English-speaking Protestant fanaticism of the incoming Canadians in the

1860s drive a wedge between French and English Métis, thus provoking a "civil war" in 1869-70 (that is, far from a resistance of old settlers against incoming settlers, was the uprising of 1869-70 a consequence of internal divisions in Red River)?[13] Did the Canadian government, after annexing this western empire, set out intentionally to deprive the Manitoba Métis of their lands in the 1870s?[14] Or was the behaviour of the English-speaking, Protestant immigrants so offensive that it drove the French-speaking, Roman Catholic Métis from those lands?[15] Or is there a third explanation (beyond government actions and Orange fanaticism), perhaps based on the old assumption of a voluntary Métis exodus, for the unquestioned eclipse of the Métis in Manitoba society in the 1870s?[16] When many Métis settled 800 kilometres farther west, along the banks of the Saskatchewan River, did the federal government persecute them, pigeonhole their land claims, perhaps even deliberately push them into an armed rebellion in 1885, which it could then crush, to the advantage of the larger white community but also to the advantage of the Canadian Pacific Railway?[17]

Too often, there is a sub-text in these debates: Who is the best and truest defender of the Métis today? Of the federal government? Which interpretation is least influenced by white racist assumptions or, alternatively, which interpretation is most biased by allegiance to the Aboriginal or the federal government cause? This terrain has become a battleground; indeed, the 1870s land questions and the Métis *diaspora* are the subject of an important court case.[18] Though much has been learned and much discarded as a result of the disagreements among historians, it is time to move on if we are to avoid a new partisanship as sterile as the old French- and English-Canadian historical solitudes.

The approaches of labour history offer a different and fruitful perspective upon the Métis experience in the nineteenth century. By emphasizing the matter of production, labour history insists, first, that close attention be paid to the circumstances of the Aboriginal economies. Second, by raising the subject of "household commodity production," recent labour histories have asked about the gendering of work and the economic terms by which "distant" staple-producing societies were integrated into the increasingly global trade in natural resources. Third, by pointing to the emergence of a single international capitalist economy, and of workers' "agency" and "resistance" as responses to this system, labour historians have introduced questions concerning the degree of difference and commonality in the experience of western Canadian Métis families in relation to that of other indigenous peoples within the global economy.

The Indians of the western interior of Canada operated in pre-contact times as extended families – hunting bands – for most of the winter season and congregated in larger communities only in the summer and early autumn when resources were sufficient to feed denser populations. Therefore, Aboriginal life was marked by seasonal movement through resource zones – winter moose hunts in the boreal forest, spring fowl and fisheries and maple syrup harvesting along water courses, summer berry and bison hunts on the plains, autumn wild rice gathering – depending on the group, the diplomatic circumstances, and the resource supply itself. The entry of the European fur trade into these cycles altered some band movements, but it did not disrupt Aboriginal continuity in this region before the mid-nineteenth century. In the case of many individuals, a version of this resource cycle has continued into the twentieth century and, to a degree, still exists.[19]

As the fur-company labour needs increased in the late eighteenth and early nineteenth centuries, the simultaneous increase in Métis population offered a supply of indigenous workers who could be hired and released as the companies required. Although some Métis were employed permanently by the fur companies – after 1821, the HBC was by far the largest operation – many, perhaps most, Métis worked from time to time as wage labourers but combined this activity with farming and hunting, and especially with participation in the increasingly important buffalo hunts. This varied economy was the essence of Métis life throughout most of the nineteenth century and ended only with the near extinction of the buffalo.

The Métis should be distinguished from their prairie Aboriginal contemporaries. They spoke different languages, often a combination of French and Cree or Ojibwa called Michif.[20] They often espoused a Protestant or Roman Catholic Christianity, though elements of an Aboriginal perspective were also part of their religious inheritance.[21] Their dress was different – more European – and they customarily lived in houses made of logs rather than lodges made of skins, though this did not apply to the periods when they travelled on the spring and fall buffalo hunts.[22] They often were employed as intermediaries between Indians, on the one hand, and Europeans and European Canadians, on the other, whether as guides, translators, traders, interpreters, or even negotiators of treaties between the two sides.[23] Perhaps most telling, they adapted more completely than did Indians to the changing demands of European and North American trade and export opportunities in the nineteenth century.

When the Métis moved into the nascent Red River Settlement from their scattered fur-trade locations during the 1820s and early 1830s, they were, in economic and social terms, as close to European peasants as they were to Aboriginal hunting bands. Rather than seeking to accumulate great wealth, they supplied the needs of their households and probably worked no more than was necessary.[24] They were not participants in a purely subsistence economy because they did engage extensively in market activities (wage labour and the sale and purchase of provisions), but accumulation was not a prominent aspect of their existence. In sum, the

Métis should not be seen as a European-Indian "blood" mixture but rather as an inchoate ethnic group whose material culture, economic niche, and social function placed them between European and Indian worlds.

The subsequent economic transition of the Metis in the mid-nineteenth century represents a second approach to the Métis story that can be associated with the historiography of labour and working people. In the 1840s and 1850s, Métis "peasant" families began to specialize in the buffalo-robe trade, in transportation, and in the "free trade" in furs. The families that adopted these occupations spent more and more time away from their Red River farms, acquiring the title of *hivernants* (or "winterers") as they hunted buffalo and traded with Indian bands from their sheltered winter camps on the prairies. In the hunt-based Métis groups, there was even a specialization of labour by gender and age as a household factory system evolved: young adult males were the hunters, other males skinned the carcasses, women and children stretched, staked, and scraped the skins and robes.[25] Whole villages, ranging in size from thirty to 1,500 people, sprang up at these wintering sites during the 1860s and 1870s. In the last years of this system, several of these vital communities possessed the services of a priest and even a church and school of sorts, and were enlivened by dances and weddings and council meetings.[26]

What is pivotal about this new Métis activity is its reliance on trade and on external markets. Some of these Métis had passed from a near-subsistence peasant economy to a household "putting-out" system, as it has been described by historian Gerhard Ens. Others in this Métis group traded the products of the fur trade and the goods required by the Indians. Still others earned the bulk of their living as freighters. All those Métis who engaged in trade had crossed a crucial divide: they had started out consuming and selling a commodity and were now selling their labour power as well; significantly, like wage labourers in a factory, or on a railway, they did not own the fundamental resource, the "means of production," as it might be described in another economy. However, the Métis did not attempt to introduce the capitalist concepts of private property in land and resources into their economic arrangements.[27] Instead, they relied on open access to God-given, community-controlled animal resources, and, increasingly, they established independent "franchise" operations based on carts and trade goods supplied by an elite of merchant capitalists, many of whom also identified themselves as Métis.[28]

The buffalo herds were destroyed by 1879-1883. It might appear that the Métis who had chosen the *hivernant* alternative had been unwise and even had been blind to the changing times. From such ruminations came historical interpretations that emphasized personal fecklessness or some fatal strain of nomadism in the Métis "blood" that had doomed them to inferiority. But to advocate an individual or race-based interpretation is to ignore a third theme from labour history that deserves greater emphasis in Métis history – the overwhelming evidence of industrial capitalism's victorious campaign to conquer the globe. These very decades, from the 1840s to the 1890s, saw the extension not simply of a European and American capitalist economic system, but also of a cultural framework to almost every corner of the earth.[29] One of the fundamental changes was the introduction of concepts of private property.[30] In the Northwest of America, two formerly public resources, land and animals, thus became private possessions. Like the Indians, the Métis were aware of the change and had considered how to respond to it, but they were too late to control this fateful transition in the dominant approach to property.[31]

Two additional concepts borrowed from labour history – "resistance" and "agency" (concepts often applied to struggles on the shop floor) – can be seen to have a place in these cultural discussions. The Métis, first, did assert their rights and resist the incursions of the new order. Métis communities convened numerous councils of resistance in the 1860s and 1870s as well as the 1880s. At Batoche, on the South Saskatchewan River, the Métis actually established conservation laws in 1875 to alleviate the pressure on animal resources. In contrast, a year earlier, in 1874, another Métis community, this one at Buffalo Lake near Edmonton, decided that any attempt to prevent the ultimate extermination of the buffalo was futile and chose to obtain whatever share of the dwindling herds was possible.[32] Each of these actions was apparently based on careful consideration and democratic discussions. However, no local decisions would have had an appreciable effect on the rate of destruction of the herds. The slaughter was too widespread, and, perhaps, too closely linked to biological factors that have yet to be fully examined, to have been reversed by the actions of a few thousand Métis in the Canadian prairies.

The issue of land was more complicated. Like the Indians, the Métis recognized the significance of the economic transition and debated how to come to terms with it. The most complete statements of their conclusions probably were those developed by Louis Riel in the 1880s; one succinct illustration was his "Pétition à 'votre excellence en conseil'" (St-Louis-de-Langevin?) dated September 1884.[33] It assumed that the Métis were a distinct nation, enjoyed a right of national self-determination, were prepared to give up their claims to prairie lands in exchange for compensation from Canada, and could place a reasonable price on the compensation. It is apparent from these calculations that the Métis had adapted to the rules of the capitalist economy. Riel was actually proposing to establish a fund from government contributions and, with the interest accrued, to build institutions like schools and orphanages that would aid the Métis transition to the new economic order. He would use capitalist tools to tame the excesses of capitalism. Riel's plans were ignored or rejected by the federal government, however, and an armed confrontation was provoked in 1885. Thus, the Métis attempt to control the introduction of the new order, an expression of their determination to control their own destiny – to exercise "agency" – received another setback.

Some Métis did not follow the course of the winterers and the buffalo trade. Rather, they stayed on their farms in Red River or in the communities that were developing in other parts of the prairies such as Victoria on the North Saskatchewan and Batoche on the South Saskatchewan. They were making the transition to the new order by pursuing the occupations of the future: trade and agriculture. In Red River, these "persistent Métis" – the ones who stayed in the district during the 1870s and 1880s – were more likely to be those who in previous decades had moved beyond subsistence to acquire more land and larger herds. They were often wealthier traders who did *not* participate (or no longer participated) in the actual production of buffalo robes or in the trade and freighting on the prairies. It is noteworthy that this phenomenon of persistence was much greater among the English- than the French-speaking Métis, a measure of the Ontario Protestant bigotry that drove the French-speaking Catholics out of Manitoba during this generation.[34] The persisters, expressing a different kind of agency, had made the transition to the new capitalist order and were now ready to embark on larger mercantile experiments or to participate in the wheat export economy. It is questionable, however, whether all of them remained Métis, as that community defined itself in the succeeding generation. Instead, some of the successful entrepreneurs had become simply Canadians; they were defined, like other Canadians, by their linguistic and religious choices (French or English, Catholic or Protestant), but they were not significantly affected by race-based categorization. They may even have put their Aboriginal ancestry behind them, denying it in order to pass for "white" in the not-so-tolerant world of twentieth-century Canada.[35]

The Métis community has survived. It finds its membership among the descendants of the economic adventurers of the 1840 to 1880 era. No one can deny the power of this heritage. The Métis themselves laboured between the 1890s and the 1930s to ensure that elders were interviewed and that their version of the past was published in A.-H. de Trémaudan's *Histoire de la nation métisse*.[36] They also campaigned for collective political recognition, a strategy that produced the Alberta Métis settlements (founded in 1938-39), and, in 1981-82, inclusion in the patriated Canadian constitution.[37] This tradition, this consciousness of what the elders described as a "nation," has been a foundation of Métis identity in the twentieth century.

It is time to emphasize the new departures in Métis history. Having rejected the race-based and frontier interpretations of an earlier generation, students of the Métis need not be limited by research into land claims.

They will find fruitful approaches in social history and, in particular, in the Métis' mediating role in economic and social relations in the northwestern interior of North America. They have already noted the relevance of the Michif language and Métis material culture to this transitional status. They have also employed the analogy of European peasant households to clarify the Métis shift to a "proto-industrial economy" in the 1840s and 1850s. In so doing, they emphasize the international context of capitalism in this era and, in looking at the expanding world-economy from below, note *both* the lack of control in *all* local economies *and* the strategies for resistance to the new rules about property and power in this particular community. By assessing the political factions and differing economic activities in Métis society itself, this new historical writing will arrive at new estimates of the degree to which the Métis people made their own history (or, as labour historians would put it, the degree of Métis agency), including the differences in interest and behaviour among the merchant-farmers, hunters, and freighters, the differences in perspective between men and women, and the accommodation and conflict that marked relations between the Christian church and Aboriginal spirituality. Finally, such a history can re-examine the emergence of a group identity – a consciousness rooted as much in heritage as in language or economy or "race" – that survives to this day.

NOTES

This paper was prepared for the Australian-Canadian Labour History Conference, December 1988. I would like to thank Jean Friesen for her comments on it.

1. Olive Patricia Dickason, "From 'One Nation' in the Northeast to 'New Nation' in the Northwest: A Look at the Emergence of the Métis," in *The New Peoples: Being and Becoming Métis in North America,* ed. Jacqueline Peterson and Jennifer S.H. Brown (Winnipeg: University of Manitoba Press, 1985); another perspective is in Carl N. Degler, *Neither Black Nor White: Slavery and Race Relations in Brazil and the United States* (New York: Macmillan, 1971).
2. Jacqueline Peterson, "Prelude to Red River: A Social Portrait of the Great Lakes Métis," *Ethnohistory* 25 (winter 1978); Jacqueline Peterson, "The People in Between: Indian-White Marriage and the Genesis of a Métis Society and Culture in the Great Lakes Region, 1680-1830," Ph.D. dissertation, University of Illinois at Chicago Circle, 1981.
3. John E. Foster, "The Home Guard Cree and the Hudson's Bay Company: The First Hundred Years," in *Approaches to Native History in Canada,* ed. D.A. Muise (Ottawa: National Museums of Canada, 1976); and John E. Foster, "Some Questions and Perspectives on the Problem of Métis Roots," in *The New Peoples,* ed. Peterson and Brown; Sylvia van Kirk, *"Many Tender Ties": Women in Fur-Trade Society in Western Canada, 1670-1870* (Winnipeg: Watson and Dwyer, 1980); Jennifer S.H. Brown, *Strangers in Blood: Fur-Trade Families in Indian Country* (Vancouver: University of British Columbia Press, 1980).
4. Though the community's boundaries have never been fixed and are often crossed, the concepts of Métis people and Métis nation have significance for an unknown proportion of the 750,000 people in modern Canada who might claim membership in the group (Jennifer S.H. Brown, "Métis," *The Canadian Encyclopedia,* 2nd ed. [Edmonton: Hurtig, 1988], 1,343-46).

5. Marcel Giraud, *Le Métis Canadien: Son rôle dans l'histoire des provinces de l'Ouest* (Paris: Institut d'Ethnologie, 1945; translated by George Woodcock as *The Métis in the Canadian West*, vol. 1 [Lincoln: University of Nebraska Press, 1986]), 211. The volume was also reprinted in French (St. Boniface: Les Editions du Blé, 1984).

6. The main works include: Alexander Ross, *The Red River Settlement* (London: Smith, Elder and Company, 1856; reprinted Edmonton: Hurtig, 1972); R.G. Macbeth, *The Making of the Canadian West: Being the Reminiscences of an Eye-Witness* (Toronto: William Briggs, 1898); George F.G. Stanley, *The Birth of Western Canada: A History of the Riel Rebellions* (London: Longman's Green, 1936; Toronto: University of Toronto Press, 1960).

7. D.P. Benoit, *Vie de Monseigneur Taché, archevêque de Saint-Boniface,* 2 vols. (Montreal: Librarie Beauchemin, 1904); A.G. Morice, *History of the Catholic Church in Western Canada,* 2 vols. (Toronto: Musson Book Company, 1910).

8. Recent review essays include: Jennifer S.H. Brown, "People of Myth, People of History: A Look at Recent Writings on the Métis," *Acadiensis* 17 (fall 1987); and, J.R. Miller, "From Riel to the Métis," *Canadian Historical Review* 69 (March 1988). Other publications include: Peter Erasmus, *Buffalo Days and Nights: As Told to Henry Thompson,* edited and with an introduction by Irene Spry (Calgary: Glenbow-Alberta Foundation, 1976); Mary Weekes, *The Last Buffalo Hunter* (Saskatoon: Fifth House, 1994; first published 1939); Diane Payment, *"The Free People – Otipemisewak": Batoche, Saskatchewan, 1870-1930* (Ottawa: Minister of Supply and Services, 1990); Guillaume Charette, *Vanishing Spaces (Memories of a Prairie Métis)* (Winnipeg: Editions Bois-Brûlés, 1976); Donald Purich, *The Metis* (Toronto: James Lorimer, 1988).

9. Sylvia van Kirk, "Fur-Trade Social History: Some Recent Trends," in *Old Trails and New Directions: Papers of the Third North American Fur Trade Conference,* ed. Carol M. Judd and Arthur J. Ray (Toronto: University of Toronto Press, 1980).

10. The most vivid portrait is in Maria Campbell, *Halfbreed* (Toronto: McClelland and Stewart, 1973). Another important study is Murray Dobbin, *The One-and-a-Half Men: The Story of Jim Brady and Malcolm Norris, Métis Patriots of the Twentieth Century* (Vancouver: New Star Books, 1981). An important report was, J.H. Lagassé, *A Study of the Population of Indian Ancestry Living in Manitoba* (Winnipeg: Queen's Printer, 1959). See also, Ken Zeilig and Victoria Zeilig, *Ste. Madeleine: Community without a Town: Métis Elders in Interview* (Winnipeg: Pemmican Publications, 1987).

11. Philip Goldring, "Governor Simpson's Officers: Elite Recruitment in a British Overseas Enterprise, 1834-1870," *Prairie Forum* 10 (autumn 1985); C.M. Judd, "Native Labour and Social Stratification in the Hudson's Bay Company's Northern Department, 1770-1870," *Canadian Review of Sociology and Anthropology* 17, no. 4 (1980).

12. van Kirk, *"Many Tender Ties";* Frits Pannekoek, "The Anglican Church and the Disintegration of Red River Society, 1818-1870," in *The West and the Nation: Essays in Honour of W.L. Morton,* ed. Carl Berger and Ramsay Cook (Toronto: McClelland and Stewart, 1976).

13. Frits Pannekoek, "The Rev. Griffiths Owen Corbett and the Red River Civil War of 1869-70," *Canadian Historical Review* 57, no. 2 (1976); Pannekoek, "Some Comments on the Social Origin of the Riel Protest of 1869," *Historical and Scientific Society of Manitoba,* series 3, vol. 34 (1977-78); and, Pannekoek, *A Snug Little Flock: The Social Origins of the Riel Resistance of 1869-70* (Winnipeg: Watson and Dwyer, 1991).

14. D.N. Sprague, "Government Lawlessness in the Administration of Manitoba Land Claims, 1870-1887," *Manitoba Law Journal* 10 (1980); and, Sprague, "The Manitoba Land Question, 1870-1882," *Journal of Canadian Studies* 15 (1980); and, Sprague, *Canada and the Métis, 1869-1885* (Waterloo: Wilfrid Laurier University Press, 1988).

15. Allen Edgar Ronaghan, "The Archibald Administration in Manitoba, 1870-72," Ph.D. dissertation, University of Manitoba, 1987.

16. Gerhard Ens, "Dispossession or Adaptation? Migration and Persistence of the Red River Métis, 1835-1890," Canadian Historical Association, *Historical Papers,* 1988.

17. Sprague, *Canada and the Métis;* Thomas Flanagan, *Riel and the Rebellion: 1885 Reconsidered* (Saskatoon: Western Producer Prairie Books, 1983); and, T.E. Flanagan, "Métis Claims at St. Laurent: Old Arguments and New Evidence," *Prairie Forum* 12, no. 2 (1987); F. Laurie

Barron and James B. Waldram, eds. *1885 and After: Native Society in Transition* (Regina: Canadian Plains Research Center, 1986).

18. The Manitoba Court of Appeal ruled on aspects of the case in 1988. That ruling has been appealed to the Supreme Court of Canada.

19. Arthur J. Ray, *Indians in the Fur Trade: Their Role as Hunters, Trappers and Middlemen in the Lands Southwest of Hudson Bay* (Toronto: University of Toronto Press, 1974); Hugh Brody, *Maps and Dreams* (Vancouver: Douglas and McIntyre, 1981).

20. John C. Crawford, "What is Michif? Language in the Métis Tradition," in *The New Peoples*, ed. Peterson and Brown. See also: Margaret Stobie, "Backgrounds of the Dialect Called Bungi," Historical and Scientific Society of Manitoba, *Transactions*, 1968; and, Peter Bakker, "'A Language of Our Own': The Genesis of Michif, the Mixed Cree-French Language of the Canadian Métis," Ph.D. dissertation, University of Amsterdam, 1992.

21. Peterson, "Prelude to Red River."

22. Maurice F.V. Doll, Robert S. Kidd, and John P. Day, *The Buffalo Lake Métis Site: A Late Nineteenth Century Settlement in the Parkland of Central Alberta* (Edmonton: Provincial Museum of Alberta Human History Occasional Paper No. 4, 1988), 22-3.

23. Peterson, "Prelude to Red River"; and, Irene M. Spry, "The Transition from a Nomadic to a Settled Economy in Western Canada, 1856-96," *Transactions of the Royal Society of Canada*, series 4, vol. 4 (1968), section 2.

24. Ens, "Dispossession or Adaptation?"

25. Ibid.

26. Doll, Kidd, and Day, *Buffalo Lake*.

27. E.J. Hobsbawm, *Labouring Men: Studies in the History of Labour* (London: Weidenfeld and Nicolson, 1964; 1968), 276.

28. Irene M. Spry, "The Tragedy of the Loss of the Commons in Western Canada," in *As Long As The Sun Shines and Water Flows: A Reader In Canadian Native Studies*, ed. Ian A.L. Getty and Antoine S. Lussier (Vancouver: University of British Columbia Press, 1983); Robert M. Gosman, "The Riel and Lagimodière Families in Métis Society, 1840-1860," Parks Canada Manuscript Report No. 171 (Ottawa: Parks Canada, 1975; 1977).

29. E.J. Hobsbawm, *The Age of Capital, 1848-1875* (New York: Charles Scribner's Sons, 1975); and, Hobsbawm, *The Age of Empire, 1875-1914* (London: Weidenfeld and Nicolson, 1987). Donald Denoon, *Settler Capitalism: The Dynamics of Dependent Development in the Southern Hemisphere* (Oxford: Clarendon Press, 1983).

30. Spry, "The Tragedy of the Loss of the Commons."

31. Jean Friesen, "Magnificent Gifts: The Treaties of Canada with the Indians of the Northwest, 1869-1876," *Transactions of the Royal Society of Canada*, series 5, vol. 1 (1986); Thomas Flanagan, "Louis Riel and Aboriginal Rights," in *As Long As The Sun Shines*, ed. Getty and Lussier.

32. Doll, Kidd, and Day, *Buffalo Lake*, 47.

33. Thomas Flanagan, ed., *The Collected Writings of Louis Riel / Les écrits complets de Louis Riel*, vol. 3 (Edmonton: University of Alberta Press, 1986), 27-9.

34. Ens, "Dispossession or Adaptation?"

35. Provincial Archives of Manitoba, Manitoba Historical Society Papers, "Programme, 28 October 1947 . . . John Norquay," and Société Historique de Saint-Boniface, Reverend Dr. A. d'Eschambault to Honorable Ivan Schultz, 27 November 1947, re: debate over Norquay's ancestry; also, *Winnipeg Tribune*, 16 October 1954, and Legislative Library of Manitoba, Norquay file. I discuss the Norquay episode in the penultimate paragraph of the essay entitled "River Road" in this volume.

36. Auguste-Henri de Trémaudan, *Histoire de la nation métisse dans l'ouest canadien* (1936; reprint Saint-Boniface: Les Editions du Blé, 1979).

37. T.C. Pocklington, *The Government and Politics of the Alberta Metis Settlements* (Regina: Canadian Plains Research Center, 1991).

The Manitoba Historical Society:
A Centennial History

IN THE LATE FALL of 1879, the Historical and Scientific Society of Manitoba, then about six months old, convened to hear an address by John Macoun, who was just returning from a summer on the prairies of the western interior. The event is a convenient occasion by which to take the measure of the Society, to analyze its origins and to assess its achievements in the intervening 100 years. On the appointed night, the old City Hall on Main Street was "completely filled" by a distinguished audience that was said to include "much of the worth and intelligence of Winnipeg." The citizens parked their carriages and tied their horses on either side of the wide, rutted street and stepped onto the board walkways, boot heels ringing in the frosty air. Ignoring the shouts from several nearby taverns, they entered the lamplight at the door and mingled with the other leaders of Manitoba society. It was an exciting evening, precisely because it was all so new. Manitoba itself seemed a new world. Of the oldtimers, McTavish of the Hudson's Bay Company (HBC) was gone, James McKay of Deer Lodge was on his deathbed, and Louis Riel, now in exile somewhere near the Missouri River, was little more than a name. With few exceptions, these citizens had arrived in the province within the decade. To them an old-timer was John Christian Schultz, who had come to Red River in 1859, or Jim Ashdown, who had walked from St. Cloud to Red

River in 1868. The number of native-born Red River citizens in their midst, such as the Métis Premier, John Norquay, was tiny. This audience crackled with excitement because John Macoun would provide the first real assessment of the worth of their empire.

As the members settled in their oak armchairs, Chief Justice Wood introduced their guest in his inimitable style. Wood's brief message reflected the local assumptions about economic development: "We are now waking up to the conviction," he said, "that our North-West is destined to be one of the most important parts of the globe, . . . and with the older eastern Provinces . . . will soon be the right arm of the British Empire." John Macoun took up this theme where the chief justice had left off. He responded to the hearty applause with a few jokes, told stories about his trek across the vast plains and, as everyone hoped, provided enthusiastic reports about the potential of the prairie soil and the salubrity of prairie climate. Here was the confirmation of the best features of the Hind and Palliser reports that Winnipeggers had awaited. Macoun was assuring them that the West would soon constitute an agricultural empire. His concluding comment, a statement attributed to Lord Beaconsfield, described this imperial frontier as a land of "illimitable opportunities." His words provoked cheers from the audience.[1]

In this event can be seen three important reasons for the foundation of the Historical and Scientific Society of Manitoba in 1879. First, the leading citizens of the prairie province were proclaiming that theirs was the next great frontier of opportunity. Like Nova Scotia historians a half-century earlier, the founders of the Society wished to correct the false impressions prevailing in a national and international audience about their distant land.[2] They wanted investors in the world's financial centres to see that the global wave of economic development had reached the western interior of Canada.

Second, by conducting thorough historical and scientific analysis, the Society's leaders would demonstrate that, as scholars and gentlemen, they were ready to take their places as partners in the international pursuit of truth. Thus, for a few brief years, the Manitoba Historical and Scientific Society corresponded with members of Britain's Royal Society and Washington's Smithsonian Institution. It enquired into the physical and social foundations of the region. Members classified its fauna and flora, defined its geological strata, estimated its potential fertility, solved such engineering problems as sanitary water supply and hard-surface roads and, of course, recorded its past. Members devoted many hours to the collection of specimens that were exchanged with museums across the continent. They wrote learned papers, sought reference works, and went on field trips that could best be described as scientific expeditions. The Society was, thus, both a booster of investment and a central institution in the advancement of western claims upon international attention.

A third important reason for the foundation of the Historical Society lay in the exigencies of a relatively unsettled Victorian community situated on what was perceived to be the frontier of empire. Living in a world accustomed to metaphors that compared the "arts" of London with the "savagery" of various hinterlands, recent arrivals in Winnipeg were very much aware of the delicate state of their transplanted civilization. The Historical Society's leaders accepted the responsibility for ensuring that the new way of life would be established upon the firm foundations of a millennium of British achievements. These self-appointed "better elements" in local society were responsible for the definition and promotion of cultural standards. The Historical Society, with its elected members, its comfortable club rooms, and its large library stacked with current newspapers, journals, and reference books was thus an expression of their social concerns and of their sense of mission to the less prosperous members of the community.

Analysis of the membership further confirms the central place of the Society in prairie public and cultural life. This was not an egalitarian community of rustics with limited education and rough-hewn manners. Fully one-half of the members in its first and most active period (1879 to 1886) could be described as professionals – doctors, lawyers, teachers, clergy, accountants, civil engineers – and another one-third were clearly members of the business community, whether merchants, real-estate dealers, bankers, or small-scale manufacturers. Thus, over eighty percent of the members were businessmen and professionals. Of over 500 individuals who were members at some time in this era and whose occupations can be identified, only one was a labourer, one a farmer, one a dressmaker, and five were railway engineers or conductors. Given that, in the entire city of Winnipeg in 1886, only one quarter of the population was engaged in professional or business pursuits, the select nature of the membership is even more apparent. In those days, when professions were just beginning to create formal rules for the training of their members, and when such training was still not available in this capital city of 20,000, a surprising proportion of the papers presented to the Society and the research trips that it sponsored were undertaken by qualified professionals: Reverend George Bryce on history, Ernest Thompson Seton on animal life, Dr. Kerr on public health, and J. Hoyes Panton on the geology of the Red River Valley. These men, by training or by a period of apprenticeship, were specialists in their fields.

Another way to express this emphasis upon education and exclusivity is to note that, as far as can be determined, only eleven women joined the society in this period. This might seem unusual, given that women on North American frontiers were expected to take a special interest not only in educational institutions such as schools and libraries but also in community activities such as musical and dramatic performances. Why the men did not automatically rely on women's help in the case of the Manitoba Historical Society must be related to their own perceptions of gender and especially to the priority they attached to the Society's economic and scientific, as opposed to its social, roles. Thus, when defending the admission of the first two women in 1883, the executive explained the recruitment of Dr. Lillian Yeomans and Miss Sinclair was "not for the purpose of swelling the numbers of the society, nor yet out of mere compliment. . . . It is believed that there are ladies of education, literary habits and good powers of observation who might be of much service. . . . All workers will be cordially welcomed."[3] This was a serious public agency and, like the Board of Trade and the City Council, was treated by its male leaders as a largely male preserve.

Though the Society was almost entirely middle-class in its social composition, its statement of purpose suggests that it wished to be seen not simply as a vehicle of class interest but also as an educational agency for the entire community. Like the Mechanics' Institutes of Nova Scotia in the 1830s or the public museums that sprang up in England in the 1840s, the Historical Society was expected to elevate the character and raise the aspirations of all classes of citizens.[4] The Society's leaders accepted their responsibility as secular missionaries to the lower classes, but they did not expect the labourers to use their new-found knowledge for class advantage. To this end, the Society sponsored lecturers, organized an archaeological and geological museum, presented the first art exhibition in western Canada and, most important of all, established a public library. Each of these endeavours was marked by the strong sense of purpose that distinguished the presentation of learned papers. The library collection of magazines, for example, despite the odd title like *Punch* or *Grip*, was said to contain "the very marrow of intellectual life." The book-selection policy was to acquire "not only works of fiction to attract the idle, the inquisitive and frivolous but works which invite the scholar, instruct the diligent enquirer, and detain the serious." One can sense the pride of Reverend George Bryce when he announced in 1886 that, as a result of the Society's initiative, "almost any important book on the North West is now within reach of the historian without leaving the Provincial boundaries." The library held over 10,000 volumes by this time, including many gifts from the Smithsonian Institution and the American government, the 4,000-volume Isbister collection (on loan from the University of Manitoba), and 300 works on Canada and the North West provided by the HBC and individual donors. The library, like the other initiatives of the Society, demonstrated the determination of these newcomers to create a vital literate culture as quickly as they built an agricultural economy.[5]

The three-fold role of the Historical Society as public-relations agency, scientific institute, and cultural standardbearer (or educational vehicle) was attested by the financial statements of the early years. The numerous publications, the expeditions, the comfortable rooms, and the growing museum collection were paid for from two principal sources: a membership fee and government grants. The actual work of the society was carried out by volunteers, except for that done by a hired clerk-librarian. Thus, in a budget that ranged from $1,000 to $3,000 per year, the Province of Manitoba contributed about $250 and the City of Winnipeg about $500, this latter specifically to support book purchases and the clerk-librarian's salary. Naturally, a society that counted the premier and most of his Cabinet in its membership was not bashful when it found itself short of funds. At the end of 1881, for example, the executive announced that "in view of the work undertaken, . . . a fair obligation rests on the Provincial Government to increase the annual grant." The grant was doubled.

Hard times and changing circumstances undermined the Society just as it seemed destined to lead cultural developments in Manitoba for the next generation. Within a decade of its creation, it foundered. Where, in the early 1880s, it could count on 200 to 400 active members to undertake commitments and to pay full membership fees, by the end of the decade only about fifty to seventy active members paid their fees in any given year. The recession of 1887 must have had some influence; the creation of associate memberships ($2 rather than $5) gave library privileges but not voting rights and undoubtedly encouraged many to ignore the public meetings; grant of free library access to University of Manitoba students, part of the arrangement that placed the University's prized Isbister library on the Society's shelves, was blamed for a drop in interest because students could borrow books for the whole family. Above all these reasons was the fact that Winnipeg had passed beyond the frontier stage of social development. Though the committed scholars and the more prominent business leaders retained their memberships, no doubt out of interest but also from a sense of duty, many others ceased to feel responsible for support of the Society. The era when any scientific knowledge was welcome – when John Macoun could pack a hall simply by describing the vegetation and climate of the plains – had been succeeded by the regular rhythms of an established community. The role of the Society as a crucial pillar of Manitoba's economic aspirations and scientific analysis had come to an end. With many clubs and institutions to claim their attention, with regular working hours to keep and an income to earn, and with the prospect of increasingly esoteric topics of research at its meetings, numerous citizens had come to see the Society as simply another voluntary interest group among many.

This second era lasted from the late 1880s until the utter collapse of the group in 1910. In these two decades, the important institutions created by the Society either separated from it or disintegrated. The pride of the Society – its library – underwent a series of organizational changes, from joint City-Society sponsorship to City control. And, finally, when the Society was asked to leave the overburdened City Hall in 1905, most of the library was moved to the new Carnegie Library Building. At this point, part of the reference collection was placed in Manitoba College under the supervision of Reverend Bryce. Part of the Society's geological collection was moved to the University of Manitoba, and much of its museum collection was placed in the basement of a member's house. With the move out of City Hall, home for almost two decades, the Society was without a permanent office for the first time since its establishment. It seems an appropriate image for this trying period. The executive toyed with the idea of building a reproduction of the Upper Fort around Fort Garry Gate that might serve as a headquarters, and they even sent George Bryce to ask Lord Strathcona for the money, but, in the end, this scheme, too, evaporated.[6]

The Society had lost the sense of purpose that it had in 1879. Its function as public relations and scientific research institute had been taken over by a dozen agencies including the government experimental farms, the University, the many local newspapers and other journals. Its function as a public educational service had been assumed by the civic library and the school system or was being shared by other specialized interest groups such as the Manitoba Society of Artists.[7] Indeed, when some upstarts founded a new Natural History Society in apparent competition with that section of its own group, the Historical Society executive dispatched one of its members to set the matter right. He returned with the sobering news that the upstarts had no intention of giving way.[8] Finally the Society's function as a cultural standardbearer was not being fulfilled to the satisfaction of the younger leaders of Winnipeg. In the view of a Dafoe or a Woodsworth, the city's social problems no longer revolved around the assertion of "civilized" standards of behaviour in the face of frontier roughness, as might have been the case in 1880; now the crucial issues concerned European immigrants and their children, the use of alcohol, the relations between capital and labour, and the place of women in political life.[9] An historical society led by the old men of an earlier era – George Bryce of Manitoba College, the retired fur trader Isaac Cowie, and HBC Chief Factor Camsell – was not attuned to the new language, nor was it equipped to respond to the new needs.

If the Society was failing as an agency of social action, it was also discovering a new role in this era. Like historical societies in other parts of North America, it acquired a broader purpose in the last years of the nineteenth and the opening decades of the twentieth century. These groups continued to act as collectors of documents and preservers of sites and artifacts, a role that had always been theirs, but they also assumed an aggressive stance in the definition of the community's particular character. In Ontario, for example, the reorganized Ontario Historical Society embarked upon an ambitious publication and education programme in 1898. In the following sixteen years, it devoted an extraordinary amount of energy to the stimulation of Canadian patriotism and imperial loyalty through Empire Day celebrations and gifts of Union Jacks to the schools, the publication of numerous volumes of central Canadian history, and the sponsorship of public festivals.[10]

The Manitoba Historical Society was unable to match this energetic public campaign, but it did respond to the intellectual challenge of defining the community's character. Particularly through the lectures and books of George Bryce, but also through the work of R.G. MacBeth and others, a Society consensus on the peculiar place of the western interior within Confederation – separate from eastern Canada and British Columbia and yet still an inheritor of the British tradition – was established. This was the first significant historical interpretation of the region to be written within the prairies. It emphasized the British-ness of the West and especially the debt to Lord Selkirk's pioneer colonists; it preferred the HBC of England to the Nor'Westers of Montreal, and thus underlined western independence from eastern economic organization in an age – the opening decade of the twentieth century – when eastern power seemed oppressive. It treated the Native people as little more than ciphers who moved at the commands of the European newcomers; the Métis and Riel were seen as dupes of the Roman Catholic Church; and, not surprisingly, the schools question was said to be further proof of priestly designs upon Manitoba. The Historical Society may not have been a leader of the local community after the mid-1880s, but, thanks in particular to the work of George Bryce, it had contributed to the popularization of a "western interpretation" of Canadian history.[11]

The closing phase of this chapter of the Society's existence was even more difficult. Attempts to assemble a program in 1910 apparently collapsed and the plan for a great exposition on the centennial of the Selkirk settlement produced little enthusiasm. Nothing more was heard of the Society until 1913, when a few loyal souls tried to reorganize it. This effort, too, came to naught, and, once the Great War began, it was simply allowed to disappear.[12] The students of natural history twice re-established their own separate movement, in 1915 as an Audubon society and in 1920 as a natural history society (forerunner of the present Manitoba Naturalists), but the historians were unable to regroup.[13] Thus, from 1910 to 1926, the Historical Society was moribund.

In 1926, as a result of the efforts of Dr. D.A. Stewart, C.N. Bell,

W.J. Healy, and Professor Chester Martin, a revival of the Society was attempted. Though it survived for a decade, the inter-war version of the Historical Society was much weaker than its predecessor. Its declaration of purpose emphasized not research but the collection and preservation of historical records. The study of local history was to be encouraged not because it was a respectable discipline but rather because it would foster "local patriotism." Publication of Manitoba studies was noted in the declaration but, to judge from the three slim papers that were produced, was not important. In an age when professional historical studies had risen to prominence, when membership in the Canadian Historical Association and research in Ottawa's Public Archives and publication in the *Canadian Historical Review* had been made hallmarks of professional achievement, local historical societies suffered a corresponding reduction in scholarly status. The Manitoba Historical Society had thus become an agency for public historical education.[14]

When one considers the times and the resources at its disposal, the record of the Society in the inter-war years was certainly respectable. Though operating without government assistance (the Bracken government refused a request for aid in the late 1920s), and with a nominal membership fee of one or two dollars, it stretched its annual budget of several hundred dollars to support a variety of activities. Chief among these was the annual series of public lectures, now aimed at popular surveys rather than original scholarship. To cite the example of 1930, Manitoba's Diamond Jubilee, members heard such programs as J.W. Dafoe's review of "Sixty Years of Journalism" and Dean McKillican's "Sixty Years of Agriculture."

Another prominent activity was the placement of plaques to commemorate certain sites and events in Manitoba history. The Society had sponsored only one plaque in its early years (the Seven Oaks Monument, 1891), but it now joined with its French equivalent, La Société Historique de Saint-Boniface, and the national Historic Sites Board to hold elaborate unveiling ceremonies as part of its public education program. La Vérendrye's Fort la Reine (Portage la Prairie, 1928), the first western Indian Treaty (Lower Fort Garry, 1928), the Dominion Land Survey (near Headingley, 1931), the first grain export from Winnipeg (Lombard Street, 1933), and a number of other sites were marked in this fashion.[15] Thus, as the Depression deepened, the Society continued to operate on a reduced scale.

Regular meetings ceased around 1936. Explanations for the failure are not obvious aside from the general circumstances of the time. A close examination of the membership demonstrates little significant change in social composition since the late nineteenth century. As in the early years, three-quarters of the members, or seventy-five of 100, were business and professional people. Teachers now played a much more prominent part, twenty-five percent instead of about five percent, and the proportion of women had increased to twenty percent from one percent, but the membership rolls tell us little else. One might conclude that the Society was sustained by teachers and interested laypeople in this era and that, lacking a larger purpose than the diffuse goal of historical education, having no fixed headquarters nor office staff nor material expression of government support, it withered in the face of hard times.

The spirit of the Society in this era was epitomized by the most important Manitoba provincial history of the inter-war period, Margaret McWilliams's *Manitoba Milestones*.[16] The author, a leader in voluntary associations and cultural activities, was a dedicated lay historian whose balanced view of society contrasted sharply with the Scots-ness of George Bryce and R.G. MacBeth. Like them, it is true, she commenced her book with European "discovery," and, like them, she ignored Native history, but her treatment of post-1870 Manitoba was detailed and balanced. Her discussion of ethnic immigration was not marred by the overt racist sentiments of Reverend Wellington Bridgman. Her outline of the 1890 schools issue explained the Roman Catholic position and avoided the militant tones of Bryce. Even in her treatment of the 1916 debates over language in the schools, where she obviously supported the Norris government decision to establish a unilingual English system, she explained the concerns of Norris's opponents with clarity if not sympathy. This concern for both sides of an issue was not quite as evident, however, in her treatment of the 1919 general strike. The sweep and balance of *Manitoba Milestones* were measures of McWilliams's wide perspective and suggested the intellectual sophistication of Manitoba society in the 1920s. The work undertaken and sponsored by the Historical Society in the preceding half-century might be given some of the credit for the maturity of McWilliams's study.

The modern era of the Manitoba Historical Society began at an informal meeting in the Legislative Building in 1944.[17] Professor W.L. Morton, of the University of Manitoba, and J. Leslie Johnston, Provincial Librarian, collaborated with Margaret McWilliams to reconstitute the organization. Despite the adverse circumstances of wartime, they were very successful. Joined by a number of distinguished citizens in the following years, they imparted an enthusiasm and a sense of purpose to the Society that sustained it in the following decades. Why these individuals should have come together at this time and should have experienced such success is not explained by any obvious circumstance, and yet one is struck by similar experiences in other communities. The Ontario Historical Society disintegrated in the late 1930s and was revived in 1944. The American Association for State and Local History was founded in 1940. Perhaps most striking of all, state aid for cultural activities became popular in many jurisdictions in the 1940s. Janet Minihan discovered that "in a single decade, during and after the Second World War, the British Government did more to commit itself to supporting the arts than it had in the previous century and a half."[18] Canada experienced this same awakening of state interest in culture; out of the House of Commons Committee on Reconstruction and Re-establishment of 1944 (the Turgeon Committee) had come the interest in government assistance for the arts that eventually led to the Massey Commission.[19]

While it is beyond my purview in this paper to explain this revolution in state activity, some of the reasons for the new government stance might be noted. The war itself had made evident the vast size of the audience available for government-sponsored artistic and cultural events and suggested that the state could define cultural ideals. The prospect of building a new society after the war encouraged citizens to consider policy innovations. The place of radio in the development of cultural policy cannot be ignored. In Canada, as in Britain, radio opened the eyes of the state to the importance of culture in national life and to the manipulative powers of this new communications technology. State regulation followed quickly, and, once begun, its extension into new realms of cultural expression was only a matter of time. The growth of government activity in all realms of life was parallelled by the development of what is now described as the "leisure culture," and the availability of free time, in turn, made possible mass interest in the arts. Thus, one might have predicted that governments would see the advantages of using art to foster "national identity," to encourage "loyalty," and to create "the symbols of integration" in their societies.[20]

Such explanations can be related to the re-establishment of the Manitoba Historical Society. History had been an important source of moral and patriotic lessons in Canada as elsewhere, and there is little doubt that the three leaders of the Historical Society looked upon it in this light. Moreover, their alliance with a Manitoba cabinet minister should be noted. The interest of the Honourable Ivan Schultz in Manitoba's ethnic composition and his decision to contribute government funds resulted in the first scholarly enterprise of the new society, a series of historical works on provincial ethnic groups.[21] Thus, one can conclude that a change in the relationship between state and culture occurred in the mid-twentieth century.

Government interest in cultural activities was supplemented in this era by strong academic support for local historical activity. Under the direction of Johnston and Morton, for example, the Society had pressed for the establishment of a proper provincial archives. In 1946, a part-time archivist, James A. Jackson, was appointed to supervise archival operations, and in 1952, after Jackson's departure for the Winnipeg schools system, Hart Bowsfield was named as full-time Provincial Archivist.[22] Agitation for proper space and an aggressive collections policy were maintained thereafter, and, in 1975, the present handsome facility was opened. That it contained as well the archives of the HBC was a stroke of fortune unprecedented in the history of scholarship in the province.

Another of the Society's research responsibilities in the post-war years was the result of Chris Vickers's devotion to scholarship. A lay student of archaeology, Vickers was so determined to preserve artifacts and to further the study of Manitoba prehistory that the Society and the government agreed to sponsor his work for a number of years. The result was the creation of a Department of Anthropology in the University of Manitoba, the establishment of a Manitoba Archaeological Society (1960), the appointment of a provincial archaeologist (1974), and the general acknowledgement of Vickers as the "father of Manitoba archaeology."[23]

Yet another Society contribution to research in this era lay in the realm of publications. Through its annual volume of *Transactions,* revived in 1944-45, its aid to the Manitoba Record Society (1960 to the present), its sponsorship of the *Historical Atlas,* the *Centennial History,* and the popular *Extraordinary Tales,* the Society has made available a wealth of historical material to professional and lay students within the province and beyond its borders. Archival development and primary research were thus important aspects of the Society's work after 1944. Their success prompted W.L. Morton to recall the ambitious purposes of its founders in 1879 and to suggest that Manitoba was coming of age as a community and a culture.[24]

The impetus for the 1944 reorganization of the Society may have come from a librarian and two historians, and one focus of its activities may have dealt with professional scholarship, but another, equally prominent, purpose of the leadership was popular education. This involved interviews with pioneers and the collection of papers for the archives in the first instance, but it soon moved on to encompass plaque unveilings, an essay contest (the Margaret McWilliams awards), and encouragement to groups wishing to prepare local historical studies. In 1956, the award-winning magazine of local history, *Manitoba Pageant,* designed for use in the schools, was launched by Alice Brown, among others, and in 1960 a program to assist small museums, particularly to provide curatorial training, was begun. The rapid development of rural museums and, indeed, of local branches of the Historical Society, and even of student societies, resulted from this outpouring of activity in the late 1950s and early 1960s.[25]

Scholarship, archival collections, and public education were supplemented by renewed efforts in another realm. Historic preservation had been an interest of the Society since Fort Garry Gate began to disintegrate in the 1880s, so it was only fitting that the revival of interest in that structure should have occurred in the 1940s. Ross House, the first post office in the Northwest, became the property of the Society in this era, and as a modest museum it attracted many visitors. There were failures, such as the destruction of Nellie McClung's house in Manitou (1964), and, inevitably, there were moments when projects seemed beyond the resources of the Society. On these occasions, other jurisdictions were encouraged to take on such tasks as the restoration of Lower Fort Garry and of Riel House in St. Vital.[26] As it happened, however, the greatest enterprise in Society history was one that should have been too large for this small group. The professional restoration of Dalnavert (Premier Hugh John Macdonald's house) resulted from the determination of Society members to preserve the provincial architectural heritage and from their faith that a Victorian museum could be built upon the resources of this community. Kathleen Richardson, Kathleen Campbell, Steward Martin, and their many helpers created a monument to a way of life and a considerable force for historical education. It is fitting that the capital debt of over a half-million dollars, a sum far larger than the entire revenue of the Society in its first 100 years, should have been retired in 1979, the Society's centennial year.

The scholarly work of W.L. Morton, like that of George Bryce and Margaret McWilliams, can be taken as representative of an era of Historical Society activity.[27] Morton's *Manitoba: A History*, first published in 1957, immediately was recognized as Canada's finest provincial history, and his perception of his native province was undoubtedly the one espoused by his contemporaries and presented to a generation of students. Morton's concern for agricultural history, his awareness of the very different societies created in rural and urban Manitoba, his interest in cultural developments, and his sensitivity to ethnic identities, all of which were reflected in the book, were also important strains in the new provincial historical consciousness. Morton's was the first truly "professional" history of the province and its academic value reflected the changing nature of historical study in Canada. One of Morton's strengths was his desire to explain relations between local events and broader historical developments. Thus, his careful attention to the particulars of Manitoba life did not blind him to the historical themes of region, nation, empire, and beyond: in his work, one had the sense that Manitoba's past was a part of the history of the world.

Interest in history has not flagged in recent years; indeed, it seems to have increased dramatically, but the funding of the Society has not kept pace. In the 1940s, when the ethnic history scholarships were its chief financial responsibility, the Society received $3,000 to $5,000 annually from the government and raised a small additional sum from its membership. In 1953, when the Honourable Ivan Schultz tired of this imbalance, he instituted a system of matching grants, dollar for dollar to a maximum of $3,000 per year in government aid. The Society more than met the challenge in the 1950s and 1960s, so the government always paid the maximum, but the Society executive began to feel limited by this arrangement after it hired a part-time secretary (1956) and especially as it contemplated its extensive publishing program and the increase in historical activity associated with the national and provincial centennials. In an important brief to the minister in 1964, Society President H. Clare Pentland raised the example of certain American state historical societies, noting the grants of hundreds of thousands of dollars (exclusive of aid to state parks), and he encouraged a reconsideration of the entire parks, tourism, and cultural policy of the province. This has taken place, at least to some degree, but the annual government grant did not raise the Society above the status of a small voluntary interest group.

In Manitoba, as in other jurisdictions in Canada and abroad, the 1960s constituted another watershed in government cultural policy. Increasingly, as the decade proceeded, government interest in and support for the arts was translated into the creation of state-directed "ministries of culture" as distinct from departments of education. The emergence of the concept of tourism as industry, and particularly the recognition of the boom in North American travel to historic sites in Europe, led governments to think of history as an adjunct of economic planning and to expand the functions of historic sites boards and historic parks. Thus, the revitalization of the historic sites program in Manitoba in the late 1960s resulted in increased funding for the "history industry" but did little for the Historical Society. Indeed, once the celebrations associated with the 1967 and 1970 centennials were past, the Historical Society was left with a diminished role. Government cultural aid would henceforth be channelled into large, highly publicized agencies like the new provincial museum, the capital city's art gallery, and various performing arts organizations rather than the smaller voluntary societies.[28]

A pessimist might conclude that the Historical Society was, once again, doomed. The Provincial Archives and City Library now functioned on their own. The plaque program and historic sites were handled by provincial and federal government agencies. Local museums, perhaps as many as 100, had been opened across the province and now found their leadership in the Museum of Man and Nature and the Manitoba Museums Association. Heritage associations, ethnic group historical societies, archaeological and genealogical associations had taken on constituencies where once the Society's members were pioneers. The Manitoba Record Society was autonomous, the *Atlas* was published, Macdonald House was opened to visitors. However, the Historical Society continues to serve the

community as a lobby group dedicated to provincial historical consciousness. Its purposes – education, preservation, scholarship – are unending.

NOTES

This paper was written at the invitation of W.L. Morton, chairman of the Manitoba Historical Society's Centennial Committee, and presented to the Society's birthday party at Government House, Winnipeg, in October 1979. I would like to thank Dr. Morton for his generous assistance, and particularly for several conversations about the Society's activities. I
would also like to thank the Society's executive director, Rosemary Malaher, and secretary, Areen Mulder, for their assistance on numerous occasions. The time-consuming business of analyzing membership rolls, as well as the investigation of the Society files, was
undertaken by two graduate assistants at the University of Manitoba, Louella Friesen and
Erna Buffie. They deserve special thanks for their unstinting help. The article was published in the Society's journal, *Manitoba History* 4 (1982); it is reprinted with the permission
of the editors of *Manitoba History*.

1. *Manitoba Free Press,* November 1879.
2. D.C. Harvey, "History and its Uses in Pre-Confederation Nova Scotia," Canadian Historical Association, *Report,* 1938. I would like to thank D.A. Muise for this and other references to the Nova Scotia experience.
3. Provincial Archives of Manitoba (PAM), Manitoba Historical Society (MHS) Papers,
Annual General Meeting Minutes, 13 February 1883. One American view of this topic is
Louis B. Wright, *Culture on the Moving Frontier* (New York: Harper Torchbook, 1955; 1961),
12, 225-32.
4. C. Bruce Fergusson, "Mechanics' Institutes in Nova Scotia," *Bulletin of the Public Archives
of Nova Scotia,* no. 14 (1960).
5. PAM, MHS Papers, 8 February 1882; 9 February 1886; 8 February 1881; and 13 February 1883. See also, George Bryce, "A Great City Library," Historical and Scientific Society
of Manitoba (HSSM), *Transactions,* no. 70 (1906).
6. PAM, MHS Papers, Executive Council Minutes, 9 November 1906: "His Lordship was
of the impression that Winnipeg was not getting along well enough if the people could not
manage themselves in such an affair," Bryce reported.
7. Angela Davis, "Laying the Ground: The Establishment of an Artistic Milieu in Winnipeg, 1890-1913," *Manitoba History* 4 (1982).
8. PAM, MHS Papers, Executive Council Minutes 1903, Annual General Meeting Minutes, 9 February 1904.
9. Kenneth McNaught, *A Prophet in Politics: A Biography of J.S. Woodsworth* (Toronto: University of Toronto Press, 1959); Murray Donnelly, *Dafoe of the Free Press* (Toronto: Macmillan,
1968).
10. Gerald Killan, *Preserving Ontario's Heritage: A History of the Ontario Historical Society* (Ottawa: 1976).
11. Doug Owram, *Promise of Eden: The Canadian Expansionist Movement and the Idea of the
West, 1856-1900* (Toronto: University of Toronto Press, 1980).
12. PAM, MHS Papers, Executive Council Minutes, 28 March and 15 April 1913.
13. H.M. Speechly, "In Celebration of the Twenty-first Anniversary of the Natural History
Society of Manitoba," *Natural History Society of Manitoba, 21st Anniversary Bulletin* (1941-42).
14. Carl Berger, *The Writing of Canadian History: Aspects of English-Canadian Historical Writing: 1900-1970* (Toronto: Oxford University Press, 1976).
15. PAM, MHS Papers, Annual Meeting Reports and Minutes of Meetings, 1926 to 1934.
16. Margaret McWilliams, *Manitoba Milestones* (Toronto: J.M Dent and Sons Ltd., 1928).
17. PAM, MHS Papers, Minutes of Meeting, 9 February 1944.

18. Janet Minihan, *The Nationalization of Culture: The Development of State Subsidies to the Arts in Great Britain* (New York: New York University Press, 1977), 215; also, Killan, *Preserving Ontario's Heritage*; and, William T. Alderson, "The American Association for State and Local History," *Western Historical Quarterly* 1, no. 2 (1970).

19. Bernard Ostry, *The Cultural Connection: An Essay on Culture and Government Policy in Canada* (Toronto: McClelland and Stewart, 1978), 41-64.

20. Ostry, *The Cultural Connection*, 5; also, Frank W. Peers, *The Politics of Canadian Broadcasting, 1920-1951* (Toronto: University of Toronto Press, 1969).

21. Six volumes were eventually published under the direction of the series editor, W.L. Morton. They are discussed herein (see, "Romantics, Pluralists, Postmodernists: Writing Ethnic History in Prairie Canada," pages 185-86).

22. PAM, MHS Papers, Executive Council Minutes, 1945-1947; "President's Reports," in *Transactions*, 1945-1953; and Manitoba Legislative Library, *Annual Reports*, 1947-1975.

23. Fischel J. Coodin, "Introductory Message," *Manitoba Archaeological Society Newsletter* (1964); interview with L. Pettipas, Provincial Archaeologist, October 1979; MHS Papers.

24. W.L. Morton, "President's Address on the Occasion of the Seventy-Fifth Anniversary of the Historical and Scientific Society of Manitoba, 1879-1953," *Transactions*, series 3, no. 9 (1954).

25. PAM, MHS Papers, Administration Files 1944-1964; see also the reports of the presidents and secretaries in the annual *Transactions*.

26. MHS, Winnipeg; office files on projects of recent years remain in the Society offices.

27. Carl Berger, *The Writing of Canadian History*; and, A.B. McKillop, ed., *Contexts of Canada's Past: Selected Essays of W.L. Morton* (Toronto: Macmillan, 1980).

28. For a discussion of the "bias in favour of bigness," see, Frank T. Pasquill, *Subsidy Patterns for the Performing Arts in Canada* (Ottawa: Canada Council Information Services, 1973). On the state, see, John Meisel, "Political Culture and the Politics of Culture," *Canadian Journal of Political Science* 2 (1974). Recent surveys of cultural history include: Maria Tippett, *Making Culture: English-Canadian Institutions and the Arts before the Massey Commission* (Toronto: University of Toronto Press, 1990); Tippett, "The Writing of English-Canadian Cultural History, 1970-1985," *Canadian Historical Review* 67, no. 4 (1986); Paul Litt, *The Muses, The Masses, and The Massey Commission* (Toronto: University of Toronto Press, 1992). The province's files are housed in the Department of Cultural Affairs and Historic Resources; see especially the Minutes of the Historic Sites Advisory Board, 1946-1970. The Board was organized in 1946 and revitalized in 1969.

Principal J.H. Riddell and Wesley College: Sane and Safe Leadership

THE CHARACTER OF A COLLEGE is an elusive thing, and the role of an administrative leader in shaping the tone of its dormitories and class-rooms is even more obscure. No one would deny, however, that differences of character do distinguish colleges, or that administrators can alter the atmosphere of an institution. Wesley College, the centre of Methodist higher education in the Canadian prairies (it became United College in 1938 and the University of Winnipeg in 1967), was a hotbed of reform doctrine during the western boom between 1900 and 1914. It was a quieter place in the inter-war years. The exciting pre-war atmosphere of debate stimulated by Reverend J.S. Woodsworth's work on immigration, W.F. Osborne's critique of the Methodist Church, and Salem Bland's advocacy of political change had given way (though it never disappeared) to a less-oppositional, more-accommodating approach to the wider world in the 1920s and 1930s. New teachers such as Watson Kirkconnell and Arthur R.M. Lower imparted a more scholarly tone to college life. Students were exhorted to develop "character" and to display an interest in scholarship but were not pressed to become crusaders for social reform. Though subtle, the change was decisive. The pre-war radicals, whose social gospel roots encouraged a critique of the capitalist economic system, gave way to moderates whose evangelicalism demanded personal repentance and whose political caution required that reform be gradual and respectful of tradition. John H. Riddell, Principal of Wesley College from 1917 to 1938, represented the forces of "sane and safe" reform. His influence was crucial in establishing the political and social tone of College life in the interwar years.[1]

Riddell was born in the Humber Valley near Bolton, Ontario, on 1 November 1863. Raised in the disciplined manner of the age, he was accustomed to daily morning worship, in which his father led in prayer and read a passage of Scripture, and he accepted the firm Methodist prohibitions against theatre, card games, drink, tobacco, and unnecessary activity on Sunday. He graduated from Victoria University in 1890, having won a silver medal in general proficiency and a gold medal in mental and moral philosophy, and he was posted to Manitoba, where he had served previously for one summer as teacher and supply minister. He travelled throughout the Cartwright district, meeting his new parishioners and holding Bible classes and church services wherever the opportunity arose. In 1892, after two years on the circuit, he was granted the bachelor of divinity degree by his college and invited to become assistant minister at Grace Church, Winnipeg, with responsibility for a new charge, Young Church, and also to lecture in Latin and Greek at Wesley College. The Manitoba and North-West Conference of the Methodist Church offered another challenge to Riddell in 1907, when he became the founder and first principal of Alberta College in Edmonton. He returned to Wesley as the College principal in 1917 and served for twenty-one years as its senior administrative officer.

The job of the Wesley College principal was a demanding one. Riddell was expected to supervise the faculty and students and to teach as many hours as his colleagues did, but he was also responsible for the boilers and the roof and the repair of the steps. He arranged for the rinks and the playing field. He also acted as fund raiser and public relations officer.[2] After his first year as principal of Wesley, Riddell reported to the Manitoba Conference of the Methodist Church that he had taught twelve hours each week in Church history and New Testament, had travelled 15,000 miles on College business, had spoken on forty public occasions, preached ninety times to seventy-five different congregations, and acted as chief administrator of the College.[3] What kind of mark could he leave upon College life when he was preoccupied by so many responsibilities? A quite considerable mark, indeed, as a survey of his work shows.

Wesley College during Riddell's tenure as principal was a small and closely knit family of about 400 to 600 students and twenty-odd faculty members. Its academic year opened in late September, ended in April, and was punctuated by the examination periods and student celebrations that had been a part of university life for several generations. The social calendar started with a formal reception for students and the initiation of first-year students. It was marked, next, by the flags and pennants and cheers of the Halloween parade and, then, by skating and hockey and basketball. All too soon, the students were dispatching Wesley Christmas cards and studying feverishly for their mid-year examinations. After Christmas, there were meetings of the drama and literary and history and choral clubs, a few curling matches and skating parties, and then it was time for class photographs and preparation for the biggest events of the year: the seniors' dinner and grads' farewell. The rhythm seemed unchanging throughout the two decades of Riddell's principalship and, indeed, differed little from the pattern of the late nineteenth or even the late twentieth century.

An air of predictability was also evident in the daily round. When the first bell sounded at 7:30 in the morning, noise erupted in the men's and women's residences as 100 students rushed to claim toilet facilities and sinks with plugs. Doors banged and warnings were left with sleepy roommates – "two minutes left" – and then the second bell announced breakfast. By 8:30, when the early mail was distributed, the students who resided (or "boarded") in city homes were streaming up the walk, and the serious business of the day commenced. There was a pause between lectures for daily chapel service from 9:45 to 10:00, and then classes resumed until the lunch bell rang at 12:30. The residence students headed off for such favourites as corn soup and shepherd's pie, while the rest unpacked sandwiches and bought a cup of coffee in the canteen. Afternoon lectures and study would give way to recreation and talk, perhaps a skate on the rink or a gathering to hear a saxophone recording. After dinner, residence students met at the Sparling Hall reading rack where, it was said, they read the comics pages of the newspapers more readily than they did the editorial sections. Secluded corners of the lounge were sometimes in short supply, but the 7:30 study bell recalled the diligent to the task at hand. The last bell, at 11:00, prompted an outburst of noise and argument but, within half an hour, all was silent again.[4] There was nothing here, it might seem, to distinguish this small college from several dozen others in Canada or, indeed, hundreds of others in North America.

The distinctive traits of Wesley College, the Methodist Church, and Riddell himself were evident, nonetheless, in several aspects of College life. Chief among these characteristics were faculty caution in the face of the students' misbehaviour, faculty concern for the academic progress of individual students, and faculty resolve that the College should develop the character as much as the intellect of its charges. The ideal was expressed in a resolution of the Wesley College Board, a resolution that Riddell himself had sought: "The final end of education is character making, not the imparting of information. We believe that toward this end an

invaluable contribution is being made by our Church through the maintenance of such institutions as Wesley College, where not only high standards of scholastic achievement are preserved, but distinct assistance and
impulse to Christian living."[5]

Faculty worries about student behaviour were expressed annually during autumn initiation rites, when the professors tried to regulate the rougher
activities or to abolish them altogether, but they were also evident when
such issues as smoking, drinking, and dancing arose.[6] The Wesley College
Board, in line with the rules of the Methodist Church, expressed "its strongest disapproval of the use of tobacco by students and wishes as far as
possible to guard its students against the formation or continuance of a
habit which it regards as injurious."[7] Alcoholic beverages were forbidden; if unwary undergraduates were caught breaking the rule, they were
dealt with severely. In April 1922, when province-wide prohibition was
still in force, a committee chaired by Riddell held twenty hours of hearings into a case in which several residence students took liquor to their
rooms. The committee recommended to the College faculty that two of
the young men be dismissed and never again permitted to enroll in Wesley.
At a formal evening session of the entire faculty, Riddell delivered repri-
mands to six others involved in the disturbance, warning them "firmly
and kindly and with a depth of feeling, of the dangers which lay ahead of
them should they continue to pursue the course which had brought them
to the place where they now found themselves."[8] A similar case in 1932
inspired an investigation in which the board of directors sought to establish "if there was genuine sorrow for their [the students'] actions, and a
desire to live so that such a thing would not occur again so far as they
were concerned." In the end, three Wesley students were forbidden to
enroll in 1933. After a more serious disturbance in 1934, three students
were told that they would never again be permitted to enter the College.[9]
The rules in these cases were clear, and the punishment for infractions
was severe.

Dancing was a more difficult problem, as Riddell was to discover. He
had been raised in a home where dancing was forbidden, and his opposition had never relented, despite the changing social atmosphere in the
early twentieth century, because he feared that dancing encouraged "un-
wholesome conduct."[10] As late as 1926, Wesley College officially forbade
dances. Indeed, when a group of graduating students in the class of 1926
arranged that the annual senior dinner at the Fort Garry Hotel be followed by a dance, the Wesley faculty issued a public statement dissociat-
ing the College from this "informal event." The professors recognized
that such questions of behaviour were "largely matters for individual conscience," the statement declared, but they did not wish to offend "the
convictions and traditions of many good friends of Wesley College." The

conclusion of the faculty statement, probably written by Riddell and Professor Watson Kirkconnell, was a stern admonition: "The President and Faculty trust, however, that the recognized and cherished loyalty of the students to their college will induce them on this and on every occasion to so conduct themselves that they will help the College that they love to do her best work in the world."[11]

Riddell could not prevent students from dancing. Dismayed by the number of student social activities, he and his faculty colleagues resolved in 1929 to require that students "spend at least four evenings per week in pursuit of their studies." Despite these strictures, the principal received another unwelcome petition from the students in October 1928 requesting that "mixed dancing" be permitted in the music room between 7:00 and 8:00 p.m. on Wednesdays. In 1931, the faculty acceded to the request for one dance hour per week but were still concerned about students' socializing and had established yet another committee: "The end to be achieved is the regulation or the restraint of social activities." One casualty of this student campaign was Riddell's rule against dancing. In 1930 he issued a formal statement to the faculty acknowledging his defeat. In this unusual document he agreed that dancing might not be wrong – "I quite readily recognize that many people just as good as I and perhaps better, dance with a clear conscience" – but he maintained that the College was "a sacred place for the reasons that it has been intimately associated with the religious ideals of a great denomination." Changing students' views and perhaps the Methodist union with the Presbyterians had altered the situation: "For the purpose of securing better control and thus preserving in the highest degree possible the honour of the College and the students," Riddell said he would accept the faculty's decision to recognize and to supervise dances.[12]

Drinking and dancing among the students were just two of the difficult social questions faced by the Wesley College staff. Faculty attention to student deportment was also evident during regular reviews of student performance. The extraordinary concern for the students' academic and social development was, indeed, one of the most striking features of staff meetings during Riddell's administration. It appears that attendance forms were regularly filled out by the instructors and that absenteeism elicited a written warning to the students and, on occasion, to the students' parents. Christmas examination results were reviewed and, where appropriate, students were placed on probation for one month. Students who "failed to respond" to several warnings were "asked to discontinue." The parents of delinquent students were also contacted and, on occasion, were invited to be present when their children were reprimanded.[13] The Wesley College record in the annual university-wide competition for grades and scholarships was a matter of great interest to the faculty and was monitored with

careful attention. Because awards, punishments, and progress were discussed in full-scale meetings of the faculty, the career of every student was
reviewed once or twice a year during Riddell's administration.

The spiritual life of the students was a matter of even greater College
concern. In his letter of appointment to a new staff member, Riddell noted
that Wesley students must do well in the University of Manitoba final
examinations (the University of Manitoba was the examining body for
the colleges), but he added that the arts faculty at Wesley existed "primarily for the spiritual contribution it may be able to make to the life and
well-being of the community."[14] After several years of debates among students and faculty over compulsory attendance at chapel services, a new
calendar entry was drafted: "As an educational institution under Christian
auspices, Wesley College is primarily concerned with the moral and spiritual welfare of its students. With this end in view students are expected to
attend morning worship as part of their regular daily program; and they
are expected to attend Divine Worship on the Lord's Day at such churches
as their parents or guardians may direct."[15]

Though Riddell failed in his attempt to secure Board participation in
the disciplinary activities of the College, he did win a Board statement
that might serve as a statement of the College aim: to cultivate "a sane,
wholesome, intelligent attitude to the principles and organizations of the
Christian religion, with a view to securing the finest type of leadership for
the people."[16] He also instituted the custom of welcoming each College
graduate into his office after Recognition Day, the annual awards ceremony in the spring, to convey "his sincere blessing and the Book which
may be carried through life as a guide."[17] Bible study was compulsory in
the high-school branch of the College, and four Bible classes were convened weekly in the university branch. The principal interviewed every
student personally and, together with the faculty, tried to ensure that students would face the "great moral and spiritual issues" of life during their
College years.[18] Wesley College under Riddell provided a carefully supervised and thoroughly religious experience for its students.

If Riddell emphasized personal discipline and the character-building
qualities of student life, he was only accentuating what had always been
strong points in the Methodist institution. He differed from his predecessors, however, in other aspects of his educational and political philosophy. As is the case with any educational leader, his views were implicit in
his teaching and scholarly work, on the one hand, and in his administrative practices, on the other. In each sphere, Riddell possessed such positive attributes as energy, determination, self-confidence, and a cautious
reforming spirit. But to this catalogue should be added less attractive characteristics, including stubbornness, high-handedness, complacency, and
a strain of anti-intellectualism. The result of this combination of qualities

was a less radical, less adventurous Wesley College than had existed before 1914.

Riddell himself believed that the two outstanding achievements of his administration were his defence of a downtown location for undergraduate arts instruction within the University of Manitoba and his financial management of Wesley College.[19] He acted with tact and diplomacy in these matters, it is true, and could take pride in the results. In his memoirs, he also emphasized his role in the construction and renovation of College buildings and the development of the College library. Again, his contributions were important.

Riddell's attitude to scholarly inquiry is less easy to discern. He was not a scholar himself, as he sometimes acknowledged, and he seemed uneasy with that aspect of College life. His speeches on ceremonial occasions tended to stress such virtues as self-discipline, perseverance, and independent judgement. He regularly taught Latin, Greek, and the New Testament, but he had little advanced training in those fields. When he founded the discipline of sociology at Alberta College, it was after a single summer of sociological studies in Chicago in 1911.[20] He pursued this interest in Winnipeg,[21] taking a special study leave in the summer of 1927 to visit the eastern Canadian provinces and to examine their social legislation, but the demands on his time were undoubtedly too great to permit further research while he remained principal.[22] When he turned to writing after his retirement, he chose such topics as the penal system, the community responsibilities of church leaders, the social history of Canada, and the history of the Methodist Church in western Canada.[23] These studies bore witness to his remarkable energy and industry, but they were the work of an intelligent lay observer, not a scholar or specialist. Two of them, the social history and an autobiography entitled, significantly, "Gateways to a Life of Service," never found a publisher. Riddell was simply too busy to develop the scholarly interest and skills usually associated with university leaders.

His record as an administrator of scholars was similarly uneven. The faculty of Wesley College had undergone a period of crisis when Riddell was appointed, as could be expected. The abrupt departure of a well-loved principal, Reverend Eber Crummy, in June 1917, and the simultaneous dismissal of a famous radical, Salem Bland, left prairie Methodists in turmoil. Bland and his followers believed forever after that "moneyed interests," including J.H. Ashdown (the hardware merchant and millionaire) and men who shared his social philosophy, had threatened to withdraw their financial support and close Wesley College rather than endure its association with the radical social gospellers. Subsequent Church investigations did not sustain Bland's charge: a financial shortfall was said to be justification enough for his departure. But Riddell's appointment

had indeed been facilitated by his old friend J.H. Ashdown.[24] The connection was logical. Riddell shared Ashdown's conviction that one person, not a committee of social gospellers, should be responsible for the
day-to-day administration of the institution. And Riddell was not a political radical. His cautious – even evangelical – views on social reform and
personal conversion were undoubtedly more congenial to Winnipeg's
Methodist businessmen than were Bland's denunciations of individual
profiteers and the capitalist system in general.

Riddell's political caution and religious evangelicalism were revealed
during the most serious academic crisis ever faced by Wesley College.
When two of Wesley's most able scholars, W.T. Allison and D.C. Harvey,
resigned in the summer of 1920, Riddell was sufficiently conscious of his
own shortcomings to launch a search for academic staff who might restore Wesley's credentials as a respectable university-level institution. By
chance, the leading Methodist candidate in what must have been a small
field was Dr. W.G. Smith of the University of Toronto. Smith had laboured
for ten years to separate the discipline of psychology from the Department of Philosophy at Toronto and had just started work in experimental
psychology that, he hoped, would establish the subject as a proper "science." At this stage in the development of Canadian arts faculties, when
psychology and sociology were not widely recognized as distinct disciplines, Smith's enthusiasm for laboratory work and reliance upon scientific measurement were advanced or, at least, unconventional. Thus, his
decision to leave Toronto, where the new approach had finally been accepted, was unexpected. He agreed to join the Wesley faculty because he
thought he was being asked to shape not just a discipline or a faculty but
also to have a leading part in the rebuilding of the post-war West. This was
the era of the Winnipeg General Strike and the Progressive movement in
politics, and the community must have seemed open to new approaches;
moreover, having just completed a survey of Methodist colleges in Canada,
Smith would have perceived the importance of Winnipeg as the metropolis of the prairies and of Wesley as the leading Methodist institution west
of Toronto. He assumed that he was being invited to direct Wesley's contribution to the new order in Canada.

Riddell did not have a clear plan for Smith's work at Wesley and did
not understand the range of his new colleague's ambitions. The misun-
derstandings were apparent in the letters of appointment in the spring of
1921. Various combinations of teaching and administrative responsibilities were canvassed, and it was eventually concluded that Smith would be
professor of philosophy and sociology, a position fraught with difficulties
because the University of Manitoba did not utilize the narrower approach
to the social sciences; and he would be a senior administrative officer with
the resounding but potentially empty title of vice president in "charge of

the academic side of the work of the College."[25] In neither position would Smith find a secure, comfortable, or defined role. What is worse, perhaps, Riddell was having second thoughts even while he was arranging Smith's responsibilities. In inviting Smith to join the small group at Wesley, Riddell was hiring a professor who would take over his own specialty of sociology; he was offering the "academic leadership" to this new man; and he still did not know Smith's political views or even his religious perspective. The unanimous opinion of Methodist leaders in Toronto seemed to be that Smith was a "brilliant psychologist and inspiring teacher" but also that he had been an unreliable radical a few years earlier and was still inclined to that side of the theological spectrum. As Reverend J.H. Arnup of the Methodist Foreign Missions Office told Riddell, "There seems nothing in common in your views on evangelical religion. . . . One [Smith] would be like a fish out of water (as it seems to me) in a red hot revival meeting, and the other [Riddell] perfectly at home."[26]

During the appointment negotiations of 1921, Riddell revealed his concerns to Smith. One can see wider implications in his comments about the teaching of sociology: "The general situation [in Winnipeg] . . . requires very careful study and very sane handling," both because of the 1917 crisis at Wesley involving Salem Bland and "because of the general situation in the City." He suggested that "the recent strike, with its peculiar emphasis and its unfortunate developments coupled with the vigorous propaganda carried on in the parliamentary session in favour of what is generally regarded as an extreme social and industrial programme, make for us a very sensitive people." Riddell said that he was committed, by contrast, to what he called "sane and safe leadership." He wished to hear Smith's views on the "industrial, social and economic propaganda" being aired in Winnipeg. He would welcome "sane constructive social and economic policy," Riddell wrote, but he wished to emphasize that "any unwise advocacy of radical measures would at this juncture here be fatal to us and to the larger cause we seek to advance in this new land."[27] Riddell was a cautious reformer, in short, and would do nothing to reinforce the labour radicals at City Hall or to alienate close friends like J.H. Ashdown.

His caution and his alliance with Ashdown saved Riddell from a severe personal reverse in the following year. Smith arrived at Wesley with great plans for change and proceeded to implement them with little or no reference to his principal. Riddell's friends feared that he was being bypassed by the newcomer and were doubly concerned when Smith's reforms roused opposition within the philosophy-sociology examining committee at the University of Manitoba. Soon, factions formed around Riddell and Smith within the Wesley College faculty. The Board was forced to intervene. In the end, Smith refused to accept Riddell's leadership and commenced an attack upon him and the College. In one dramatic episode,

Smith convened a luncheon meeting at Eaton's cafeteria in which he told a number of Methodist ministers of his concerns about the moral conditions and the scholarly atmosphere at Wesley and produced a "French safe" (condom), presumably from the residence, as proof of his allegations.[28] The Wesley College Board did not accept Smith's arguments about Riddell's alleged laxness. It terminated Smith's contract in July 1922 and then endured a year of legal actions, first in the Methodist Court of Appeal, then in the Court of King's Bench, and finally in the Winnipeg District of the Methodist Church, where Smith charged Riddell with having uttered falsehoods.[29] The Board supported Riddell throughout the battle, despite the dissatisfaction of a minority within its ranks and despite the resignation of several highly respected faculty members. Riddell remained principal, Smith left in disgrace, and the annual round of lectures and meetings and student events resumed as if they had never been interrupted. The confidence that Ashdown placed in Riddell in 1917 had been reciprocated by the support of those Board members who shared Ashdown's perspective in 1922-23.[30]

Riddell displayed greater decisiveness but no better judgement a decade later. In 1932, three years after hiring two promising historians, Arthur R.M. Lower and Jack Pickersgill, the principal informed Pickersgill that his services were no longer required. Riddell explained that "the welfare of an institution was greater than that of its members" and that Pickersgill's position would be better filled by Riddell's own son, Gerald, who was then studying at Oxford. Pickersgill stood his ground and, in a remarkable letter to the principal, wondered "whether the principle of reasonable security of tenure for its [Wesley College's] staff could be compensated for by an incidental advantage." Pickersgill won and the principal lost face.[31] The episode was an unfortunate reminder of his informal approach to higher education.

Riddell continued to be principal of Wesley College until its complete merger with Manitoba College in 1938. After his retirement, he spent his time addressing the social issues that had always interested him. In one of these works, he wrote something approaching his own epitaph: "My highest interest in life found expression in a longing to make men and women, boys and girls, capable of fulfilling their divine mission in the world. . . . I was never a brilliant student, never a great scholar. I knew something about a lot of things, but was never an authority on any one thing, but I did love my fellowman and was always ready to toil and sacrifice that his well-being might be promoted."[32] The statement was characteristic of his self-deprecation, but it did not do him justice. Riddell was a vigorous, hearty, hard-working, efficient, and courageous man. In his younger days, his great popularity was due, as one observer recalled, to "his spiritual passion and deep sympathy, so that he was a great-hearted comrade to many a student." His personality did not change in later years, but the demands on his time became nothing short of extraordinary.[33] He continued to labour for a better world. He had no patience with "idle, careless, thoughtless time-serving" students;[34] his sympathy rested with those who displayed "courage, kindness, constancy and candour coupled with an undying determination to make life better."[35] And how would this be achieved? Riddell was an evangelical Christian, not a social gospel advocate. He believed that the crucial institutions of society were the church, the school, and the home rather than the social class or the trade union or the political party.[36] He believed that, in the end, individuals were responsible for their own fate. He believed that "joy in life consists in serving, in being hopeful. Of my difficulties I can say they've all been helpful in the end."[37] These were the opinions of a "sane and safe" administrator. Wesley College was a competent, cautious institution under Riddell's leadership because its principal was a dedicated, cautious, respectable Methodist.

NOTES

This is a revised version of an article that was first published in Garth Butcher et al., eds., *Prairie Spirit: Perspectives on the Heritage of the United Church of Canada in the West* (Winnipeg: University of Manitoba Press, 1985).

1. John H. Riddell, "Gateways to a Life of Service: An Autobiography" (manuscript, ca. 1941 to 1943). Further details on his career can be obtained in: David Owen, "Dr. J.H. Riddell," *Winnipeg Free Press*, 13 November 1952; Alberta College Board of Directors Minutes, Provincial Archives of Alberta; "Obituary by George B. King," biography file, United Church Archives (UCA). A study that contains some revealing parallels is Michael Bliss, *A Canadian Millionaire: The Life and Business Times of Sir Joseph Flavelle, Bart., 1858-1939* (Toronto: Macmillan, 1978). The Wesley College years are best examined in A.G. Bedford, *The University of Winnipeg: A History of the Founding Colleges* (Toronto: University of Toronto Press, 1976).
2. Executive Minutes, 23 December 1919, Wesley College (WC) Board of Directors, WC-5-5, University of Winnipeg Archives (UWA).
3. Minutes of Proceedings of Manitoba Conference, 1918, Methodist Church.
4. W.M.S., "Residence Life," *Vox Wesleyana*, March 1931; Minutes of WC Students' Representative Council (SRC), WC-5-26, UWA.
5. Executive Minutes, 30 May 1925, WC Board of Directors, WC-5-6, UWA.
6. They wished that "a higher type of life" be pursued at the College (Minutes, 19 October 1921, WC Faculty Committee, WC-5-12, UWA).
7. Executive Minutes, 5 May 1922, WC Board of Directors, WC-5-12, UWA.
8. Minutes, 20 April, 20 April (evening), and 27 April 1922, WC Faculty Committee, WC-5-12, UWA.
9. Executive Minutes, 27 April 1932, 6 February 1933, 23 February 1934, WC Board of Directors; Minutes, WC 5-6, 21 February 1934, Faculty Committee, WC-5-15, UWA.
10. Minutes, 6 February 1930, WC Faculty Committee, WC-5-14, UWA.
11. Minutes, 11 March 1926, WC Faculty Committee, WC-5-13, UWA.
12. The issue can be followed in the Minutes, 11 March 1926, 16 May 1928, 30 October 1928, 6 February 1930, 31 December 1930, 19 January 1931, and 28 April 1932 of the WC

Faculty Committee, WC-5-13 and WC-5-14, UWA.

13. Minutes, October 1919, 5 January and 19 January 1923, WC-5-12; 6 March 1925, WC-5-13; 12 January 1933, WC-5-16, WC Faculty Committee; Executive Minutes, 6 February 1933, 23 February 1934, WC-5-6, WC Board of Directors.

14. Executive Minutes, Riddell to Reverend J.N. Anderson, History Department appointee, 11 June 1927, WC-5-6, WC Board of Directors.

15. The debate is joined in the Minutes of 28 February 1919 and 10 March 1919 of WC, SRC (WC-5-26). It is noted in the Minutes of 14 March 1919 of the WC Faculty Committee (WC-5-12), and the above "solution" was drafted and passed at the 15 April 1924 faculty meeting.

16. Executive Minutes, 12 May 1924, WC-5-7, WC Board of Directors.

17. *Vox Wesleyana,* March 1930; Minutes, 1928, WC-5-13, WC Faculty Committee; Minutes, 17 February 1933, WC-5-15, WC Faculty Committee, which note that "Hebrew" students would be given a copy of "their own scriptures."

18. Minutes of Proceedings of Manitoba Conference, 1921, Methodist Church, UCA, Manitoba and Northwestern Ontario.

19. W.L. Morton, *One University: A History of the University of Manitoba, 1877-1952* (Toronto: McClelland and Stewart, 1957); Riddell, "Gateways to a Life of Service"; Bedford, *University of Winnipeg.*

20. Riddell, "Gateways to a Life of Service"; Methodist Church, Minutes of Manitoba Conference, 1918, Methodist Church, UCA-MNO.

21. Minutes, 19 October 1921, WC-5-12, WC Faculty Committee.

22. Executive Minutes, 10 June 1927, 11 July 1927, WC-5-6, WC Board of Directors.

23. For example: J.H. Riddell, "A Synopsis of the Report of the Royal Commission Appointed to Inquire into and Report upon the Penal System of Canada" (manuscript, Winnipeg, n.d.); *The Eldership: A Study in Official and Individual Privilege and Responsibility in the Christian Church* (Toronto: United Church of Canada, 1940); "Gateways to a Life of Service"; "Living Together: A Study in the Social Life of Canada" (manuscript, ca. 1946); *Methodism in the Middle West* (Toronto: Ryerson, 1946).

24. Executive Minutes, 1917, WC-5-4, WC Board of Directors; Bland-Irwin File, UWA; Minutes, 1917, 1918, 1919, Manitoba and Saskatchewan Conferences, Methodist Church. A conditional bequest by J.T. Gordon was said to have been involved (Riddell, "Gateways to a Life of Service," 275-6). The context is discussed in Richard Allen, *The Social Passion: Religion and Social Reform in Canada, 1914-28* (Toronto: University of Toronto Press, 1971); and, Richard Allen, "Children of Prophecy: Wesley College Students in an Age of Reform," *Red River Valley Historian* (1975):15-20.

25. Smith Case Correspondence, Riddell-Smith letters, January to May 1921, and Smith Case miscellaneous file, WC-10-1, UWA.

26. Arnup to Riddell, 7 February 1921, Creighton to Riddell, 3 February 1921, T.W. Neal to Riddell, 16 February 1921, all Smith Case Correspondence, WC-10-1, UWA.

27. Riddell to Smith, 14 March 1921, Smith Case Correspondence, WC-10-1, UWA.

28. Undated Riddell memorandum outlining his view of the issues, Smith Case miscellaneous file, WC-10-1, UWA; Smith Case, Examination of Plaintiff for Discovery, 7 February 1923, and Examination of Dr. Riddell for Discovery, 17 February 1923, Court of King's Bench.

29. The trials are discussed in Vera Fast, "Smith, Riddell and Wesley College" (manuscript essay, University of Manitoba, 1976).

30. Ashdown to Smith, 24 March 1922, Smith Case Correspondence, WC-10-1, UWA.

31. J.L. Granatstein, *The Ottawa Men: The Civil Service Mandarins, 1935-1957* (Toronto: Oxford University Press, 1982), 208-12. Lower's memoirs provide an interesting perspective upon Wesley College but do not mention this episode (Arthur R.M. Lower, *My First Seventy-Five Years* [Toronto: Macmillan, 1967]). A different view of the College is given by Watson Kirkconnell in *A Slice of Canada: Memoirs* (Toronto: University of Toronto Press, 1967).

32. Riddell, "Gateways to a Life of Service," 457.

33. A.E. Vrooman, memorandum, Smith Case miscellaneous file WC-10-1, UWA; Committee and Church Reports, Board Committee re: Principal, 10 January 1923, Smith Case miscellaneous file, WC-10-1, UWA.

34. J.H. Riddell, "The Student and World Problems," *Vox Wesleyana,* December 1922.

35. J.H. Riddell, "Popularity," *Vox Wesleyana,* November 1923.

36. J.H. Riddell, statement at funeral of T.A. Burrows, *Vox Wesleyana,* March 1929.

37. "Wesley College Portraits: The Principal," *Winnipeg Tribune,* 30 April 1935.

Bob Russell's Political Thought: Socialism and Industrial Unionism in Winnipeg, 1914 to 1919

WHEN BOB RUSSELL walked under the great portico at Stony Mountain Penitentiary near Winnipeg on Boxing Day, 1919, he had just passed his thirtieth birthday and had been in Canada less than nine years. Despite his relative youth, his recent emigration from Scotland, and his occupation – machinist and union executive member – he was during the months after the Armistice one of the best-known figures in Winnipeg. As he placed his signature on the register at Stony Mountain, he commenced a two-year term for seditious conspiracy – for conspiring to overthrow lawful authority – though he insisted that he was innocent. What made Bob Russell so dangerous?

THE EARLY YEARS

Robert Boyd Russell was born in Springburn, a district of Glasgow, on Halloween, in 1889. He did not continue his formal schooling beyond the age of ten or eleven. Instead, he went to work at the John Brown shipyards when he was twelve, adding his small wage to the family income. He proved to be an alert apprentice, and, after acquiring the basic skills with lathe and cutting tools and drill, he became a fully qualified "mechanic," or, in North American terms, a machinist. He joined the Amalgamated Society of Engineers, a strong British union, and there he learned about the local union movement. He also was an attentive bystander at the political harangues around Glasgow Square, and he was an active participant in the "Clarion Scouts," which met weekly to promote socialist causes and which became a favourite Sunday outing for the young labourer and his neighbour, Margaret Ritchie Hampton. He liked football games and horse races on Saturday afternoons and he enjoyed other aspects of Glasgow life, such as the libraries and the newspapers, but, having concluded that the Clydeside industries offered a mechanic little hope for the future, at the age of twenty-two he joined the wave of Scots emigrants to Canada.[1]

Russell arrived in Winnipeg during the economic boom of 1911. With his Scottish background, his widely recognized union card, and his articulate, forthright style, he won a permanent job in the huge Weston shops of the Canadian Pacific Railway (CPR). He then married Margaret Hampton and moved into an apartment in the working-class area of Winnipeg's West End, and later into a small house not far from the Weston shops. He and Peggy found good friends and plenty of support among workers and neighbours in the rapidly growing metropolis of prairie Canada.

Lodge 122 of the International Association of Machinists (IAM) in Winnipeg's Canadian Pacific shops soon absorbed much of Bob Russell's extra time. He made his mark in the shop-floor discussions at Weston and, despite his relative youth, became a leader within months of his arrival. In 1913, he was named to the shop grievance committee and, by the end of the year, chaired the committee. He then was elected to the schedule and negotiating committee, the crucial body that represented workers in talks with management concerning wages, hours, and conditions of work. By 1914, he was the Lodge correspondent for the Canadian machinists' monthly newspaper, the *Machinists' Bulletin*, and also a member of the local executive. A year later, he was sent to Vancouver as the Lodge 122 representative at the national convention of Canada's Trades and Labor Congress (TLC). In 1917, he became the chairman of the executive that represented all the machinists employed by the CPR and a member of another executive board, which guided the activity of all members of the IAM in Canada. By this time, as he entered his thirtieth year, he was one of the country's most prominent machinists. In February 1918, he was appointed IAM organizer for western Canada and, two months later, to a more senior post, secretary treasurer of District Two, which represented all railway machinists in Canada. He was managing the journal and all boards, organizers, and negotiations in Canada as well as chairing the machinists' union in the Canadian Pacific system. He left the shop floor forever in 1918 and set up a new workplace in Winnipeg's Labour Temple. Russell's rise in the union hierarchy had been rapid. It demonstrated his ambition, ability, and diligence.

To lead a national institution within seven years of arrival in Canada was surely unusual and suggested that broader circumstances, not just Russell's personal attributes, played a part in his achievement. Why did he achieve such power in so short a time? The relative openness of union locals in the burgeoning prairie metropolis of Winnipeg was part of the explanation. So, too, was the prominence of the Weston shop, one of the largest in the Canadian Pacific system. Russell's British background and working-class assumptions were also important. In a community dominated by British habits and customs, Britons assumed patterns of behaviour, re-established networks of friends, and entered into the governance of public institutions as if they belonged to the people. Central Europeans might be members of the union local, but, as Russell later noted, "the fellows who took the lead in the thing were mostly Old Country English and Scotch."[2]

Russell was supported by his shop mates during these years in part because he was a warm, enthusiastic man, but also because he was a thoroughgoing union loyalist. He enjoyed boosting the union and attacking "the capitalists." He had nothing but contempt for the company unions that awarded "little gold striping" to uniform-wearing employees as a tribute to service – "five years of servitude" for every stripe, Russell commented – or for the CPR attempts to establish company-based recreation activities such as the Saturday night social club at the Royal Alexandra Hotel where "the common stuff from the jobs would go down there and dance with the foreman or the foreman's wife, you understand, and the manager would look in." Russell and his union friends "were having none of this kind of stuff," as he said, because "we had been through all that . . . experience in the Old Country, you see?" Russell understood the politics and culture of Britain's industrial capitalist system. Who better to lead the union?[3] (*MB* April 1916; August 1917).

Another reason for Russell's rapid rise to power was his pugnacious, even vituperative, debating style. During a heated dispute in the columns of the *Machinists' Bulletin*, he addressed some angry words to those "low curs who were not men enough to make any insinuations they had to make in my presence or through the *Bulletin*, where one would have an opportunity to put the dirty lies down their throats, all I have got to say is that unless they retract these statements . . . at their next meeting in the same manner as they retracted them to me I will take the opportunity to visit their next meeting and make them retract them in public" (*MB* August 1917).

Russell entered the machinists' debates as a partisan of the "socialist" faction. Indeed, his first dispatch to the *Bulletin* in 1914 was an argument in favour of admitting apprentices to membership. His second dispatch urged union members to be active in politics: "Let the capitalist class see that by these hard times . . . they have taught us to . . . wonder why they should have the best that can be bought while we and our families starve. Now, boys, our organization is alright [sic] but without political action it is useless" (*MB* June 1914). In his third report, Russell tackled the moderate reformers in Winnipeg, lamenting that in the 1914 provincial election many Weston workers voted for such "dopey stuff" as direct legislation and female suffrage and temperance. In his view, the biggest political issue was how "to remove the causes of poverty, or the wage system" (*MB* August 1914), and the socialists alone among the political campaigners had addressed this issue. Bob Russell knew where he stood in political and economic debates; he did not hesitate to let his views be known. His move to western Canada during its boom years was a stroke of fortune, and he soon reaped the rewards made possible by his diligence and energy.

CANADA'S UNIONS IN 1914

The Canadian labour movement was relatively weak before the Great War. Fewer than one in ten members of the Canadian work force belonged to unions in this period, and, of those who did possess a union card, most worked in the skilled trades in urban centres or in a few other industries, such as coal mining, where workers' organizations had a long tradition. The movement was deeply divided by craft loyalties. The metal trades, including machinists, represented about ten percent of the national union membership. These metal crafts included engineers, blacksmiths, boilermakers, moulders and sheet-metal workers, but, of the total, the machinists' 4,654 members (forty percent of the total in the metal trades in 1914) constituted the single most powerful union. Given the division within the movement and its geographical dispersion, the relative influence of a large skilled group such as the machinists was not surprising.[4]

A further source of division within Canada's organized labour movement was the influence of American, or "international," craft headquarters. Most of the local lodges of individual crafts in Canada were affiliated with these international bodies – for example, Russell's IAM – and, thus, took their direction on many important policy matters, including jurisdictional rulings, sickness and death benefit funds, and decisions on strikes, from American-run, craft-based organizations. The loyalties that developed with membership in one particular fraternity, which were burnished by the inevitable debates about jurisdiction and job conditions, and which deepened with continent-wide friendships and alliances, were sufficient to bind most members to an exclusive code and community – the international craft union. This was the club that Bob Russell entered when he signed his IAM card.

Two issues that affected the American labour movement were also noteworthy in shaping the Canadian union movement. The first was the struggle between the craft principle of organization as enunciated by the American Federation of Labor (AFL) and the broader, industry-wide approach – known as industrial unionism – advocated by some opponents of the AFL. The second was politics: should organized labour establish its own political party, endorse one socialist movement, or remain aloof from parties except, perhaps, to reward "friends of labour" at election time? Samuel Gompers, President of the AFL, was suspicious of political action by trade unions and, indeed, of any government intervention. He had barred party politics from AFL conventions and opposed state regulation of industry or government-run social programs such as unemployment insurance. Gompers's principles became paramount in Canada's TLC after a brief dispute at the 1902 Congress convention. Gompers and his allies in the international unions prepared the ground carefully for that convention and were able to win an historic victory for the AFL approach to labour issues in Canada. Henceforth, AFL craft jurisdictions alone would be recognized by the Canadian Congress. TLC membership would be denied to dual organizations and to labour or socialist political parties. By 1914, when the internationals were affiliated with eighty percent of Canadian union locals, Gompers's principles were, in effect, the official policies of Canada's labour movement.[5]

Canadian labour presented contradictory images to the world in the decade before 1914. It was intensely local, and yet it was aligned with powerful "international" unions. It often debated "political" subjects, and it spawned several labour and socialist parties, yet it seemed incapable of establishing a single national party to represent its interests. It had a national parliament, the TLC, but that body was too divided and too closely aligned with one American union perspective to provide a satisfactory forum for all shades of opinion. Still, the TLC retained its pre-eminence because it was the official mouthpiece of AFL craft union affiliates north of the border and because the differences of opinion among Canadian unionists seemed capable of resolution. Reformers had won provincial autonomy in political action, for example, though a national labour party still eluded their grasp. The role of unions in national life was slowly being acknowledged by Canadians, even if management's recognition of unions was far from universal. Union locals and national craft federations were growing stronger, though in most cases they still looked to American headquarters for guidance and accepted American financial control. National debates on the utility of craft unions and of union activity in politics were also becoming more intense, as if a uniquely Canadian labour movement, independent of the American model, might soon overcome the obstacles of regional and craft divisions. This was the uncertain state of the Canadian labour movement when the Great War commenced in August 1914.

ORGANIZED LABOUR DURING THE GREAT WAR

The First World War precipitated great changes in labour-management relations in Canada. The very fact of war intensified political divisions among workers. Union leaders found their influence increasing with the boom in war-related industries, but they found, too, that they were under greater pressure to accommodate rapid "modernization" of the workplace. The role of government in the regulation of the economy was also substantially increased during the war. With his machinist colleagues, Bob Russell daily reported to work in shops that bore the brunt of the war-related changes.

The outbreak of the war revealed deep tensions within labour and socialist movements around the world. As in a number of other countries, unionists in Canada could not agree on the causes of the war or on the appropriate response to it. Bob Russell was one of the first machinists to publish his opinions, and, by the style as well as the substance of his remarks, he raised a small storm in his union. Russell's October 1914 dispatch to the *Bulletin* commenced with the flippant remark: "Not being willing to join the army and having no reason to curse the Kaiser, I will talk about the war." He then blamed the conflict not on German or Prussian autocracy but, paraphrasing the poet Edward Carpenter, on the "insane commercial and capitalist rivalry, the piling up of power in the hands of mere speculators and financiers, and the actual trading for dividends in the engines of death, all these inevitable results of our present capitalist system." He concluded: "This is a capitalists' war, so why should we let ourselves be gulled to fight their battle?"

Conservative machinist leaders had no sympathy for Russell's inflammatory style and no patience with opponents of the British and Canadian war effort. They put a stop to such discussions in the *Bulletin* because, as they explained, such comments did not have "any bearing on the trade" (*MB* October, November 1917). Russell discovered the influence of the TLC conservatives during his visit to the TLC in 1915. Confident of their position, Canadian labour leaders had introduced a resolution at the Congress convention that expressed support for the British war effort but, as a sop to the left wing, opposed the use of war as a means to settle disputes. Some socialists took advantage of the obvious equivocation in the resolution to introduce an amendment condemning the capitalist aggression alleged to be responsible for militarism. Such Congress stalwarts as Secretary Paddy Draper, Vice President Fred Bancroft, and Toronto's James Simpson responded with attacks upon Germany. "Prussianism was out to dominate the world with the sword," shouted Draper. Far from establishing a compromise, the resolution inspired further dispute within the labour movement. The pro-Britain resolution passed by 103 votes to twenty-eight; of the twenty dissenters who asked that their names be recorded, nineteen, including Bob Russell, were from western Canada.[6] Those whose first loyalty lay with Crown, Empire, and the Canadian army confronted those whose first loyalty was to the international working class. It is significant that, at this early stage of the conflict, only one in five labour leaders at the Congress was critical of Canada's war policy and that most of the dissenters resided in western Canada.

The radicals' dissatisfaction with the TLC won greater sympathy in the union movement as the military conflict dragged on and the threat of conscription grew. In the winter of 1916-17, Canada's TLC executive endorsed the national work-force registration scheme. A number of city labour councils, including Winnipeg's, immediately repudiated the TLC initiative. Unease increased in the summer of 1917, when several labour leaders rejected the federal government's proposed conscription legislation on the grounds that it could be used "to control the boys in the trenches of industry." Once again, however, the protesters were overwhelmed by popular support for the war effort. Thus, the TLC executive instructed union members to obey the law of the land and to accept conscription. Russell and his fellow radicals were furious.[7]

American entry into the war in the spring of 1917 and Samuel Gompers's support of the war effort only heightened the tension among Canada's labour leaders. For Canada's AFL loyalists and their socialist opponents, the conflict over participation in the war and over conscription complicated the disagreements concerning Gompers's approach to unions and politics. Thus, the war exacerbated the factionalism within the Canadian union movement.

If military issues and work-force policy provoked disagreement in union circles, the rapid economic transition necessitated by the war was even more contentious. Indeed, the development of a huge Canadian munitions industry should be seen as a crucial factor in the post-war labour crisis. In 1917, about 250,000 Canadians, one-third of the industrial labour force, were employed in munitions work. This number included, for the first time in the history of Canadian machine shops, a substantial number of women. The presence of these 35,000 women in the shops, about one in seven of the arms makers, irritated many of the union leaders, including Bob Russell, but it was just one of many extraordinary changes in the work process itself.[8]

To make the industry efficient, the new leaders of Canadian shell production on the Imperial Munitions Board instituted drastic changes. "Using time-and-motion studies, comparative production ratings, and roving trouble-shooters," historian Michael Bliss has written, "the IMB's production staff standardized shell-making at levels of efficiency far beyond anything that individual manufacturers working in isolation and secretive competition could have hoped to attain."⁹ The result affected not only shell casings but also went to the very heart of the machinists' craft. Payment by piecework, long anathema in railway shops, was one point of contention but so, too, was the actual work on lathe and press, according to one of Russell's brothers in the Weston shop: "Skill, at one time a necessary requisite of the working man, is now a lost art. The few remaining mechanics, like relics of the past, are fast disappearing, and in their place appear[s] the modern machine with its 'Made while you wait' operator. This system is fast reducing the workers to one level of skill." As in the United States, so in Canada the time-motion studies and labour-saving inventions increased workers' productivity while reducing their control over their jobs and eliminating thousands of positions. "Look back over the last four years," wrote an anonymous machinist, perhaps Russell, in early 1919, "think of the development of the modern machine, you men who work in the railroad shops. How many men does the Acetylene Torch displace? The Electric Torch? The Automatic Turning and Screwing Machines? The Modern Lathe? The Automatic Hammer? and the thousand and one other modern developments. . . . Thousands of your class have been displaced" (*MB* April 1919; November and December 1917; February 1915). In the view of union leaders, these fundamental changes in the workers' environment required significant alterations in union organizations.

The boom in munitions production, driven by the extraordinary degree of government regulation and supervision, also affected the status of unions. To assure high standards of shell quality, efficiency in the allocation of raw materials, and punctuality in the completion of contracts, Canadian entrepreneur J.W. Flavelle of the Imperial Munitions Board exercised unprecedented regulatory powers. He was supposed to act as an intermediary, too, in smoothing relations among government, military, capital, and labour bodies. In this delicate balancing act, compromise and accommodation were Board watchwords, and that philosophy, in turn, ensured that unions would at least be heard. The union leaders did not win all they sought, by any means, and were especially disappointed by their failure to secure the "fair wage clause" in munitions contracts, but they did win greater recognition than ever before and remarkable gains in union membership. By 1918, there were about 250,000 union members in Canada, as opposed to 166,000 members in 1914. The IAM membership trebled from under 5,000 to over 15,000 in the same period. For the first time, machinists were able to organize the Grand Trunk Railway shops, for example, as well as many private or "contract" shops.

In an official climate dominated by a sense of sacrifice and urgency, the use of centralized, government-controlled supervisory agencies to solve problems of production and distribution seemed increasingly appropriate. In the summer of 1917, both food and fuel control programs were instituted, and, several months later, the rail systems voluntarily banded together under the Canadian Railways War Board to promote greater efficiency in the allocation of resources for the shipment of shells and fuel. This, too, was a crucial step in the evolution of the Canadian industrial relations system and, in particular, in the history of Canadian machinists.[10]

If the business climate changed significantly during the war, so did the machinists' domestic circumstances. The most obvious change was in the cost of living. The price of a loaf of bread or a bottle of milk doubled during the war, and, though it is difficult to establish a clear picture of the relative levels of prices and wages, it is nonetheless certain that workers were keenly aware of inflationary forces. Bob Russell and his fellow correspondents referred regularly in the machinists' journal to the high cost of living, worker poverty, and capitalist wealth. As in other nations, hotly contested wage negotiations increased workers' political consciousness (*MB* March 1915; October 1916; September 1917; May 1918). Thus, the Great War changed the life of the metal worker. It was especially noteworthy that the introduction of new machines, the production of shells, the scientific management, and the wage-price spiral were crowded into the brief space of four years.

BOB RUSSELL'S UNIONISM

In responding to the new circumstances, Bob Russell had to consider two perspectives. On the one hand, as an increasingly powerful executive member in the IAM, he bore some of the responsibility for the smooth operation of an important military facility, Canada's railway system. On the other, he was a political party member dedicated to radical change in Canadian politics and society. How should his union adjust to the changed climate? How should his political party approach the prospect – a seemingly likely prospect, given the Soviet revolution in Russia – of a social revolution in Canada? The IAM presented more immediate and pressing problems during the war, but, in 1919, the union's pre-eminence was briefly challenged by a second, equally persuasive, force in his life, the Socialist Party of Canada (SPC).

Union structure changed rapidly during the war, but not without heated debates. Russell confronted such issues with enthusiasm because he believed they presented opportunities to increase union strength. Should the union admit apprentices to its ranks? What about the helpers and the shop maintenance workers? Could the IAM organize successfully in the munitions shops? Would coalition with other metal trades, such as plumbers and steamfitters and boilermakers and blacksmiths and sheet metal workers, create a more powerful bargaining unit? Was it possible to unite

all the rail workers in a single union that served one of the national railway corporations, say, the CPR? Russell had answers for each of these
questions. Amalgamation into larger, more inclusive, and more effective
unions was his guiding principle.

Bob Russell was strongly opposed to the craft exclusiveness of the AFL.
He labelled it the "aristocratic tendency." Reliance on skill as the basis of
the union, he wrote, turned "the most efficient division of the workers
against those whose position as unskilled workers make[s] them least capable of defence." His argument was based on technological change. With
the introduction of new machines, he wrote, "one craft after another tum-
bles into the abyss of common labor." The workers' only resort, he claimed,
was "the strength of the working class as a whole." His conclusion was
much more ambitious than a mere offer of assistance to helpers in the
Weston shop, however, and seemed to propose nothing less than a blue-
print for a union-based, party-led revolution: "Machinists are ready to
amalgamate with the other crafts, and in the end [this] will result in the
amalgamation of all the workers in one big army, and when we have
educated ourselves to that point we will be alive to the fact that the present
system of capitalism, or production for profits, is the cause of all the evils
in present-day society, and only by abolishing capitalism can the coop-
erative commonwealth be realized" (*MB* April 1915).

The machinists debated various proposals for greater centralization
of their membership between 1915 and 1918. One proposal would have
created a single organization for all railway *machinists* in the country.
This would be acceptable to the IAM and the AFL, of course, because it
did not alter existing craft organizations. It was not sufficiently radical,
however, to satisfy Bob Russell and his allies, who called for an *independent Canadian industrial* union for all *railway employees*. Russell's proposal was significantly different from that of his colleagues because it
envisaged independence from American craft union headquarters in the
crucial matters of negotiations and strikes. Thus, Russell would no longer
try to convince the Americans of the advantage of industrial organization and would sidestep the problem of craft autonomy that handicapped
the loose federation of railway trades in Canada: "I feel that if we ever
intend to have joint negotiations on a successful scale it will only be
accomplished when we realize the necessity of doing away with our
present affiliations and putting in their place one central body which would
have jurisdiction over all" (*MB* November 1917; see also, October 1917,
and Johns's report in February 1919; the discussion occurs in *MB* in 1916
and 1917).

Russell called this a "nearer attempt at the one big union idea." It was
an unusual phrase to use in 1917, in view of what happened two years
later. The term *one big union* described an important alternative to the

loose federation that would require each union to seek international head-quarters' approval for strike action and would waste valuable energy as each of the seven crafts negotiated with each of Canada's railway companies. Russell's proposal was calculated to appeal on economic grounds, too, because a single national railway union with a single executive would cost much less than the current web of officers. The importance of this change in Russell's thinking cannot be exaggerated. He was calling for a new organization to supersede the AFL craft system, but it was based on a *Canadian* secession from the internationals, and a railway rather than a metal trades constituency for the new industrial union (*MB* November 1917; see also, October 1917 and February 1919).

The emphasis on Canada should not be mistaken for nationalist sentiment on Russell's part, any more than his preference for a railway constituency should be seen as an expression of affection for the CPR. Rather, Russell had been in Canada for only seven years, and, though he was slowly learning about his new home, he remained – in his own view – a member of an international proletariat. No, Russell was being a careful political strategist when he advocated a national industrial union. He could see that Canadians' chances of influencing American unionism, either at the machinist headquarters or in Gompers's AFL offices, were tiny. On the other hand, change in the Canadian political environment was much more likely. Winnipeg, Manitoba, and the West seemed ready for his radical message. And even the TLC might be swayed by a united western faction. Moreover, Canada's rail companies operated on east-west lines; a nation-wide union made sense in railways, if not in the manufacturing – often branch-plant – communities of central Canada.

Creation of the AFL-sponsored Railroad Employees' Department in the United States in 1918, a response to President Wilson's United States Railroad Administration, must have surprised Russell. He greeted the news of the federation of American railway carmen, boilermakers, blacksmiths, and machinists as a great advance, but he did not think the American initiative should also absorb Canadian railway workers. When Canadian railway metal workers met in Winnipeg in March 1918, however, they resolved to follow the American example by creating Division Four, the fourth group in the AFL's Railroad Employees' Department. Russell was not happy with this continent-wide amalgamation, but he did not have sufficient influence to win a reorganization based on national lines and on a unitary concept (*MB* February, March 1918).

The Canadian machinists entered negotiations in the spring of 1918 with high expectations. Talks between the Railways War Board and the amalgamated unions of the major Canadian railways continued for several months, and, finally, the bargaining teams agreed to accept a Canadian equivalent of the settlement reached in the United States, known there as the McAdoo Award. This result, which was released in July, was a great disappointment to Canadian machinists.

The story of the 1918 settlement is unwritten. It seems clear, however, that the Canadian union negotiators had originally decided to reject the Railways War Board's offer and call a strike. In accordance with the rules of the international craft unions, each of the crafts should then have applied to its headquarters for approval of the strike. This did not happen. Instead, one of the Canadian representatives, perhaps a member of the carmen's union, wired secretly to Washington to inform the AFL of the looming danger of a large Canadian strike. The AFL, committed by Gompers to support the war effort, then forbade the strike and threatened the Canadians with expulsion from the internationals if they walked off the job. It is said, too, that the Canadian government warned the railway unions that a strike would bring about the imposition of martial law and a wage based on army pay. The Canadian negotiators then knuckled under and signed the McAdoo Award (*MB* August 1918).[11]

The immediate response among many of the rank and file was that they had been betrayed and that the officers in the IAM headquarters, if not the AFL and Gompers himself, were responsible. In Winnipeg, the machinist lodges refused to send in their dues. Criticism of the international officers was voiced in a number of other lodges. President Johnston of the IAM made a special tour of Canadian cities in October to quell the unrest. At Johnston's mass meeting of machinists, specialists, and helpers in Winnipeg, Bob Russell declared that "the so-called International Organization" was international in name only. However, Russell was unable to win support for further action (*MB* August 1918).[12]

A small dispute in Winnipeg was representative of the tense atmosphere among prairie unionists. The CPR had hired a new employee in June 1918 who was regarded as "obnoxious" by the other workers at the Weston shops. Rather than accept the man, Lodge 122 walked out, and locals in several Saskatchewan towns joined them, though their actions disrupted the national contract negotiations. The strike was brief, the issue apparently small, but the victory – the workers on the floor won their case – was sweet. As the Lodge 122 correspondent reported, machinists believed they should have "a say in who they will associate with when they are grinding out their existance [sic] in the sweat shop." Moreover, this dispatch said, the strike illustrated "the passing of the present social system; . . . this system of society will be relegated to the scrap heap and a new civilization will spring up in its place, a civilization for the mutual benefit and protection of the working class, a social system that will demand production for use and not for profit." Such vast conclusions and such unusual militancy over an issue of worker control in the shop suggested the extraordinary atmosphere of 1918 (*MB* October, November 1918).

The use of strikes as a weapon in bargaining was widespread in 1918 but so, too, was a new weapon, the threat of sympathetic walkouts. Both in Winnipeg and in Calgary, limited confrontations between management and union grew into extensive strikes that involved many locals. It was noteworthy that, in each case, the unions won important victories that they attributed to their new-found power as a "class" (*MB* July, November 1918).[13]

Winnipeg's private metalworking or "contract" (the non-railway companies) shops were involved in bargaining talks in 1918. Rather than confronting the employers over the issue of union recognition, as they had done unsuccessfully in 1915 and 1917, the workers created the Metal Trades Council, which was like those in other Canadian cities, and they presented their proposals to all the contract shops as one. Wages were ostensibly the issue, but recognition of the Metal Trades Council by the big shops – Manitoba Bridge, Vulcan Iron, Dominion Bridge – was really at stake. The owners refused to budge, a strike ensued, and after two hard months – for this was the second strike in the shops in just over a year – the workers drifted back to their jobs without a union contract. Once again, the Winnipeg machinist lodges had suffered a bitter defeat. But there was a difference in this strike. One new target of Winnipeg machinists' anger was their international grand lodge, which had forced them to wait eight weeks before granting approval of the strike. That, too, played a role in the events of the next year (*MB* June, August, October 1918).

The first union crisis of the post-war era occurred on 12 December 1918, and, fittingly, it was at a national machinists' convention in Winnipeg. After three days of strenuous debate, the leaders decided to seek the abolition of craft lines among the railway unions and the creation instead of an industrial union, the Federation of Railway Employees of Canada. It was an extraordinary victory for the machinist opponents of the AFL and must have seemed all the sweeter to men like Russell because it was approved despite the opposition of the International union's officers, especially James Somerville of Moose Jaw.

The victory was short-lived. In the following week, all the railway crafts in Canada met in convention in Winnipeg, where the ground was covered again. This time, the resolution to unite the Canadian railway workers in an industrial union while "retaining their affiliations with their International and National organization" (*MB* January 1919), as was prudently specified, was lost by a vote of sixty-two to forty-four. A majority of delegates preferred to stay in their international craft unions and to retain their amalgamation with the Railroad Employees' Department of the AFL. The delegates also chose to negotiate "in Washington" for a new wage contract that would cover all *North American* railway trades.

Russell and his colleagues must have been bitterly disappointed. They blamed the labour "skates" of eastern Canada for the decision and were especially angry with the entrenched international union officers in such groups as the carmen. For the next month, Russell and his allies had to endure jeers aimed at the "Winnipeg clique" and accusations that their group was trying to destroy the railway labourers' best ally, Division Four of the AFL's Railroad Employees' Department. Russell could scarcely deny the charge, for that indeed had been his goal (*MB* January 1919). Having failed for the moment, however, Russell moved on to the next battles.

BOB RUSSELL'S SOCIALISM

How would the workers' extraordinary energies and deep dissatisfaction be managed? Who would provide the leadership and establish the goals? Bob Russell and his friends in the SPC, a revolutionary socialist group, were ready with answers. For the previous several years, Russell and his radical colleagues had despaired of the political guidance provided by the international craft unions, but they had also been frustrated by the Canadians who controlled the TLC. Now, they attempted to control and guide the militancy of Canadian workers on their own terms. Russell may have been a strong union supporter, but, as his membership in the SPC made clear, he was more than simply a bread-and-butter union man.

Russell had often explained to his fellow machinists that "labour power" was a commodity. When applied to "natural resources," he said, labour power created all wealth, "the wealth of the rich, the wages of the poor." Though unions raised the price of workers' labour power, they could never ensure that workers received "the full product of their toil." Rather, as Russell expressed it, wages would never be raised above the average price of labour. This average was determined, he wrote, "by the average cost of living necessary to maintain the standard of productive efficiency required of them." This thesis may have been a depressing conclusion, but it did demonstrate that Russell had little faith in the ultimate value of wage increases and the typical union victories at the bargaining table (*MB* October 1918; see also, September 1917).

Bob Russell had a different reason for union activity and political party membership. This was his deep conviction that capitalism would eventually be defeated by a social revolution. In his discussion of politics, for example, he offered a message of hope. "Those of us who have taken the time to study Marx and Engels and thereby become conscious of the position in society the workers are in," he wrote, know that revolution is "the stepping stone of progress" (*MB* September 1917; see also, February 1915). Russell took pains to point out to the sceptical that revolutions need not be violent, that human history was "a series of revolutions," and that the revolutionary worker "does not worry about guns; nor does he engage in wild and illegal acts. The movement is a peaceful one; it accepts the civilized weapons of political and industrial action, propaganda and agitation. The revolution is already begun; its crucial period will be marked when the workers perform the act of taking and holding industry, but it will not end there. It will go on and become a constructive movement that will not stop until its aim is accomplished and the socialist republic established" (*MB* November 1918).[14]

In Russell's thinking, the workers' goal was not higher wages or shorter hours. It was not even nationalization of industry. Indeed, Russell believed that in a state-owned, state-controlled economic system, which he called "state socialism," the individual "ceases to count; . . . he is bound hand and foot by the red tape of bureaucracy. The State becomes the Engine of class rule." Instead, he sought to "take and hold the means of life, and control and administer same on a true and democratic basis of industrial ownership." This was the commonwealth of the true revolutionary socialist (*MB* December 1918).

Bob Russell was a special type of socialist, as these statements suggest. He was a member of a small band of Marxists who belonged to the SPC. By the last year of the war, Russell was the Manitoba secretary of the Party and was in regular contact with its leaders in Vancouver. He hewed closely to a party line and had a clear view of the relative place of political movements, union organizations, and strikes in the establishment of the coming socialist commonwealth. He was an important figure in Manitoba debates, and he contributed, through letters and his union work, to the larger socialist cause. On the basis of his work and union experience and his observations of socialist activity around the world – for Russell was a keen reader and a student of public affairs – he had concluded that revolution was inevitable, just as Marx had predicted. His party membership was important in 1919 because it gave him an alliance with a revolutionary cadre several thousand strong. He drew personal strength from this association, and he acquired influence as well. Alone, he might alter the Winnipeg union movement. Together with his dedicated colleagues in the SPC, he might alter the course of Canadian labour.[15]

The SPC revised its tactics in 1918-19 and thereby permitted Bob Russell and his colleagues to assume a greater role in radical politics. Revolutionary socialists in western Canada had formerly sneered at union attempts to improve the workers' lot because their greatest oppressor, according to orthodox revolutionary theory, was the "wage system," which could be changed only by revolution. In the debate over whether parties or unions were more effective as instruments of change, the SPC leaders had always come down on the side of the party because they believed that only a political organization could govern the community. The consequence of their reliance on the party was a relative lack of interest in unions. However, the circumstances of the war, especially the increasing power and membership of unions, changed the attitude of many SPC members. Men like Russell, who were wholehearted supporters of the union movement, then assumed greater influence (*MB* February 1919).

THE SPRING OF 1919

Bob Russell became a popular hero in 1919, his cheery face and stormy rhetoric well-known in Winnipeg and beyond. He was a central figure at the Western Labour Conference in March, in the Winnipeg General Strike in May and June, and in the formation of a revolutionary industrial union, the One Big Union (OBU). He was subjected to immense pressure in his new public role, was taken from his family by the police in the dead of night, endured a long and frustrating trial, and, finally, as the year ended, he was sentenced to a term in the federal penitentiary. It is generally conceded today that Russell did not seek to foment a revolution by means of the Winnipeg General Strike. It is also suggested, however, that, in supporting the OBU movement, he was a naive and even foolish individual who was part of a "children's crusade."[16]

Russell's purposes in advocating industrial unionism have been misrepresented and misunderstood. As he had been in his earlier union activities, Russell remained in 1919 an advocate of inclusive, more centralized, unions. His disdain for craft-union exclusiveness, his concern for greater worker control in the workplace, and his determination to establish effective working-class organization for the coming revolutionary era, lay behind his drive to secede from the internationals and the AFL and to create an industrial-union movement in Canada. In the final analysis, these three forces – industrial unions, worker control, and revolutionary socialism – explain his actions.

A crucial shift in the rhetoric of Russell and his SPC colleagues occurred in December 1918 and January 1919. Before that time, the revolution had been discussed as an event in the distant future; from the Armistice, however, it seemed to be just around the corner. As Russell explained in January 1919: "We have passed into the most important stage of Capitalistic development, namely the period of Revolution, wherein we witness in some of the European countries the passing of the Capitalist system of production and the introduction of the Co-operative Commonwealth which reminds us of the not long distant past when we were reading our histories about the passing of Feudalism and the introduction of the Capitalistic system" (*MB* January 1919).[17]

One target of the SPC leaders was the conservative leadership of the TLC. The radicals' dissatisfaction, which had been evident in the 1915 TLC debate on participation in the war, had won greater popular sympathy as the military conflict dragged on and the threat of conscription grew.

This discontent, especially evident in western Canada, became outright rebellion in September 1918, when the TLC again rejected a series of radical proposals, this time on the question of whether the Canadian labour movement should discard craft unionism in favour of union reorganization along industrial lines.[18] Though the ranks of the dissatisfied included many who were not western Canadians, Russell and his colleagues returned from the convention with the belief that Canada's labour reform would have to begin in a regional constituency – the West. They immediately began a carefully orchestrated movement to convince western labour organizations to participate in a regional union convention.

The SPC members used their seats in the provincial and urban trade councils to dominate the campaign for a western labour conference and to win appointment as delegates to that conference. In Winnipeg, Russell was in constant battle with the labour conservatives and moderates. He was optimistic, however, as he explained to the SPC secretary: "The movement here is developing rapidly and we are fast knocking hell out of the Labor Party." By mid-February, he could claim to have "killed the Labor Party for sure" and, with his selection, along with Dick Johns, his friend and colleague in the SPC, to represent the Winnipeg TLC at the Calgary Western Labour Conference, to have nearly won control of the Winnipeg movement. His goal, he told Edmonton SPC member Joe Knight, remained the same: "I see arising out of the unemployment that is now beginning to make itself manifest, the most glorious opportunity to show the plug [worker] the only solution to the question is by continually pointing to him (as you say) the situation in Russia."[19]

The Western Labour Conference in Calgary was a stunning success for the SPC. The 240 delegates approved the revolutionary program that Russell and the SPC had been advocating, including a referendum on secession from the AFL and the international craft unions. In their place, if the workers approved in the referendum vote, a Canadian – or, if necessary – a western Canadian organization known as the One Big Union would be created.[20]

Russell exulted when he prepared his monthly article for the machinists in April 1919. "At last? The Crisis!" was the headline of his analysis of labour's pivotal era. He attacked the conservatives of the TLC and the AFL. He scoffed at the international unions, noting that, in confrontations between labour and capital in 1918 in Winnipeg, Edmonton, Calgary, and Vancouver, "in every instance a strike by a single organization . . . necessitated . . . a general strike in order to win and each of which had to be pulled off in defiance of the various Internationals." Canadians had the advantage, according to Russell, of being more aware of the British labour example, "where the rank and file found it necessary to take concerted action in spite of the threats of their International [sic] officers . . .

which has been partly responsible for the development of the Shop Steward movement. If ever there was a time when workers in Canada, as in Britain, could attain the "Overthrow of the Wages System," he concluded, this was it. His argument was not that some mystical revolution would occur but, rather, that the workers could take control of industry as the British shop stewards had done and establish factory governments that actually bypassed the "wage system" (*MB* April 1919).

Co-ordination of the machinists' wage negotiations and the OBU campaign was not an easy matter, especially when the day of revolution seemed so close. On the one hand, the machinists were committed to contract talks with Canada's Railways War Board. On the other, Russell and Johns wanted to bring their machinist colleagues into the OBU. Johns pressed for a Canada-wide vote of Division Four (the Railway Employees) on the OBU issue and, in the meantime, decided to campaign in eastern Canada on the imminence of revolution: "We must get those Railway organizations in the East, it is an impossibility for us in the West to break from the East, they could successfully fight us with Locomotives in case of a strike." The SPC leaders also wondered about sending Bob Russell to Minneapolis: "You see, we must rouse the mass in the U.S., and the nearest home must be approached first." Even if the revolution were not likely to spread, consolidation of labour gains in western Canada was considered essential. Victor Midgley, who co-ordinated the SPC campaign from Vancouver in the spring of 1919, told a Calgary union leader that the committee elected by the Calgary conference "was definitely instructed while taking a vote of the whole of Canada, to separate the ballots east and west, with Port Arthur as the dividing line, and if the west voted in favour and the east against, then it was understood that the west would go it alone." The SPC tactics in April were evolving with the situation and, if not entirely settled, were still reliant on a western Canadian base for radical change.[21]

Russell spent his time during March and April at meetings on local bargaining issues and in the preparation of broadsides and other items of political education. His friend Dick Johns carried on the lecture tour in the East. When Johns talked in Toronto about the general strike as bargaining tactic, the workers shouted (he wrote Russell excitedly), "Come on Wpg. give us the O.B.U. Oh say, Bob! I sure rose to the occasion. . . . Gee, when I concluded they gave such a shriek out of them. I never experienced a meeting with so much interest in the question."[22] In the days of expectation between March and May, Bob Russell and his friends encountered no serious checks in their campaign for a new industrial union and secession from the AFL.

One crucial flaw in the revolutionary socialists' plan was their failure to co-ordinate their activities with sympathetic radicals among eastern Canadian craft unions. On this topic, their correspondence had a rueful air.

Johns, who was almost alone in conducting the OBU advertising east of the Great Lakes, perceived quickly enough where the problem lay: "Our difficulty up to date has been, we haven't done sufficient spade work in Eastern Canada. . . . The general idea prevailing here is, that the West ignored the East, and because they did not get the opportunity to participate in the [Calgary] Convention they are refusing to comply with our request." Johns had not given up: "I was always advised that if I ever went East I would soon lose my optimism. But I wish to emphasize that I am more optimistic now than I was before I left Wpg." Nonetheless, neither Johns nor Russell nor anyone else had a specific plan to overcome these obstacles.[23]

Insofar as the revolutionaries had a plan, it was to build the OBU as quickly as possible and then, perhaps, to take over Canada's TLC. That this would provoke a confrontation with the AFL and the internationals – since the OBU would be regarded as a "dual union" – the revolutionaries must have known. They were not deterred. Russell told an ally, Tom Cassidy, that socialist preparations in Toronto were proceeding well: "They are anxious that the West turn out solid to the Congress at Hamilton [in September 1919], and I believe that it is the best thing we can do – get down and force and capture it and I agree with you that it should be started at once. I will write Pritchard and the bunch [in the Vancouver SPC] to-night . . . and see how they feel. Personally I feel that we ought to get control and it would give the Government an awful shake."[24]

One wonders whether the revolutionary socialists ever had a chance of success in Ontario and Quebec, Canada's labour heartland. The internationals were well regarded and well entrenched among so many workers – the carmen, for example – that they would have been hard to dislodge. As a leader in the telegraphers' union advised Russell, an OBU vote in international locals in central Canada would be a disaster and "would be taken full advantage of by the Powers That Be and their Lieutenants to discredit the West. . . . You go on and make the plunge and the East will follow, but it hasn't the necessary knowledge to intelligently join you now."[25] In this sense, the extension of government regulation into the metal trades and the railway industry had, paradoxically, both a radical and a conservative impact: by encouraging the unionization of workers and the amalgamation of craft unions, it had radicalized the movement; but, by consolidating the influence of the international lodge officers, who adhered to the "win the war" philosophy of Prime Minister Robert Borden and AFL leader Samuel Gompers, the government had ensured that workers' protests remained within safe limits.

The SPC leaders' campaign to take over the TLC, if that was indeed their plan, would depend on a summer of labour peace and intense politicking within the unions. The creation of the OBU fit in well with this goal. As an anonymous machinist, probably Russell, explained, the radicals had no wish to precipitate an early confrontation with the forces of capital: "Say, fellow-workers, you can't initiate any prepared plan to start a revolution. . . . We claim the One Big Union is the next steps [sic] in progress for the workers, and, instead of precipitating a revolution, will prevent it coming before we could make good" (*MB* April 1919).[26]

Another aspect of the Calgary conference made the hopes for labour peace less than likely, however; that was the enthusiasm for "joint action" or "direct action," which was expressed in workers' willingness to employ the general strike in cases of confrontation with capital. The Calgary conference had actually approved a nation-wide referendum on whether to call a general strike to press certain demands, including the thirty-hour week, but the measure was outstripped by rapidly changing events. The threat of a general strike arose again, however, because a number of long-running disputes in Winnipeg's metal and building trades were reaching the boil. Such was the optimism and aggressiveness in union circles that these battles were adopted as their own by the delegates to Winnipeg's TLC and boosted into a city-wide general strike. It was a fateful decision.

BOB RUSSELL IN WINNIPEG, 1919

Bob Russell advised against a Winnipeg metal trades strike[27] and probably had mixed feelings when the Winnipeg workers raised the general strike threat. The conflict itself, and the workers' unity, delighted him. But were the other western cities, and even more important, the union members in the rest of the country, ready for a crucial confrontation with business and the state? Surely, that was exactly the concern that had been worrying the SPC leaders for the previous two months. Russell could only hope that this general strike threat, like the one over the Winnipeg civic employees' contract a year earlier, would bring a prompt settlement.

It was not to be. The contract shop owners dug in their heels and refused to budge. The workers could not appreciate the owners' fears for the stability of the capitalist system, whether because they thought such talk was without foundation or because, like Russell, they saw the change as inevitable. The workers genuinely believed that the general strike was merely an extension of the principles of union amalgamation and direct action – thus their phrase, "joint action" – into the sphere of industrial relations. Many members of the wider community regarded the general strike as a political weapon – an attempt by the workers to usurp the powers of legislatures and, ultimately, to take control of the state. The simplification of the issue divided the city into two camps and was tantamount to a declaration of class war.

On 15 May 1919, the Winnipeg General Strike began. Thousands of workers, many of them not even members of a union, walked out in support of their colleagues in the metal and building trades. Bob Russell became a crucial figure in the central strike committee and spent his days in meetings that directed both strike policy and a considerable share of the civic administration. It was probably Russell who raised the strategic problem of food supply and argued that, given the reports from the Seattle general strike of February 1919, the strikers should endorse the operation of milk- and bread-delivery vans under placards reading Permitted by Authority of the Strike Committee.[28] The message provoked outrage among business leaders across the country and became a rallying point for the strikers' opponents. As the Winnipeg strike dragged on, workers in other Canadian centres walked out in sympathy. In a number of cities, strikes took place as a result of local disputes. Thus, the Winnipeg strike was just the most dramatic event in these months of unprecedented worker hostility to the Canadian economic and political system.

After six weeks of turmoil, the combined forces of government and business succeeded in bringing the walkout to an end. The unions lost the immediate confrontation in Winnipeg but they also lost a larger battle. While the Winnipeg workers were on strike and while the associated chain of sympathetic strikes taxed the energies of union leaders across the West and, to a lesser degree, the East, the radical socialists had neither time nor resources to organize the OBU or otherwise confront the AFL loyalists in the international unions. Russell and Johns tried to push the machinists and the other railway crafts into the OBU camp but met with only limited success. They became labelled as the "Winnipeg Bunch & Co." and were said to be "grasping at every little chance" to call a rail strike. The unions in Division Four could not be moved quickly enough. The collapse of the Winnipeg strike at the end of June and the arrest of important figures like Bob Russell gave the international union loyalists a breathing space during which they could regroup.[29]

Russell was soon preoccupied by legal problems. He had been remanded three times, he told his fellow machinists in July, while private homes and Labour Temples across Canada were raided for evidence to convict him and, especially, to show that the Winnipeg strike had been fuelled by "Bolshevik" money channelled through the United States. He appealed for donations to fight the "hundreds of cases" soon to be brought before the courts (*MB* July 1919).

In the interim, Russell's opponents, the international loyalists, fought back. They were led by such men as James Somerville, the Moose Jaw machinist who had climbed the union ladder to become a vice president of the IAM. Somerville had fought the socialists from the beginning of this revolt. He defended moderate campaigns for legislative reforms, and he stood firmly for Gompers's approach to unions. In the spring of 1919, after the Calgary conference, he had warned: "For every one born to wear the exalted crown of a martyr in support of a new cause, thousands upon thousands are forced to suffer martyrdom in degredation [sic] wives and families as well" (*MB* April 1919). Somerville agreed that amalgamation of craft unions was a wise step but opposed a break with the internationals because, in his opinion, the OBU secession would deprive workers of their strongest defence, the power and money of their American colleagues. Somerville could count on considerable support from the AFL leadership. Within weeks of the collapse of the Winnipeg strike, he and at least six other paid organizers were campaigning against the revolutionary socialists for the hearts and votes of Winnipeg workers.

Winnipeg was the key to the Canadian socialist revolt, according to the AFL. As another AFL organizer, R.A. Rigg, noted, "The other side apparently are of the same opinion and the heavyweights, Pritchard, Knight, Johns and Russell are all here."[30] Russell had considerable success in the railway shops in this early stage of the contest, but, inevitably, the court cases and the failure of the strike itself eventually undercut his efforts. He raged against Somerville: "You are like Politicians, very slippery and just as tricky, but the rank and file today can't be fooled as in the days of old, so wake up and play a man's part; don't crawl around like a snake in the grass trying to sting someone" (*MB* July 1919). Russell's anger was futile. The local railway unions split, and Russell was replaced by Somerville as officer of the local branches of the IAM.

SOME CONCLUSIONS

Russell's court trial on charges of seditious conspiracy culminated in a guilty verdict and a sentence of two years to be served in Stony Mountain Penitentiary. He was a candidate in the federal election while in prison and emerged to a hero's welcome on 13 December 1920. Russell then became the head of the OBU, which included a substantial number of Winnipeg workers and a rapidly declining number of workers in the rest of the country. After six years of exhausting and ultimately fruitless organizational work, he retreated to the OBU office in Winnipeg, from which he administered the local transit union and a few other small groups of workers. The OBU disbanded in 1956. By the time of his death in 1964, Bob Russell was regarded fondly by many Winnipeggers, and almost all of the union movement, as an elder statesman. Nevertheless, the central point of his life's story must be the events of 1918-19 and the failure – his and others' – to establish a significant alternative to the AFL-TLC alliance. A crucial opportunity had been missed.

Opportunity for what? At his flamboyant best, Bob Russell might have said that the workers had lost the opportunity to cause a social revolution and to abolish the wage system. Despite his periodic outbursts of inflammatory rhetoric, however, he did not perceive the OBU campaign of 1919, or the Winnipeg General Strike itself, to be the pivotal attempts by Canadian workers to overthrow capitalism. Russell was usually careful to distinguish short-term tactics like strikes and union organizing from long-term "scientific predictions" about the fate of the wage system. In his view, revolution would occur without prompting and without violent acts when the proper historical moment had arrived. Thus, Russell's true goal in the period from 1914 to 1919 was to reform the structure of organized labour, to increase the political activity of union members, and to promote socialist education.

Though Russell had only these relatively modest ambitions, the events in the spring of 1919 should be seen as a watershed in Canadian union history and, thus, in the political history of the Canadian nation. At this decisive moment, an important segment of the nation, its unionized work force, faced a choice between two paths, one continental and based on integration within the increasingly continental economic system, the other national and based on the consolidation of a national union movement. The greater proportion of Canada's union movement chose the AFL approach and relinquished one of the rare opportunities to create an independent, country-wide political focus for union leadership.

The choice of the OBU as the vehicle to implement industrial union ideas was not as foolish as is sometimes suggested. The OBU might have become an effective union and a force in politics in time, given enough room, but it simply never had a chance to get on its feet. Its failure was due to the extraordinary opposition of an AFL-government-business alliance. It was also due to an accident of timing: the OBU was organized too late to prevent the Winnipeg General Strike and the sympathetic strikes associated with that event, and too early to unite Canadian craft unions in a nation-wide secession from the AFL on the basis of industrial union principles.

The war should be seen as the catalyst in this crisis. In this article I have only sketched the impact of shell production on the relationship between labour and capital; however, it is important to note that machine shops witnessed a revolution in technology and management during the war years. This revolution must be juxtaposed with the remarkable changes in the bargaining system for the "non-operating" (largely shopcraft) employees of Canadian railways. Taken together, the new circumstances on the shop floor and at the negotiating table precipitated a crisis in the Canadian machinists' locals.

The cautious craft unionism of pre-war Canada was confronted by the militant industrial unionism of Bob Russell and other revolutionary socialists in 1919. Russell and his SPC colleagues were important at this moment of decision because they translated a myriad of grievances into an integrated critique of the capitalist economic order. Russell was not defending his "craft," it should be emphasized, but rather was propagating a Marxist interpretation of the "inevitable collapse" of the "wage system." Nor was Russell's campaign the mere application of Scottish or British socialist principles to the Canadian scene; on the other hand, neither was he propagating some new-found sense of Canadian nationalism. Rather, he and his colleagues had adapted their youthful socialism to North American political, business, and trade union exigencies and had utilized *local* institutions – the SPC and the OBU – to consolidate the working class while they awaited events of the sort predicted by Karl Marx. Russell and his socialist colleagues in the IAM were opposed by "conservatives" within their union, within the other shopcraft unions, within the Canadian TLC and the AFL. They also confronted the problem of communicating their program to workers, whether members or not, in a dozen other important industries. The wonder is not that their secession drive failed but, rather, that it attained so much and that it was prepared to risk so much more.

Bob Russell had been in Canada only nine years when he entered Stony Mountain Penitentiary, but he had been at the centre of events that shaped the history of the nation's labour movement and, perhaps, of its political system. His most lasting influence was his contribution to Canadians' awareness of class. As Donald Creighton once wrote, "Before the war, Canada had believed herself to be a land of equality of opportunity; but the war increased the social stratification of the country and deepened the class consciousness of its component groups."[31] Bob Russell was at the centre of that cultural transformation.

NOTES

This essay was initially prepared for a collection of biographical articles on Canadians during the First World War; the collection was never completed. The project was intended to honour Roger Graham, professor of history at Queen's University and formerly, when he was my teacher, at the University of Saskatchewan. The essay is dedicated to his memory. I would like to thank the faculty and students of Macquarie University, North Ryde, New South Wales, for the invitation to present a version of this paper, and Dr. B.D. Dyster of the University of New South Wales, whose generous assistance made its preparation such a pleasure. Greg Kealey, Ken Osborne, and Nolan Reilly kindly read the manuscript.

1. Mary Jordan, *Survival: Labour's Trials and Tribulations in Canada* (Toronto: McDonald House, 1975); Provincial Archives of Manitoba (PAM), Historical and Scientific Society of Manitoba Papers, Orlikow Tapes, Lionel Orlikow interview with R.B. Russell; PAM, Russell Papers, *King v. Russell*, Examination of R.B. Russell, December 1919; Mrs. Mary Sykes, interview with the author, 14 November 1985; Kenneth W. Osborne, *R.B. Russell and the Labour Movement* (Agincourt: Book Society of Canada, 1978). A major source for this paper was the monthly publication, *Machinists' Bulletin.* It will be cited within the text as *MB.*
2. PAM, Orlikow interview with Russell. See also, Ross McCormack, "Cloth Caps and Jobs: The Ethnicity of English Immigrants in Canada, 1900-1914," in *Ethnicity, Power and*

Politics in Canada, ed. Jorgen Dahlie and Tissa Fernando (Toronto: Methuen, 1981), 38-55.
3. PAM, Orlikow interview with Russell.
4. H.A. Logan, *Trade Unions in Canada: Their Development and Functioning* (Toronto: Macmillan, 1948), 81; Robert H. Babcock, *Gompers in Canada: A Study in American Continentalism before the First World War* (Toronto: University of Toronto Press, 1974), 219-21.
5. James O. Morris, *Conflict within the AFL: A Study of Craft Versus Industrial Unionism, 1901-1938* (Ithaca, NY: Cornell University Press, 1958); Babcock, *Gompers in Canada,* 139-42.
6. TLC, *Proceedings,* 1915, 91. (Draper was quoted in the *British Columbia Federationist,* 25 September 1915, 2.)
7. *British Columbia Federationist,* 2 November 1917, 3, and 28 September 1917, 1. See also: Martin Robin, *Radical Politics and Canadian Labour, 1880-1930* (Kingston: Queen's University Industrial Relations Centre, 1968); Paul Phillips, *No Power Greater: A Century of Labour in British Columbia* (Vancouver: B.C. Federation of Labour, Boag Foundation, 1967); A. Ross McCormack, *Reformers, Rebels, and Revolutionaries: The Western Canadian Radical Movement, 1899-1919* (Toronto: University of Toronto Press, 1977).
8. Jordan, *Survival,* 25-6.
9. Michael Bliss, *A Canadian Millionaire: The Life and Business Times of Sir Joseph Flavelle, Bart., 1858-1939* (Toronto: Macmillan, 1978), 305. See also, Peter E. Rider, "The Imperial Munitions Board and its Relationship to Government, Business, and Labour, 1914-1920," Ph.D. dissertation, University of Toronto, 1974, 371, 392.
10. The story of labour in the First World War, and especially analysis of the machinists' position, is not yet clear. The context is provided by: John Andrew Eagle, "Sir Robert Borden and the Railway Problem in Canadian Politics, 1911-1920," Ph.D. dissertation, University of Toronto, 1972; Elizabeth Ann Taraska, "The Calgary Craft Union Movement, 1900-1920," Master's thesis, University of Calgary, 1975; David Montgomery, "New Tendencies in Union Struggles and Strategies in Europe and the United States, 1916-1922"; and, Melvyn Dubofsky, "Abortive Reform: The Wilson Administration and Organized Labor, 1913-1920," in *Work, Community, and Power: The Experience of Labor in Europe and America, 1900-1925,* ed. James E. Cronin and Carmen Sirianni (Philadelphia: Temple University Press, 1983). One Canadian treatment is in Myer Siematycki, "Munitions and Labour Militancy: The 1916 Hamilton Machinists' Strike," *Labour / Le Travail* 3 (1978). A broader perspective is in Craig Heron, "The Crisis of the Craftsman: Hamilton's Metal Workers in the Early Twentieth Century," *Labour / Le Travail* 6 (1980):7-48. Further background is provided by Wayne Roberts, "Toronto Metal Workers and the Second Industrial Revolution, 1889-1914," *Labour / Le Travail* 6 (1980). Finally, several provocative insights are outlined in David Montgomery, "Immigrants, Industrial Unions, and Social Reconstruction in the United States, 1916-1923," *Labour / Le Travail* 13 (spring 1984).
11. See also, Logan, *Trade Unions in Canada,* 148.
12. Ibid.
13. See also: David Jay Bercuson, *Confrontation at Winnipeg: Labour, Industrial Relations, and the General Strike* (Montreal: McGill-Queen's University Press, 1974), 58-65; Bryan Thomas Dewalt, "Arthur W. Puttee: Labourism and Working-Class Politics in Winnipeg, 1894-1918," Master's thesis, University of Manitoba, 1985; A.E. Johnson, "The Strikes in Winnipeg in May 1918: Prelude to 1919?" Master's thesis, University of Manitoba, 1978; Taraska, "Calgary Craft Union Movement."
14. This November article was signed "A.M., Winnipeg Roundhouse, C.P.R." The author of this and several other important articles in the *Bulletin* is not known. The by-lines of Winnipeg Roundhouse and Winnipeg R. House obviously suggest a common inspiration. From the context and content, I have concluded that the articles entitled "Revolution," "Industrial Ownership," "The Way Out," and "Reconstruction or Revolution" (*MB* November and December 1918; March and April 1919) were written by Russell, Johns, or their associates. In a letter to the Socialist Party of Canada secretary, Russell reported that he edited the machinists' newspaper and had "been able to get some good stuff off, but as you know, have got to handle the situation carefully. . . . [Recent articles] are not the real

thing, [but] you will realize the necessity of me leading them gently" (PAM, Winnipeg Strike Trials, *The King v. W. Ivens* [Ivens Trial], R.B. Russell to C. Stephenson, 3 January 1919).

15. Gerald Friesen, "'Yours in Revolt': The Socialist Party of Canada and the Western Canadian Labour Movement," *Labour / Le Travail* 1 (1976).

16. Bercuson, *Confrontation at Winnipeg,* 188.

17. As secretary treasurer of the IAM District and editor of the *Bulletin,* Russell presumably wrote the column entitled "Current Events."

18. Friesen, "'Yours in Revolt.'"

19. PAM, Ivens Trial, Russell to Joe Knight, 3 January 1919. See also: Russell to C. Stephenson, 3 January 1919, 22 January 1919, 30 January 1919, 18 February 1919; PAM, OBU Papers, David Rees to Victor Midgley, 24 November 1918; Victor Midgley to Dick Johns, 2 December 1918; Johns to Midgley, 10 December 1918.

20. David J. Bercuson, *Fools and Wise Men: The Rise and Fall of the One Big Union* (Toronto: McGraw-Hill Ryerson, 1978).

21. PAM, OBU Papers, Victor Midgley to W. Smitten, 31 March 1919; W.A. Pritchard to Dick Johns, 2 April 1919; Dick Johns to Victor Midgley, 29 March 1919.

22. PAM, Winnipeg Strike Trials, *The King v. R.B. Russell* (Russell Trial), Dick Johns to R.B. Russell, 30 April 1919. See also, OBU Papers, Russell to Victor Midgley, 17 April 1919.

23. PAM, OBU, Dick Johns to Victor Midgley, 17 May 1919, and Russell to Victor Midgley, 5 April 1919 and 17 April 1919. See also, Ivens Trial, J.B. Houston to Russell, 22 April 1919.

24. PAM, Ivens Trial, T.S. Cassidy to Jack Kavanagh, 28 April 1919; Russell Trial, Russell to Cassidy, 22 April 1919.

25. PAM, Ivens Trial, D. McNaughton to Russell, 24 May 1919. The context is set out in Gregory Kealey, "1919: The Canadian Labour Revolt," *Labour / Le Travail* 13 (spring 1984). The central Canadian situation is discussed in James Naylor, "Toronto 1919," Canadian Historical Association *Historical Papers,* 1986.

26. This despatch was headlined "Chairman Section One" and was probably written by Russell because he chaired the IAM's Section One (the CPR) from December 1916.

27. PAM, Russell Trial, "Examination of R.B. Russell," 134. The conflict seemed relatively innocent when it started (Russell Trial, Russell to Victor Midgley, 1 May 1919).

28. PAM, Winnipeg Strike Papers, Minutes of Central Strike Committee.

29. PAM, Ivens Trial, J. Corbet to [R. Kerrigan?], 23 May 1919; Russell Trial, Russell to W.H. Johnston, 14 June 1919 and 16 June 1919.

30. PAM, Rigg Papers, Rigg to P. Draper, 21 July 1919.

31. D.G. Creighton, "Federal Relations in Canada Since 1914," in *Canada in Peace and War: Eight Studies in National Trends Since 1914,* ed. Chester Martin (Toronto: Oxford University Press, 1941), 42.

Part Three:
Toward New Historical Syntheses

Radical History in Australia:
A Model for Canada?

AUSTRALIANS AND CANADIANS can readily appreciate each others' national circumstances. They recognize the telltale signs of colonial experience that mark life in the shadow of the British Empire and of its successor, the American Empire. Most citizens of the two countries speak English, though Canada's French minority offers one great contrast, and many recent immigrants have been recruited from the same European and Asian countries. The parliamentary and federal institutions seem instantly recognizable. The economies, with their exports of primary products from farm and forest and mine, also seem familiar. So do the party systems. The universities seem to have been built on comparable intellectual foundations, first British and then American. For historians, the prospect of dealing with a literature based on Burke and Mill, Marx and Morris, and that takes for granted footnotes to E.P. Thompson and Herbert Gutman, makes the prospect of comparison relatively attractive. Yet, the links between the scholarly literatures, especially the historical writings, of the two countries are few.

Students of Canadian history will find that the effort to learn about Australia will be repaid. Australia is home to a vigorous and rigorous scholarly discourse. It also possesses historians accustomed to ideological debate. Both the "left" and the "right" are more clearly defined than in North America. As in England, there is a strong labour history tradition and a large contingent of socialist and Marxist social scientists. As in the United States, there are numerous historians trained in liberal graduate schools. What is interesting is that the factions wage a continuing battle for control of the campuses and even of public discourse. History finds its way into the large contingent of Australian magazines, into the "quality" newspapers, and into the speeches of public figures. The 1984-85 debate over Australia's economic future, in which comparisons with Argentinian experience became commonplace, were interesting for their use of international perspectives, and the same could be said about the 1989 discussions of the Australian place in a Japan-dominated Asian economy. In each case, the assumptions and reasoning of the debates were exposed to searching criticism by adherents of other intellectual perspectives.

In an age preoccupied by international comparisons and global currents, the quest for appropriate standards of measurement is no idle ramble. The experience of Canada, like that of Australia, is often obscured by the dust raised by our "close and powerful friends" (the phrase is that of Robert Menzies, Australian Prime Minister, 1939 to 1941 and 1949 to 1966, ideological counterpart of George Drew). We who study smaller countries must stand some distance from the centre of the whirlwind if we are to see clearly the patterns of experience in our peripheral lands. This is not to disparage the study of imperial capitals and empire policy. For us in Canada, as for Australians, one external priority has always been British history and, more recently, the history of the United States. But a second level of priority must be to learn enough about comparable nations to understand what is unique and what is common in the histories of the globe's hinterlands. For Canada, the most appropriate and readily understandable foil is Australia.

The bibliography of Canada-Australia comparative studies is neither long nor encouraging. Neither country can claim to have devoted much attention to the history of the other. Readers of *Labour / Le Travail,* Canada's journal of labour history, for example, received only three reviews of Australian books, one scholarly article on an Australian subject that had special resonance in Canada, and one review article on the state of Australian labour history. This last essay, however, is worth recalling.

"Australian Labour and Labour History," by Eric Fry, former editor of Australia's *Labour History,*[1] is a useful introduction to the subject. Fry's outline of Australian labour historiography demonstrates why it is so different, and so much stronger, than Canadian. He notes the important Australian labour histories that appeared before 1960, most of them socialist or Marxist in tenor, and the relative failure of a liberal tradition or a bourgeois school of national history to dominate the conventional wisdom. As a consequence, the creation of a labour history society and journal in 1960 anticipated the boom in Australia-centred scholarship in that decade and actually led national history in the definition of subjects and themes. Populist in approach, nationalist in expression, progressive in sentiment – though ambiguous in its ideological underpinnings – this generation of labour histories paid close attention to developments in British scholarship. All this changed in the 1970s. A new group of historians, influenced by the debates among European Marxists, attacked the imprecision of the social democrat–Marxist popular front during the preceding decade and encouraged the discussion of class identity, world economic "systems," and the language of culture. In this debate, the new subjects of social history – women's history, Aboriginal history, South Pacific imperialism – also received attention.

When the Australian scholars turned their attention to the forthcoming celebration of the bicentenary of the First Fleet's arrival (1788 to 1988), they parted company over the nature of a quasi-official history project similar in intention, though not in structure, to Canada's Centenary Series. The critics, who were not happy at the prospect of a "sophisticated form of celebratory history" (their words), decided to assemble a "people's history" (*Acquisition* xi). Verity Burgmann and Jenny Lee began the editing process in 1982. Their goal was a critical history. They wished to emphasize that European settlement began with dispossession. A dominant theme in the story would be inequality. Another would be the degree of control exercised over their own lives by those "outside the magic circles of power and influence" (*Acquisition* xiii). The audience for this history would be the people themselves. And the purpose, as the editors declared, was "to suggest that we can not only interpret the world in new ways, but also use that knowledge to change it" (*Acquisition* xiv).

This people's history comes in four instalments. One volume examines the "structural" basis of social violence and racism. It asserts the class-based origins of white Australia and places the responsibility for social injustice and racial conflict on the holders of power. A second volume deals with how people fed, clothed, and housed themselves, raised children, and secured a living. The individuals' experiences with gender, the household, and the workplace take the foreground here. A third deals with popular movements of opposition against the dominant class and the barriers to the success of such resistance movements. And a fourth discusses culture, especially inter-ethnic relations, the regulation of expression by the state, and the re-direction of popular expression by capitalist enterprises. This is an ambitious agenda. Its very structure illustrates the sophistication of historiographical approach, the range of radical historians' interests, and the intensely political character of historical writing in Australia.

A Most Valuable Acquisition, one of the volumes, focusses first on aboriginal Australia, then the convict origins of white society, the many variations on the themes of immigration and ethnicity, the emergence of an Australian "empire" in the South Pacific, and, finally, war as a source of national definition and of national misunderstanding. One theme of the volume is that racism and inter-racial conflict, including inter-racial violence, are part and parcel of the past 200 years in Australia. In the key essay, Jenny Lee argues that the relationship between mother country and colony, that is, Britain and Australia, provides an epitome of the national experience. Even if Australians enjoyed living standards higher than those in Britain and Europe, she explains, they and their families lost much because of their place in the social and economic structure of empire. Australia was locked into the role of exporter of primary products; British financiers controlled the flow of investment; local manufacturing was primitive and vulnerable; in each of the key economic areas – sheep, mines, railways, urban development – there were problems. Most of these problems, including concentration of ownership, male-dominated frontiers, Aboriginal dispossession, and unequal gender relations, were direct consequences of external economic control and the class system that was its creation.

The ostensible purpose of the volume is to inquire why Europeans have lived in Australia and how they have exploited its resources. Thus, the land is seen as "a dumping-ground for convicts, a sheep-walk for the benefit of British industry, a convenient source of cannon-fodder" (*Acquisition* ix).

The white community is described as one that kept itself in comfort "by excluding other races" (*Acquisition* ix). Behind the exploitation and dispossession was not simply white racism, however, but something more pervasive: "White Australia was, and is, a class society. We need to look towards the real source of power within it to uncover the responsibility for social injustice and racial conflict" (*Acquisition* x). Which side won in the contest for profit between "mother" country and colony? In arguing that no group emerged as winner, Lee suggests that a few individuals became wealthy and that many households were caught in an exploitive, self-defeating struggle for survival.

The second volume of this people's history offers a fascinating combination of household, or gender, issues and workplace, or work process, issues. The balance between household and workplace has changed over the past century, the editors argue, and wage labour has assumed tasks formerly reserved for unpaid family members. The consequence is a shift in the role of women and children in society and a "new phase in the history of capitalism" (*Life* xi). How to tackle such themes? Start with the home: a history of food from salt pork to takeaway; a history of clothing as "one of the means of domination in society" (*Life* 28); a history of shelter for those who do not own their own homes; a history of the public sector transportation systems; a history of health, the basis of which is the probability of untimely death; a history of public and private welfare systems. In a valuable synthesis, Marilyn Lake asserts that a central theme in colonial Australian history is the dependency of women. These circumstances were the product partly of the social organization of production and reproduction, partly of the male exclusiveness of unions. Such circumstances forced women to work "a double shift." They also created a society in which men and women "inhabit different cultures: theirs was the intimacy of strangers" (*Life* 164). The volume then turns to the workplace and the working family, examining households in times of depression, employer-employee relations, unions, compulsory arbitration, and work relations in several industries. The strongest article is Peter Cochrane's survey of work processes under the strain of technological change, which asserts the "possibility of socialist organization of work" (*Life* 192). *Making a Life* is a stimulating book. By juxtaposing work and gender, the editors have illuminated the working lives of men and women in a way not usually available to labour or gender studies. Not surprisingly, much of the material is directly relevant to Canadian scholars.

Staining the Wattle is an unconventional political history. The subjects of these histories of political movements include gay men and lesbian women, the women's and green and unemployed people's movements, Communists and Aboriginal-rights activists, and anti-war and anti-bomb campaigns. In short, politics is interpreted as a contest between those with and those without power, as expressed by organized movements. Naturally, organized labour and the Labor Party come in for special attention as bases for hope and obstacles to change. Verity Burgmann and Stuart MacIntyre provide a measured analysis of the matter in "Divided We Fell." They criticize both the unions and their political advocates; they quote with approval the admission of a Labour member of parliament that it was difficult to take up radical causes in Parliament and his comment that, in the end, "we either go right or go cranky" (*Wattle* 129). But Burgmann and MacIntyre conclude on a more optimistic note by arguing that the interests of the workers are "compatible with the interests of the social movements. All share a common objective of liberating humanity from oppression, inequality and ultimate self-destruction" (*Wattle* 131).

The volume *Constructing a Culture* is similarly stimulating. It contains papers on schools, crime, prostitution, madness, gambling, churches, temperance, and sport, each of which offers a survey of the national experience. It then proceeds to subjects that might seem more properly "cultural," including the media, humour, writing, music, the visual arts, and radical intellectuals. Imagine a Canadian counterpart! These papers are useful as models, not just as a means of establishing a perspective on the Canadian experience. They offer concepts that are helpful – "cultural

cringe" and "cutting down tall poppies" (*Culture* 213, 129), for example –
and they make generalizations that sound strikingly familiar. Thus, according to John Docker, since the 1920s Australia has had a "split culture"
(*Culture* 257) in radio and television between the ABC (Australian Broadcasting Corporation), which "looks to the BBC and British high culture,
and commercial stations, which look to American popular culture. It is a
deep split corresponding to a tension between class cultures, and any account of Australian cultural history must ponder its significance" (*Culture*
257). In the most wide-ranging of these papers, Andrew Milner selects
three streams of intellectual radicalism – socialism, feminism, and nationalism – in modern Australia. Milner concludes: "If the inequalities
of race, class and gender that exist in Australia and the even more hor-
rific inequalities that exist internationally are ever to be reduced, let
alone eliminated, then that will not be brought about by specialist groups
of radical intellectuals. Rather, it will be achieved by the efforts of those
masses of people who themselves pay the price, in human misery and
suffering, for the continued existence of structured social inequality"
(*Culture* 283).

These are stimulating essays that deserve an audience in Canada. In
recommending the four volumes – seventy essays – to Canadian historians, I am conscious of the fact that they contain no footnotes and precious
few references to differences of opinion in the historical literature. Nonetheless, they are challenging and broadly representative, as far as I can
tell, of critical thought in Australian historical circles. And, for those who
are determined to go further, each essay is accompanied by a brief bibliographical note.

Wherever they are used in Australia, whether in classrooms, union halls,
or critical discussion groups, they will make the task of stimulating debate
much easier. The very design of the questions around which each volume
is organized represents an important contribution to national
historiography. That seven dozen historians could then be chivvied into
completing brief pithy essays along the desired lines might leave Canadian scholars envious or incredulous, but it should also cause them to
reflect on their own attempts to exert some influence upon the so-called
public agenda. Certainly, one leaves these volumes convinced that Canadians have much to learn from the Australian example. One feels a sense
of place and national debate in these books that may have driven Canadian historians at one time but does not appear among us with the same
intensity today. One observes in these essays an appreciation of the international context of the nation and of scholarly inquiry that is too often
lacking in Canadian historical writing. And one cannot help but be impressed by these historians' determination both to communicate to the
non-professional or lay readers in their communities and to set out a co-

herent synthesis upon which ordinary Australians can base their reflections on politics and community life.

One lesson for Canadians, I think, concerns this need for synthesis. What is the essence of a national story? Burgmann and Lee and their colleagues were determined that self-congratulation not be the only theme in Australia's bicentenary celebrations. They were convinced that a study of "well-heeled, white, Anglo-Saxon males" (*Culture* xiv) would offer only a tiny part of the people's history. They wanted to emphasize that the myths of national progress and national unity were misleading and that most citizens – Aboriginal people, women, members of ethnic minorities, the working class – would not receive adequate treatment in celebratory volumes. Hence the focus on inequality. Balancing this negative was a positive: people can affect the course of history; hence the focus on "agency." The editors wanted to "encourage people to think critically about the imagined community of the Australian nation" (*Culture* xv). They concluded: "If we think about it for long enough, we might decide to . . . open up the doors and windows and let in a bit of fresh air" (*Culture* xvi). A convincing and authoritative synthesis permits the expression of such ambitions.

In Canada, the absence of critical syntheses has impoverished discussion of public issues. Canadian historians have a lot to learn about creating a concerted critical discourse, not least from their Australian counterparts represented in this people's history.

NOTES

This article reviews Verity Burgmann and Jenny Lee, eds., *A People's History of Australia since 1788*, 4 vols.: *Constructing a Culture; Staining the Wattle; Making a Life; A Most Valuable Acquisition* (Fitzroy, Victoria: McPhee Gribble / Penguin Books, 1988). The review appeared in a slightly different form in *Labour / Le Travail* 27 (spring 1991); it is reprinted with the permission of the editor (copyright Canadian Committee on Labour History).

1. Eric Fry, "Australian Labour and Labour History," *Labour / Le Travail* 12 (1983).

Comparative History and Wheat Production: Argentina's Pampas and the Canadian Prairies

THE FIRST OBLIGATION of historians who specialize in Canadian history, it need hardly be said, is to tell the country's story. If we historians don't write it, who will? However, by spending a lifetime on research into local questions, Canadian historians run the risk of neglecting decisive forces that originate outside the country's borders or that seem striking only when placed in a broader context. To correct the inevitable tendency toward a narrowing vision, we must rely on international and comparative approaches to historical study. In this brief essay, I attempt to illustrate the advantages of such comparative enterprises by discussing two very interesting books that utilize the Canadian prairies as one part of a case study and the Argentinian pampas as the other. Ironically, the two volumes reach very different conclusions about the strengths and weaknesses of prairie society.

Carl Solberg's *The Prairies and the Pampas: Agrarian Policy in Canada and Argentina, 1880-1930* assesses the Canadian prairie agricultural experience positively. The book commences with the observation that Argentina's wheat exports occupied about twelve to twenty-five percent of the world wheat market between 1900 and 1937. Though these export volumes were not as high as Canada's wheat shipments, wheat held a similar role in the Argentinian and Canadian economies. Remarkably, Argentinian wheat exports declined to about four to seven percent of the world wheat market in the following four decades, well below the levels maintained by Canada. Of course, Solberg's purpose is to ask why. The answer, he says, lies in the "solid institutional structure that [Canadian] prairie grain growers and the Canadian state established prior to 1930" and, by contrast, in "decades of neglect . . . [that] left pampa farming in no position to expand production."[1]

The late Dr. Solberg, a specialist in the history of Argentina who taught at the University of Washington, was obviously struck by the very different roles played by "the state" in the development of these two wheat economies. Based largely on secondary sources, his illuminating work at once challenges some of the implications of dependency theory for Argentina's economic history and attempts to modify the influential conclusions of Vernon C. Fowke concerning the relative weakness of Canadian farmers in the making of Canadian agricultural policy.[2]

At the heart of Solberg's argument is an emphasis on government policy. He argues that the Argentinian government, dominated by a wealthy cattle-raising landed elite, was convinced that "the free and unregulated operation of market economics would bring the fastest possible development to Argentina." The result was disastrous: "The absence of any comprehensive government policy meant that property ownership remained highly concentrated, that the educational system was primitive, that the roads were abominable, and that the agricultural marketing system was left in the hands of grasping grain merchants."[3] Moreover, southern European immigrants who did not become citizens and who rented farms on short-term contracts, Solberg asserts, lacked the commitment to the land, the material expectations, and the political influence that might have produced agrarian reforms. This combination of forces, all of which might have been altered by government intervention, undermined the wheat economy in the pampas.

Solberg's picture of prairie Canada contrasts sharply with this sketch of Argentina. By basing its policy on the rapid naturalization of northern Europeans and on family farm ownership, the Canadian government created a vigorous agrarian community that won numerous concessions in policy, established strong co-operatives, and encouraged further research and development. The simultaneous Canadian government decision to sustain infant industries by means of a high tariff was part of an integrated national development policy – eastern industry, western grain production, railways to serve both – that demonstrated the virtues of government intervention in the economy.

The argument presented by Solberg is suggestive but not conclusive. First, he should have examined what happened in other areas of Argentina farm production (beef, linseed oil, maize, wool) and of the national economy in order to determine whether the nation merely transferred resources from wheat to more profitable activities after 1930. Second, he asserts, rather than explores, the consequences of the immigrants' cultural expectations. Third, since some Canadian scholars employ (as does Solberg) a version of dependency theory (it is called the "staple trap" in Canada), Canada's experience does not necessarily demonstrate the flaws in an approach that has been very influential in Latin American scholarship. And, finally, he would not convince Canadian farmers that they were well treated simply because they were better educated, better housed, and more successful in national political debates than their counterparts in Argentina. Rather, like their scholarly champion, V.C. Fowke, Canadian farmers would have appealed to abstract standards of "economic justice" for citizens of both nations. Solberg's discussion of Canadian history, and especially of Sir John A. Macdonald's National Policy, is old-fashioned and lacking in nuance.

The great virtue of *The Prairies and the Pampas* is its comparative framework. This might seem to be of little consequence, given that the industry itself is well aware of global trends, but it is an important departure in the history of prairie Canada. Indeed, Solberg may not have added new material to the history of Argentinian or Canadian wheat production, but, by juxtaposing the national histories, his book establishes a realistic gauge by which to measure the experience of each. Moreover, in today's political forums, where debates about globalization occur often, it is useful to see the industry in a broader perspective. Thus, a careful outline of global markets and international competition is welcome and timely. In the end, however, one must come to terms with Solberg's basic argument: should Argentina's relative failure or Canada's relative success in the wheat trade be attributed to *government's* role in the economy?

Jeremy Adelman's *Frontier Development: Land, Labour, and Capital on the Wheatlands of Argentina and Canada, 1890-1914* does not jibe with the Solberg volume. A Canadian who completed his doctorate at Oxford University and now teaches at Princeton, Adelman is interested in and familiar with contemporary Latin America. This revision of his dissertation reflects his sympathy with Spanish-speaking America as well as his training in Toronto's political economy and England's Marxist historical traditions. *Frontier Development* constitutes a significant contribution to the continuing international discussion about frontier capitalism and property rights. As such, it commands the attention of those who are following the so-called Brenner debate, the work of Douglass North, and other assessments of the relative importance of what Adelman calls "property relations" in the evolution of capitalist communities.[4]

Adelman challenges Solberg's versions of prairie and pampas agriculture. He contends that the Argentinian reliance on large estates and tenant production actually represented an efficient and flexible adaptation to local conditions. By contrast, he says, the Canadian approach

to settlement, which relied on family farms and high initial capital investment in equipment, placed great burdens on individual homesteads and,
by its very inflexibility, doomed a high proportion of these families to
failure. The consequent human wastage has never been properly assessed
by Canadian scholars, he implies. Moreover, Adelman contends that the
apparent advantages of the family farm's labour relations system and more
patient approach to capital accumulation, which have been asserted especially in Harriet Friedmann's adaptation of the "world-systems" approach,
have been exaggerated.[5]

One might take issue with Adelman on the relative success of the Argentinian and Canadian systems. Indeed, I suspect that he has opened
but not settled an important debate. In my view, he conflates two very
different stories: the effects of homesteaders' decisions upon the regional
economy, and the potentially quite different impact of these decisions
upon individual households. This ambiguity underestimates the political
influence of farm families and the degree of their success in national policy
debates, as Solberg might contend. It also foreshortens the horizon of the
householders' experience, limiting it to a twenty-year period, rather than
permitting the judgement of their lives to encompass the longer term,
including both their careers in their homelands and their accumulation of
knowledge and cultural capital over several generations, whether in Argentina or in Canada. Adelman's rational "economic" approach is justifi-
able in economic terms, of course, but it leaves little room for human
factors such as the pace of cultural change and the subjects' own assessments of their adaptation experience.

The more important issue, Adelman might reply, concerns the nature
of frontier capitalism. Adelman's thesis is that the "property relations regime" represented the crucial force shaping the very different histories of
the two communities. In each case, the internal contradictions of the capitalist system – the "latent contradictions between labour and property
ownership" – undermined the "ephemeral conditions of prosperity. Thus
[Adelman continues], rather than treat the frontier as a region of unful-
filled promises, it is treated here as a premier manifestation of the tension
between property and independent labour." And his conclusion? The rational behaviour of the economic actors in both countries – peasants and
landlords in Argentina, homesteaders in Canada – "undermined the goal
of socially healthy rapid capitalist growth."[6] This is an important and convincing argument that must be acknowledged in future studies of agrarian
capitalism.

These two books take the study of prairie agriculture out of an exclusively Canadian setting and place it in an international context. The consequence is that the reader's attention shifts to the world wheat market, to
a wide range of possible production systems (and the social arrangements

accompanying privately owned family farms or landlord-owned peasant sharecropping), and to the role of the state in market regulation and social policy.

Solberg's *The Prairies and the Pampas* is at once interesting and disappointing. Its treatment of the contrasting societies cannot but surprise Canadian students who know little of the history of wheat growing in Argentina. However, its enthusiasm for Canadian policy decisions must evoke suspicion. Solberg concludes that Canada's agricultural policies established a sound institutional structure whereas the Argentine government's unwillingness to intervene in the market permitted grasping landlords to exploit hapless peasants. This apparent evidence of Canadian wisdom and Argentinian foolishness vindicates too quickly those who take a northern, Protestant, and democratic (even social democratic) approach to hemispheric history. After all, these were the same Canadian policies that prairie farmers condemned bitterly and that resulted in a homestead failure rate estimated to be around forty percent of total applications.[7]

Frontier Development travels a quite different path to a very different conclusion. Adelman asserts that capitalism's internal dynamics take precedence in the story of modern society. Therefore, property relations and institutions governing work shaped the pattern of economic expansion. Two different systems of production evolved, a divergence that would "help us understand the differences in development between Argentina and Canada." In agreeing with Solberg that the agrarian production systems are different, however, Adelman also wishes to refute the "Jeffersonian synthesis" that prevails in the historical writing about North American agriculture. In other words, he rejects the assumption that family-owned farms are superior to all other systems of agricultural production; as he writes in his conclusion, he wanted to contest the prejudice, evident in almost all the writing about farming, that lauds "the synthesis of unfettered accumulation and bucolic prosperity of independent workers" said to have been generally attainable in North America. Inevitably, this view of North America has been contrasted with Europe, and with the "unfortunate proletarianization which accompanied capitalist industrialization" there. Argentina could only be diminished by such a standard because it followed an allegedly worse system yet – landlord-and-peasant agriculture. To this criticism Adelman responds: "It is time that the myth of North American development, predicated upon the exaggerated success of family farming, cease to be invoked as the path of capitalist development which Latin America failed to follow."[8]

The analysis undertaken by Adelman should be juxtaposed with similar studies that have challenged perceptions of labour and property in other societies. Indeed, one of the noteworthy aspects of Adelman's approach, given its insistence on the fundamental role of the property/labour

relations nexus, is its lack of interest in class conflict as the engine of historical change. In ignoring this strain of Marxism, Adelman does not mention or cite another recent comparative work, Donald Denoon's *Settler
Capitalism: The Dynamics of Dependent Development in the Southern Hemisphere.* Denoon's book, published in 1983, discusses the economics and
politics of six countries, including Argentina, during the boom of 1890-
1914. (The others are Chile, Uruguay, South Africa, New Zealand, and
Australia.) Denoon introduces the concept of "settler capitalism" as a means
of generalizing about these communities in which Aboriginal people were
pushed aside during the nineteenth century and overseas Europeans then
created staple export economies. He suggests that each of the six countries was dominated by classes committed to the imperial trade link and
to the production of such staples. Their state institutions were bulwarks of
the dominant group's class interests. Thus, though all six could be described as self-regulated (that is, they were not victims of imperial coer-
cion), their public life featured a remarkable agreement on the priorities
of economic policy. Indeed, says Denoon, formal political life in these six
countries became a contest between groups already committed to export-
led development. And the result was that all six failed to develop self-
reliant economies that were diversified and internationally competitive.
Instead, they relapsed into differing degrees of dependency, specializing
in the staple exports that reflected their initial comparative advantage when
the cards of global trade were shuffled and dealt in the 1890-1914 era.
This theme, I suspect, might offer a valuable extension of Adelman's fundamental insight.

Adelman's *Frontier Development* belongs at the forefront of the debate
about property and the frontier. Its analysis of the internal dynamics of
the capitalist system is compelling. So is his conclusion: "In both Argentina and Canada, the struggle to fashion a Jeffersonian synthesis of independent labour bonded to property through ownership did not fulfil expectations, despite each country's enviable performance in world markets. The reasons for the frontier project's demise varied. While no single
pattern prevailed, in both cases it was the collective activity of producers
and owners which undermined the goal of socially healthy rapid capitalist
growth."[9]

For readers in the Canadian prairies, the lessons are important. If
Adelman has emphasized the negatives in prairie history, expressing concern for the many families that lost their ten-dollar gamble on "free homesteads" and endured years of harsh existence in a lonely, cold climate, it is
perhaps because he has spent less time among the fortunate families who
survived and prospered, building a world that has functioned reasonably
well, just as Solberg suggests. Theirs is a capitalism, of course, that has
been modified by their own political success. Nevertheless, as one looks

at this history from today's perspective, one cannot deny that rapid economic change and global cultural forces are now challenging the stability of contemporary prairie Canada just as much as the waves of price and market fluctuation and climate variation wracked the farm family a century ago. Adelman's clear and sustained concentration on the dynamics of this capitalist impulse says as much about today's travails as it does about those of a preceding generation.

Comparative histories, especially those works that reveal the global context of local experience, can subvert hitherto unassailable myths in national historiographies. Students and citizens of the Canadian prairies are fortunate when their own society is included in such scholarly enterprises. Let us learn from them by assimilating the conclusions and then subjecting them to equally rigorous analysis.

NOTES

This paper is based on two published reviews and an unpublished paper. The first, on Carl Solberg, *The Prairies and the Pampas: Agrarian Policy in Canada and Argentina, 1880-1930* (Stanford: Stanford University Press, 1987), appeared in *The Hispanic American Historical Review* 68, no. 4(1988); it is reprinted with permission. The second, on Jeremy Adelman, *Frontier Development: Land, Labour, and Capital on the Wheatlands of Argentina and Canada, 1890-1914* (Oxford: Clarendon Press, 1994), will be published in the *International History Review* (1996-97); it is reprinted with the permission of the editor of the *International History Review*. The broader context of the discussion was developed in a seminar meeting on Donald Denoon's *Settler Capitalism: The Dynamics of Dependent Development in the Southern Hemisphere* (Oxford: Clarendon Press, 1983). I would like to thank Dr. Denoon and the Research School of Social Sciences, Australian National University (Canberra), as well as Dr. Barrie Dyster, University of New South Wales, for their encouragement of my hesitant steps into this type of study, and Dr. Jeremy Adelman, who shared his enthusiasm for comparative approaches.

1. Carl Solberg, *The Prairies and the Pampas: Agrarian Policy in Canada and Argentina, 1880-1930* (Stanford: Stanford University Press, 1987), 232.
2. Vernon C. Fowke, *Canadian Agricultural Policy: The Historical Pattern* (Toronto: University of Toronto Press, 1946); Fowke, *The National Policy and the Wheat Economy* (Toronto: University of Toronto Press, 1957).
3. Solberg, *The Prairies and the Pampas,* 15, 20.
4. Robert Brenner, "Agrarian Class Structure and Economic Development in Pre-Industrial Europe," in *The Brenner Debate: Agrarian Class Structure and Economic Development in Pre-Industrial Europe,* ed. T.H. Aston and C.H.E. Philpin (Cambridge: Cambridge University Press, 1985); Douglass C. North, *Growth and Welfare in the American Past: A New Economic History* (Englewood Cliffs, NJ: Prentice-Hall, 1966); North, *Structure and Change in Economic History* (New York: Norton, 1981); and *Institutions, Institutional Change, and Economic Performance* (Cambridge: Cambridge University Press, 1990).
5. Jeremy Adelman, *Frontier Development: Land, Labour, and Capital on the Wheatlands of Argentina and Canada, 1890-1914* (Oxford: Clarendon Press, 1994); Harriet Friedmann, "World Market, State and Family Farm: Social Bases of Household Production in the Era of Wage Labor," *Comparative Studies in Society and History* 20 (1978). The world-systems approach was developed in the 1970s by Immanuel Wallerstein. The first of several volumes is *The Modern World-System: Capitalist Agriculture and the Origins of the European World-Economy in the Sixteenth Century* (San Diego: Academic Press, 1974).

6. Adelman, *Frontier Development*, 269.
7. Chester Martin, *"Dominion Land" Policy*, ed. Lewis H. Thomas (Toronto: McClelland and Stewart, 1973; first published 1938).
8. Adelman, *Frontier Development*, 15, 266.
9. Ibid., 269.

The Prairies as Region:
The Contemporary Meaning of an Old Idea

TALK OF A SINGLE WEST, of a prairie region, and of prairie regionalism is part of Canadian popular expression. Even before Confederation, visitors to the western interior accorded a special status to this striking expanse of plain or steppe that they depicted as one of the noteworthy "wildernesses" of the globe. Métis rebellion and Aboriginal resistance and provincial rights, all of which might be said to have a regional cast, dominated published histories concerning the last decades of the nineteenth century. During the first half of this century, such labels as *prairie protest*, *agrarian revolt*, and *labour revolt* were often applied to similar expressions of discontent. This historical experience has ensured that "regional" considerations have consistently influenced discussions of prairie Canada.

In this essay I review the idea of prairie region and provide a context for discussions of the place of prairie residents in Confederation. It is constructed around several questions: First, how has the concept of prairie region been used, and has it been regarded as helpful or appropriate in the interpretation of prairie experience? Second, when we invoke "prairie regionalism" in our contemporary constitutional discussions, what is the "ism" meant to convey? Third, what is the relative importance of prairie regional identity today?

DEFINING REGION

There are three main approaches to the phenomenon of "region": the formal, the functional, and the imagined. Separately, each has been employed as a means of depicting the Canadian prairies. Together, they present problems. They tend to overlap in popular thinking, to reinforce each other and, yet, to flee from precise definition. They are often fuzzy when utilized in debates about public policy, so it is as well that the concept "region" be made clear before it is used in social analysis.

The simplest approach, on the surface, is the formal region: the prairies *look* like a separate and distinct and homogeneous place – in short, like a region. When Henry Kelsey arrived on the edge of these plains in 1690, he described them as a "barren ground" and said that they offered "nothing but short Round sticky grass & Bufillo."[1] A century later, David Thompson named this zone "the Great Plains as a general name," said they constituted a "very different formation," and placed the area in continental perspective by suggesting that they stretched from the Gulf of Mexico to the fifty-fourth parallel.[2] Another century on, European Canadian scientific observations had intensified with the extension of national boundaries and surveys. Thus, an 1884 geology textbook divided the northern half of the continent in two at the "Laurentian axis" extending from Lake of the Woods to the Arctic, arguing that the eastern and western halves were "geologically and physically distinct."[3] These generalizations represent the first level of European Canadian regional perceptions. They rely upon land forms and climate and unity of historical experience to define a separate and distinct place on the earth's surface.

The historian Goldwin Smith best encapsulated this phase of thinking about regions. Writing in the late nineteenth century, when nation building and national re-alignment were still transforming the globe, Smith evoked the power of geographical forces in suggesting that the new transcontinental Canada was far from a stable or permanent entity. He argued in the opening statement of his *Canada and the Canadian Question* that, if one wished to understand Canada's national dilemma, one must turn "from the political to the physical map." In doing so, the image of a united land would be superseded by one that featured "four separate projections of the cultivable and habitable part of the Continent into arctic waste," each separated from the others "by great barriers of nature, wide and irreclaimable wildernesses or manifold chains of mountains," and each "closely connected by nature, physically and economically" with the adjoining American region.[4] Such perceptions represent the physical interpretation of the western interior as a formal region. They underlie all the perspectives that follow, and they *will* linger in our minds, despite our best efforts to rid ourselves of such apparently simple interpretations of human society.[5]

The developing literature on the prairies, whether in fiction or the social sciences, offered further variations on this interpretation of regional difference – of formal region – in the late nineteenth and early twentieth centuries. Environment, in this view, affected and perhaps even determined human character or social behaviour. Thus, Roger Pocock, a novelist of the 1880s, described mounted police returning from patrol, "their eyes bright with the reflected breadth and freedom of the plains. . . . [They] have no flavour of the old tiresome life of the umbrella and the table-cloth."[6] In a novel by the immensely popular Ralph Connor, a character exclaims: "How wonderful the power of this country of yours to transform men!"[7]

These assertions may now appear foolish, but they once represented a significant strain in Canadian thought. Scholars shared with novelists this preoccupation with the power of the land. The geographer Griffith Taylor, for example, built a career on his environmentalist interpretations. His major work on Canada, published in 1947, distinguished twenty Canadian regions, including the Winnipeg Basin and the Western Prairie, and forecast remarkable population growth for both on the basis of his assessment of the future of world agricultural and energy production.[8] The great prairie historian of that era, Arthur Silver Morton, invoked similar assumptions when, in describing the crucial shift of Aboriginal groups from parkland to plains in the 1700s, he wrote that the "Crees wandered over into the prairies and adopted the very different manner of living which characterized the buffalo country." In such works, an implied environmental determinism assumed as much as it explained but it also offered an explanation for the presence of formal regions in the author's thought.[9]

The foregoing versions of the western interior, whether depicting the area as a natural product of physical geography (David Thompson and Goldwin Smith), or as a social phenomenon introduced by environmental forces (Ralph Connor and Griffith Taylor), asserted that the Canadian prairies constituted a definable portion of the earth's surface. No reference to other places was necessary to establish the region's character. The prairie region stood on its own, distinctive and clearly demarcated, a "formal region" that occupied an unmistakable physical place on the map. Its boundaries would not change significantly as long as the physical environment remained unaltered. It was relatively consistent internally as measured by certain self-evident and allegedly objective characteristics. The link in this analysis between formal region and environmental interpretations of human affairs will be unmistakable.

Environmentalism, pure and simple, has since fallen into disrepute, but recognition of environmental *influence* in human affairs can hardly be disputed. Ronald Rees's recent volume on the Canadian plains examines such difficult matters as the effect of an environment devoid of trees and other physical relief upon human well-being.[10] The careers of many Canadian scholars, including W.L. Morton and Harold Innis, were devoted to understanding the interplay between environment and human endeavour. Thus, environmentalism need not become determinism. Emphasis upon landscape and resource differences in regional analysis must not be dismissed today as the musings of fanatics. Students of society run the danger, ironically, of neglecting environmental influences upon human activity while, because of some atavistic mental reflex, retaining a dogged and simple concept of formal physical region – the Canadian prairies – that underlies daily life and thought. No matter how one tries, one's picture of a prairie region will always retain some degree of this plain and simple thinking, of formal regionalism.

A second kind of regional definition, also important in Canada, employs a relative, or relational, approach. In order to have one region, in this view, one must have another. Hinterland regions exist because there are also metropolitan regions, frontiers can only be distinguished from densely settled zones, areas of staple exploitation from central markets where consumers and entrepreneurs and, often, cultural and political leadership are located. These places, shaped as much by the coherent whole of which they form a part as by internal consistency or evident boundaries, have been labelled "functional regions." As Janine Brodie has suggested, they are defined by their relationships as well as by their internal characteristics, and by social as much as "natural" elements.[11]

Consider two illustrations of how this approach has influenced our thinking about the prairies. Canadians once were accustomed to describing the West as a frontier. Thus, the Queen's University academic Adam Shortt reported that his preconceptions about social organization had been "revolutionized" during his travels in the Northwest in 1894. He found in the prairies not the well-defined characteristics of business and social life he was accustomed to in Ontario but, rather, a society "in process of formation."[12] When Isaiah Bowman designed his multi-volume scholarly project, the Canadian Frontiers of Settlement series, in the late 1920s, he believed that he was creating a science of settlement that would have international application because "the pioneer belts of the world are regions of experiment – 'experimental zones' we might call them."[13] Similarly, the distinguished economist W.A. Mackintosh argued that "sectionalism is always characteristic of a new and expanding country. There is always division between the frontier and the old settlements, whether exemplified in Jacksonian democracy, or in conflict between Halifax and York currencies and between established churches and Methodism, or in farmers' movements."[14] The sociologist S.D. Clark employed comparable arguments in linking the Seven Oaks incident, the two Métis resistances, the One Big Union, the People's Church, the wheat pools, and Social Credit as "western movements of revolt," the expres-

sions of "a separate people," that would recur as the predecessor movements lost their bite.[15] Each of these examples distinguishes the Prairie
West as a type of frontier from settled zones in the rest of North America.
Each is an example of a functional region built upon assumptions about
frontier and metropolis.[16]

A second influential approach to the prairie region has been the so-
called staples, or Laurentian, school of Canadian history. As Janine Brodie
has noted, Harold Innis's work on cod, fur, timber, and wheat implies a
spatial distribution of economic activity consequent upon the export of
particular staples to a metropolis. Brodie's emphasis on the uneven spatial development in capitalist economies must be treated seriously. Her
revival of Innis and V.C. Fowke's concern for the spatial biases of government policies must, similarly, be acknowledged as sound.[17]

Both the frontier and staple approaches to prairie history entail the
use of a functional definition of region. Each assumes a relationship between at least two entities and, consequently, a larger system, one that
encompasses its component parts, and one that can change over time. In
some cases, the boundaries between the communities – and thus the identity of previously distinct regions – may actually vanish. The prairies need
not always be the prairies, or at least need not be distinguished as a separate place and society.

The third approach to region assumes that a place must be imagined
before it can exist. This approach grew out of the environmentalism associated with early novelists such as Ralph Connor. It was consolidated in
the late 1940s by the critic and novelist Edward McCourt, who argued
that prairie literature was distinctive because of prairie authors' associations with the landscape.[18] Of course, this environmentalism has been
superseded by more precise language in later decades, but McCourt's
convictions about prairie cultural differences have not been contradicted.
Rather, one could argue that more convincing articulations of the same
perception have won the attention of cultural scholars.

Eli Mandel, who wrote of these matters in the 1970s and '80s, viewed
region as "a mental construct, . . . a myth." He argued that there was a
"certain coherence or unity or identity" in the poetry and prose described
as *prairie* literature. This coherence was expressed through elements common to regional literatures: a local landscape pictured with startling clarity; a child's view of the world and of home – home being the place where
one realizes one's *first* and most memorable vision of things; a grotesque
story teller; a regional dialect; and stories of the past. Thus, in Mandel's
view, there is a distinctive regional prairie literature that creates a mythi-
cized prairie world. Prairie storytellers project onto the land their chosen
images of the environment – images of the land's redemptive powers (in
the figure of a child), and of its demonic tyranny (a hostile father), and in
that choice these writers adapt their images to a pattern that belongs to all

humankind. What images do prairie writers choose? Mandel replied that they are "images of a search for home and therefore a search for the self."[19] Mandel's conceptual language is, one would say today, more convincing, more subtle, than the environmentalism of McCourt. The conviction that drives him, and perhaps even the conclusion that he reached, may be little different, but Mandel's understanding of human society and his articulation of the processes of the human imagination convince the reader that something about this place warrants a distinct category in the company of Canadian communities.

There are three fundamental approaches to region: formal, functional, and imagined. Each has been used to distinguish a prairie social order. Together, over the past two centuries, these approaches have sustained an abiding belief that something marked the prairie place or the prairie experience or the prairie expression off from other places, experiences, and expressions. Whether observers were describing a landscape that shaped one's interests and one's mind, or minds that shaped a landscape, or political and economic interests that dominated one's outlook, the cumulative weight of thinking, illustrating, and writing about "the prairies" asserted the distinctiveness of life on this portion of the globe. There is something here that cannot be ignored. Thus, to my first questions – how has the concept of region been used and has it been regarded as helpful – my answer is that region has been applied to the prairies in three overlapping ways and that, yes, it has been regarded as helpful, even necessary, in discussing the prairie experience.

UNDERSTANDING PRAIRIE "REGIONALISM"

To this point, "region" has been discussed as a place and a proper noun. One can't have regionalism without a region or regions, presumably, but the analysis of a popular sentiment or political movement distinguished by the term *regionalism* must be different from the relatively abstract discussions about formal and functional and imagined regions. Regionalism implies protest. It speaks of injustice, of neglect, perhaps even of one community's alleged superiority or power over another. Regionalism demands that the student pay simultaneous attention to community consciousness and community behaviour; that is, regionalism speaks of outlook, on the one hand, and self-interest or needs, on the other. The term *regionalism* presumes a larger administrative, economic, and political entity, of which one's special "region" is a part. Regionalism, in Canada at least, also raises the problem of federalism, meaning such specialized topics as the distribution of powers, revenue sharing, and mechanisms for resolving constitutional disagreements between levels of government. As Northrop Frye once commented, it also raises the issue of national survival. Indeed, regionalism is often used to describe an alternative nationalism, a loyalty to place and people that is built upon the same foundations of sentiment as the nation. In short, regionalism is a messy concept.

Because of the overlap between region and province – between economic and social definitions of a community, on the one hand, and political units, on the other – such scholars as Donald Smiley and Ramsay Cook have called for an end to talk of regionalism and a focus on province in Canadian scholarly discourse concerning territory-based loyalties. Alan Cairns's landmark article, "The Governments and Societies of Canadian Federalism," probably did much to sustain this approach in contemporary political studies.[20] Nor should one underestimate the fear of national disintegration as a force in proscribing talk of regionalism from the late 1970s on.[21]

Garth Stevenson, Ralph Matthews, Raymond Breton, and Janine Brodie have rejected this conclusion. Stevenson defines *region* as a "natural and organic unity and community of interests that is independent of political and administrative barriers."[22] Matthews asserts the existence of "a socio-psychological factor that involves identification with and commitment to a territorial unit."[23] Breton has argued that regionalism is a political phenomenon in which other interests are articulated in spatial terms – that is, he offers "an interpretation of social relations that gives political priority to the condition of the territorial entity" rather than to such non-territorial conditions as gender, class, and race.[24] Brodie, too, emphasizes the political and material foundation of regions, which she defines as "*political creations* that state development strategies cumulatively impose upon the geographic landscape."[25] These scholars share a conviction that regions and regionalism exist in Canada, that they are not merely arbitrary constructs, that their origins lie primarily in material factors (associated especially with the distribution of resources and with economic development policies), and that, in the final analysis, reference to them in public discourse is a significant part of Canadian life. In the case of the Canadian prairies, it is possible to reconcile the views of advocates of regional analysis and those who believe it should be jettisoned.

The case for the existence of an identifiable political force called prairie regionalism is usually made by reference to moments of significant public protest: the Métis resistances of 1869-70 and 1885, the farm and labour and religious outbursts after 1918, the rise of third parties in the 1930s and 1940s, the emergence of provincial rights and secessionist sentiments in the 1970s and early 1980s. What do these expressions say about prairie regionalism?

The Aboriginal unrest of the late nineteenth century, whether Métis or Indian, should not be described as an example of "regionalism." Rather, the moments of violence should be seen as incidents in the painful adjustment of very different cultures. The Aboriginal protests did originate in a concern about land but not about *land as region*; rather, Aboriginal people were concerned about *land as resource* and *land as home* or *land as centre of universe*. Thus, the term *regionalism* assumes a European cultural construction of "land," whereas Aboriginal protests focussed on the legitimacy and consequences of those very cultural constructions. It is true that the conflicts arose in part because of Ottawa's failure to communicate effectively and to reconsider particular policies, and that the most visible conflicts took place in the prairies. Seen from the Aboriginal perspective, however (and they were the people engaged in the uprisings), the refusal of the government to understand the needs of the first nations was not a "regional" issue but, rather, evidence of a failure of European Canadian cultural imagination.[26]

By an unusual reversal, ironically, the Aboriginal discontents have been included in the tradition of western grievance. Given this confusion, it is important that one support W.L. Morton's perspective on the initial bias of prairie politics and reject S.D. Clark's inclusion of Métis uprisings in the tradition of western regional protests. Incoming settlers, mostly Ontarians, who had very little sympathy for the Aboriginal cause when the spectre of violence arose in the 1880s, had no difficulty separating their grievances against Ottawa and central Canada from the anti-government complaints of the Métis and Indians. The newcomers, often transplanted Ontarians, complained about federal control of lands and resources, the tariff, freight rates, federal subsidies to the provinces and the Manitoba school imbroglio. They even sustained a revisionist, western-based school of historical interpretation. They did not endorse Big Bear or Riel after the shooting started. The grievances of the incoming settlers, as W.L. Morton pointed out, arose from the initial "bias" of Confederation: this "bias" comprised the political imbalance established by the Manitoba and North-West Territories Acts and the economic policies that followed. Such causes originated in the relations of one part to other parts in a system, or of one part to the whole, and are properly described as regional. It was only many decades later, the precise issues having been forgotten, that Aboriginal leaders became the heroes of western protest.[27]

The second source of prairie bias, in Morton's interpretation, was the agrarian protest that peaked during the opening decades of this century. The agrarian campaign, driven by western unhappiness over tariffs, freight rates, and many other farm-related matters, consolidated the local and national conclusion that a distinct prairie region had come into being. To understand this complicated interpretation, one must return to the thorny question of territory-based loyalties.

In the decades between 1900 and 1930, Canadians came to believe that a new community had crystallized in the Prairie West. A formal region, a variety of functional regions, and an imagined region had coalesced into a single image. Its characteristics, aside from the all-important lines on the political map, included frontier vitality and economic griev-ance and political protest. The evidence that would sustain popular belief in the actual existence of such a regional community has seemed incon-trovertible. It included the secession of western members of the Presbyte-rian Church in such numbers that the Church (or most of it) was pro-pelled into the United Church of Canada in 1925; the secession of many trade unions from the Canadian Trades and Labor Congress and their American craft union headquarters in the events surrounding the Win-nipeg General Strike and the One Big Union; the secessions from the old-line political parties that launched the Progressive Party; and the secessions from the grain handling and marketing system that produced the co-operatives and wheat pools. *Regionalism* was the term applied to this shift in the locus of power in Canada and the development of new pressures upon national institutions. Regionalism, thus, explained the appar-ently collective assault upon Canada's fabric by western residents in these heady decades. A model of "the Canadian region," and an assumption about both the prairies and all the other parts of Canada, had crystallized.

A host of writers on the farm movement argue that these manifesta-tions of regional protest were reactions to the First National Policy.[28] This interpretation of prairie voting patterns between 1918 and 1926 is reason-able, as far as it goes. It does not explain, however, why the One Big Union should have been founded on a regional secession from Canadian and American unions, or why western newspaper editors seceded from the Canadian Press syndicate in favour of Western Associated Press, or why the establishment of the United Church should have been driven by western needs, attitudes, and individuals. In each case, the assumption that regions existed, that regional interests were primary interests in com-munity life, and that regionalism was a fundamental interpretation of so-cial organization, underlay their dissent. This cultural perspective, a sup-plement to the economic and political analysis, is pivotal to one's appre-ciation of the regional "imagined community" that had just taken shape. Not surprisingly, these "regional" characteristics coincided with the for-mal prairie region.

Why did the consolidation of the prairie "imagined community" occur between 1900 and 1930, and why did it occur within these boundaries? The lines on the map help to explain the boundaries. Such cultural icons shape the way one thinks. So, too, does the administration of the territory; boundaries are made real by the activity of civil servants who work within these limits. In prairie Canada, to a degree now forgotten, civil adminis-tration was the work of the federal government and thus was a unifying force. Ottawa treated the West, especially through the Department of the Interior, as a single administrative unit for settlement, for lands and forests, for naturalization and police and Indians and transportation and the tariff. Another explanation of the regional boundary rests upon the work of the prairie's metropolis (as it was in that period), Winnipeg, which sent its decrees from Grain Exchange and Stock Yard and newspaper print shop (the "patent insides" of common feature stories and advertisements that accompanied many prairie weeklies), and by means of an army of travelling salespeople. These metropolitan forces, too, generated a sense of a single community. The "prairieness" of this era was also sustained by the intellectual climate, a climate composed of equal parts frontier theory, staple thesis, environmentalism, and simple boosterism, which reinforced the perception that the prairies constituted a new society, one truly in tune with the times.

The relatively greater success of socialism and social credit on the prairies in the 1930s and 1940s has also been attributed to a distinctive regional outlook. W.L. Morton suggested that the rise of the two parties represented the culmination of the previous biases in prairie politics. In other words, he linked these phenomena to the National Policy era that preceded 1930 as well as to a contemporary regional fascination with "utopian" solutions. No one would wish to deny the presence of East-bashing in some of the platform rhetoric of the 1930s, but, by the same measure, CCF and Social Credit owed their electoral successes to far more than regional sentiments.

V.C. Fowke introduced a different perspective by arguing that the first National Policy had been completed by 1930 and that a second was struggling into life in these decades, commencing with the introduction of "a social net" (wealth redistribution measures) as part of a new Keynesian approach to economic planning.[29] How could the second national policy be interpreted as a regional phenomenon? One might argue (though Fowke did not) that the devastating prairie experience of depression, unique in its regional impact, drove Bracken and Dafoe and Douglas and Aberhart, unlike other political leaders, to adopt distinctive approaches to political economy, including social democratic and redistributive measures. This seems unconvincing, given the crisis in other parts of Canada, as well as the widespread willingness of political figures in many parts of the world to embark on political experiments.

Janine Brodie takes another tack by suggesting that the prairies, whether or not they may have contributed to the introduction of Keynesian approaches, actually were the creation of them, in the sense that the second National Policy, like its predecessor, reinforced regional interests. Indeed, by targeting regional disparities as a primary concern of national politics, according to Brodie, the second National Policy contributed a significant new source of regionalism to Canadian public life. This approach seems to me viable, especially if one links it to events in the 1960s and 1970s.

However, the arguments in favour of a sharp divide in prairie history around 1930 and of prairie continuity during the next half-century will require further elaboration.

Prairie unrest during the Trudeau era was focussed especially on federal government policies. Agricultural issues such as grain sales and freight rates and the temporary LIFT (Lower Inventories for Tomorrow) program to reduce crop production, control of such resources as oil and potash (indeed energy policy in general), bilingualism, metric measures, diversification of the prairie economy into secondary and tertiary sectors, multiculturalism, all could be said to have fuelled prairie protest between the late 1960s and the mid-1980s. Of course, Prime Minister Trudeau was held to be responsible for everything.[30] What was especially galling to prairie residents, as David Smith has suggested, was that many of these federal Liberal enactments rejected long-standing prairie conclusions about public policy. One official language, continuity on the family farm, the Crow's Nest Pass freight-rate agreement, and provincial control of natural resources belonged in the category of sacred trusts in prairie political life. Thus, "prairie regionalism" in this era was a means of describing the prairie revolt against federal policies and against the Liberal Party.

The regionalism of the 1970s, indeed the regionalism that had been developing from the 1930s through the 1970s, differed from its predecessor. Though it inherited the causes and the fervour of the 1870 to 1930 model, this next phase of prairie regionalism was actually expressed through the province. Prairie society became more like Ontario society in these decades. Provincial governments assumed an increasingly prominent part in defining their communities.[31] Moreover, Ottawa no longer ruled a prairie fiefdom but, rather, treated all the provinces more or less equally. Winnipeg's economic leadership was superseded by the emergence of four other "provincial" metropolises and by increasingly national and international trade flows. This was the generation of province building. Prairie regional sentiments in the 1970s simply reinforced the prevailing "provincialism."

What does such an historical review demonstrate? Popular outbursts occurred often in the prairies during the century after 1870. Some of these expressions of discontent had their roots in Aboriginal culture and in European Canadian blindness to the imperatives of that culture; such expressions should not be described as regionalism. The later protests targeted the Macdonald National Policy and probably were reinforced by the Second National Policy. These protests demonstrated the ways in which the federal structure of government and the electoral system sustained territory-based loyalties in preference to those of class, gender, or ethnicity. Changes in prairie Canada's relations with the international economy, as in the 1880s and after the First World War and again in the 1930s and

1970s, also lay behind the conflict. Rather than enter into a debate about the relative merits of regionalism and provincialism, it is wise to argue that both are territory-based loyalties, both can be plausibly invoked in discussions of prairie history, and one is the heir of the other.[32] The key question concerns the vehicle that carries and simultaneously diffuses prairie political protest: before 1930, that vehicle was the federal party system; increasingly, after 1930, it was the system of federal-provincial relations.

PRAIRIE REGIONALISM TODAY

An important problem for contemporary observers is not just to decide whether regionalism, based on the formal region or on the various provinces, has existed but to estimate how important the sentiment is. Does it play a role in public opinion in the 1990s comparable to its role in earlier decades? One way to tackle such a difficult question is to approach it from the perspective of nation and nationalism.

In Canada, discussion of region often has provoked concern about nation, especially the unity of the nation, and regionalism often is said to contradict national identity. Northrop Frye was not happy with this concatenation of the two sentiments, love of nation and love of region, and he preferred to separate them. He argued that they arose out of two very different concepts: unity and identity. In this view, "unity is national in reference, international in perspective, and rooted in a political feeling," whereas "identity is local and regional, rooted in the imagination and in works of culture."[33] Frye's perspective is interesting because he is trying to define different types of feeling. He is suggesting that one can distinguish between sentiments concerning political loyalty and sentiments concerning personal identity.

This is rather shaky ground. Some people would claim that a large part of their personal identity was bound up with – even determined by – their political and national feelings. Even if one rejects Frye's advice, however, one might feel that it required a re-assessment of Mandel's work on prairie literature and prairie region. (Mandel had posited that "region" in literature was an expression of personal identity.) If the discussion of "identity questions" is separated from political feelings and other such territory-based loyalties, then one must redefine the cultural or "imagined" region. To understand the problem posed by this line of reasoning about politics and culture, it is helpful to consult some of the recent discussions about nation and nationalism, which are both innovative and insightful.

The nation, as it has been discussed in the literature of the last decade, offers a perspective upon smaller, territory-based, community loyalties (region, province, city, neighbourhood) because it is said to be the essence of community. As Benedict Anderson has suggested, "nation-ness is the most universally legitimate value in the political life of our time." The nation, in Anderson's definition, is a limited, sovereign, imagined community: limited, in that it does not, in any single instance, cover all of humankind; sovereign within the boundaries of a given state; and a community in the sense that it is "imagined" as "a deep, horizontal comradeship."[34] The strengths of this recent and fruitful approach are that it treats communities as *political* places and that it distinguishes these political communities by "the style in which they are imagined."[35] It takes no great leap of imagination to place the region and the province on the same scale – perhaps different steps on the same ladder – as nation. We all possess a hierarchy of political or civic values associated with the imagined communities in which we live. Moreover, the standings within this hierarchy and the reasons for the ranking are probably subject to investigation. If regionalism were profoundly important in the outlook of citizens resident in the Canadian prairies, then the prairie community would tend toward nation; if province were paramount, then the three provincial communities would acquire nation-like attributes; if neither a prairie-wide nor a provincial community were as important as nation, or some other "national" alternative such as continental union, then neither would constitute an alternative nationalism. What is the relative importance of the various imagined communities in prairie society? Put another way, what is the *cultural* context of the Canadian prairie community?

"Culture" is a complicated concept in today's scholarly writing and the subject of considerable disagreement. Many scholars of culture now assert that their subject is just as likely to be as primary – and as important – as economics or technology. Their purpose is to subvert the customary Marx-derived assumption that "base," defined as material reality, determines "superstructure," which might be defined to include law and literature and social customs among other cultural matters. When they examine culture, these scholars are discussing the sense we make of our "selves" and situating that sense within our social order.[36]

Little has been written on prairie cultural identity from this perspective. Let us assume, for argument's sake, that prairie regionalism, whether expressed within 1920-era, prairie-wide boundaries or 1980-era provincial boundaries, might coincide with an imagined community. Where would it find its definition or rationale? One potential source of an imagined community is kinship.[37] Of course, prairie Canada and its constituent provinces do not possess such genealogical continuity. A second source of community identification would be religion. Again, though some students might contend that prairie people think in similar ways about transcendent questions, this is not a common view. A third base of community would be language. This is a more plausible suggestion. The experience of prairie citizens during the past hundred years constitutes a relevant and important claim to a common prairie linguistic heritage, one based on shared experience of linguistic assimilation into the English of Canada or North America.

A fourth foundation of the imagined community is a network of communications. Local newspapers and television establish a feeling of simultaneity, or of shared political experience, across space, time, and household. Region-wide communications networks did develop in the late nineteenth century in the prairies and helped to sustain a prairie regional consciousness between the 1880s and 1930s. Thereafter, the region-building institutions were replaced by more influential networks that underwrote continental and national empires, on the one hand, and provincial empires, on the other. Yet another foundation is the network of functionaries in the modern state whose pilgrimages and very existence outline the boundaries and educate the imaginations of the citizenry. The professions linked by this communications web, including lawmakers, mapmakers, museum builders, archivists, census takers, and government administrators, also shifted from a prairie-wide to a provincial constituency in this century. The Hudson's Bay Company and the Department of the Interior, two pivotal "inventors of tradition" before 1870 and 1930 respectively, gave way to provincial and city leaders in the later decades of the twentieth century. All this would suggest that a prairie-wide nationalism is a little less likely today than is a province-based alternative nation. But it offers little guidance about the relative power of a regional or provincial perspective.

The province-based communications networks and the inventors of provincial traditions have not received a great deal of attention in prairie scholarship. The failure of any single newspaper to sustain a region-wide circulation after the First World War might be seen as evidence of provincial pre-eminence in post-1920 cultural networks. This same trend is reflected in the absence of prairie-wide electronic media. Significantly, when the Canadian Broadcasting Corporation entered the prairies in 1939 and 1945-46 with its own stations, it set up *provincial* super-stations of 50,000 watts. Language and schools issues were fundamental in prairie cultural history; again, it is noteworthy that ethnic cultural distinctiveness, which in the case of many groups could have been sustained by community support drawn from across the prairies, capsized on the rocks of *provincial* education policy. After 1945, and especially after 1970, prairie cultural history is noteworthy for the rise of *provincial* museums and heritage departments and cultural policies. Thus, one might distinguish two phases in twentieth-century prairie cultural history: the first illustrates the force of prairie-wide regional consciousness before, roughly, the 1920s and 1930s, and the second is marked by the ascendancy of provincial consciousness in the next half-century.[38] Indeed, David Smith has argued that the cultural shift could be discerned even in the twenty-five years between

Saskatchewan's fiftieth jubilee celebration in 1955 and its seventy-fifth in 1980. Thus, by 1980, "when federal policies, including even cultural ones, were perceived as a threat to provincial integrity, the diamond jubilee identified the province as a distinct society. In the 1950s the emphasis was on overcoming isolation, in the 1980s it was on maintaining or developing separateness."[39]

Does this answer the question concerning the relative importance of regionalism today and yesterday? It offers this response: as prairie Canadians face the prospect of their country's dismemberment, they have few prairie-wide (regional), cultural pillars upon which to construct an alternative nation. Not that the task is impossible, just that it has not really been addressed. Rather, the cultural alternatives to the nation, at present, are the province and the continent.

Territory-based loyalty has long been important to residents of the Canadian prairies. Geography and policy choices and cultural expressions have ensured its continuity. This loyalty was once expressed in terms of a prairie-wide imagined community and later through the province, but there is no law that requires the continuation of such a cultural consensus. If a new government, or an alliance of governments, created a single prairie province, the formal, prairie-wide region and the imagined regional community would soon coincide. The power of politics, government, and the communications media that feed off them would ensure this result. But whether such loyalties really matter in the 1990s is not as clear. And whether any imagined community smaller than the continent can prevail in the days of globalization is even less certain. So much will depend on the power and ability of Canadians to establish as strong an imagined community as their forebears were able to do.

NOTES

This essay was published during the debates concerning the Charlottetown Accord. It appeared in the proceedings of a Maritime-Prairie constitutional conference organized by the Canadian Plains Research Center, University of Regina, and by the Gorsebrook Research Institute, St. Mary's University, Halifax. The proceedings were edited by James N. McCrorie and Martha L. MacDonald: *The Constitutional Future of the Prairie and Atlantic Regions of Canada* (Regina: Canadian Plains Research Center, 1992); they are reprinted with the permission of the Canadian Plains Research Center.

1. Cited in B. Kaye and D.W. Moodie, "Geographical Perspectives on the Canadian Plains," in *A Region of the Mind: Interpreting the Western Canadian Plains,* ed. Richard Allen (Regina: Canadian Plains Research Center, 1973), 18.
2. J.B. Tyrell, ed., *David Thompson's Narrative of His Explorations in Western America, 1784-1812* (Toronto: Champlain Society, 1916), 183.
3. A.R.C. Selwyn and G.M. Dawson, *Descriptive Sketch of the Physical Geography and Geology of the Dominion of Canada* (Montreal: Dawson Brothers, 1884). John Warkentin employs an earlier moment in this same generation to define the West; he contends that the exploring

parties of Palliser and Dawson and Hind between 1857 and 1860 laid "the basic conceptual framework for our present interpretation of the physical geography of Western Interior Canada" (*The Western Interior of Canada: A Record of Geographical Study, 1612-1917* [Toronto: McClelland and Stewart, 1964], 147).

4. Goldwin Smith, *Canada and the Canadian Question* (Toronto: Hunter, Rose, 1891), 1-3.

5. They are not entirely "wrong." See: Donald F. Putnam, ed., *Canadian Regions: A Geography of Canada* (Toronto: Dent, 1952); and, William C. Wonders, "Canadian Regions and Regionalism: National Enrichment or National Disintegration?" in *A Passion for Identity: Introduction to Canadian Studies*, ed. Eli Mandel and David Taras (Toronto: Methuen, 1987).

6. H.R.A. Pocock, *Tales of Western Life, Lake Superior and the Canadian Prairie* (Ottawa: 1888), 62, 56.

7. Ralph Connor [C.W. Gordon], *The Foreigner: A Tale of Saskatchewan* (Toronto: Westminster, 1909), 378.

8. Griffith Taylor, *Canada: A Study of Cool, Continental Environments and Their Effect on British and French Settlement* (London: Methuen, 1947).

9. Arthur S. Morton, *A History of the Canadian West to 1870-71* (Toronto: University of Toronto Press, 1973; first published 1939), 13.

10. Ronald Rees, *New and Naked Land: Making the Prairies Home* (Saskatoon: Western Producer Prairie Books, 1988).

11. Janine Brodie, "The Concept of Region in Canadian Politics," in *Federalism and Political Community: Essays in Honour of Donald Smiley,* ed. David P. Shugarman and Reg Whitaker (Peterborough: Broadview Press, 1989), 42; also, William Westfall, "On the Concept of Region in Canadian History and Literature," *Journal of Canadian Studies* 15, no. 2 (1980); and, Roger Gibbins, *Regionalism: Territorial Politics in Canada and the United States* (Toronto: Butterworth, 1982).

12. Adam Shortt, "Some Observations on the Great North-West," *Queen's Quarterly* 2 (1894-95):184.

13. Isaiah Bowman, *The Pioneer Fringe* (New York: American Geographical Society, 1931), v.

14. W.A. Mackintosh, "Current Events," *Queen's Quarterly* 29 (1921-22):312.

15. S.D. Clark, foreword to *The Progressive Party in Canada* by W.L. Morton (Toronto: University of Toronto Press, 1950), viii-ix.

16. For most North American historians, the shorthand version of this approach to region, an approach that assumes that one can distinguish stages of social formation, has been the frontier hypothesis of Frederick Jackson Turner. After all, it is no accident that Turner spent much of his career working on sections and sectionalism in American history (Frederick Jackson Turner, *The Frontier in American History* [1920; reprint New York: Holt, Rinehart and Winston, 1962]; Michael C. Steiner, "The Significance of Turner's Sectional Thesis," *Western Historical Quarterly* 10 [1979]). However, because the distinction between "frontier as place" and "frontier as process" has never been clear, the implications of the frontier hypothesis for analysis of prairie regionalism have been uncertain. Moreover, the idea that American theories might have relevance for Canadians has also raised the hackles of some Canadian scholars. Neither objection need detain us. Canada, like the United States, is a North American nation, after all, and the frontier is, or was in Turner's thought, *both* a place and a process. In our terms, Canadian scholars who relied upon frontier characteristics to distinguish the Prairie West were thinking in terms of a functional region.

Though not often remembered today, the "frontier" assumption was once a commonplace in Canadian discussion. Clifford Sifton observed in 1898 that party loyalty, an important basis of the Canadian community, did not prevail automatically in the newly settled regions: "One of the difficulties in politics in the West," he told Walter Scott in 1898, "is that matters do not run in well settled grooves which exist in the older communities. There is therefore extra need for friendliness on all hands" (Saskatchewan Archives Board, Scott Papers, Sifton to Scott, 20 September 1898). The region, in this view, was "the West," and was defined in relation to older communities, for which one might read "the East." The

West was different – it constituted a region – because it was a "frontier." Such attitudes became a reflex in Canadian public life between the 1880s and 1930s. The West occupied a distinct and obviously different stage of social development. See also, Henry Nash Smith, *Virgin Land: The American West in Symbol and Myth* (New York: Vintage, 1957; first published 1950), 267.

17. Janine Brodie, *The Political Economy of Canadian Regionalism* (Toronto: Harcourt Brace Jovanovich, 1990).

18. Edward A. McCourt, *The Canadian West in Fiction* (Toronto: Ryerson, 1949; 1970), 125.

19. Eli Mandel, "Images of Prairie Man," in *A Region of the Mind: Interpreting the Western Canadian Plains*, ed. Richard Allen (Regina: Canadian Plains Research Center, 1973); also, Gerald Friesen, "Three Generations of Fiction: An Introduction to Prairie Cultural History," in *Eastern and Western Perspectives*, ed. D.J. Bercuson and P.A. Buckner (Toronto: University of Toronto Press, 1981).

20. Alan Cairns, "The Governments and Societies of Canadian Federalism," *Canadian Journal of Political Science* (December 1977); Ramsay Cook, "Regionalism Unmasked," *Acadiensis* 13, no. 1 (1983); Donald Smiley, *The Federal Condition in Canada* (Toronto: McGraw-Hill Ryerson, 1986), 23.

21. Lovell Clark, "Regionalism? or Irrationalism?" *Journal of Canadian Studies* (summer 1978); J.M.S. Careless, "Limited Identities – Ten Years Later," *Manitoba History* 1 (1980).

22. Garth Stevenson, "Canadian Regionalism in Continental Perspective," *Journal of Canadian Studies* (summer 1980):17.

23. Brodie, *The Political Economy of Canadian Regionalism,* 12, where she summarizes Ralph Matthews, *The Creation of Regional Dependency* (Toronto: University of Toronto Press, 1983), 22.

24. This summary is taken from Brodie, *The Political Economy of Canadian Regionalism;* she is citing Raymond Breton, "Regionalism in Canada," in *Regionalism and Supranationalism,* ed. D. Cameron (Montreal: Institute for Research on Public Policy, 1981), 19.

25. Brodie, *The Political Economy of Canadian Regionalism,* 77.

26. Moreover, the Aboriginal cultures did not divide along territorial (east-west) lines. The distinction between resistance by military action and resistance by other means was less significant, in the Aboriginal view, than it was in European Canadian eyes.

27. W.L. Morton, "The Bias of Prairie Politics," Royal Society of Canada *Proceedings and Transactions,* Third Series, 49 (1955); Doug Owram, "The Myth of Louis Riel," *Canadian Historical Review* 53, no. 3 (1982); and, Owram, *Promise of Eden: The Canadian Expansionist Movement and the Idea of the West, 1856-1900* (Toronto: University of Toronto Press, 1980).

28. Paul Phillips, *Regional Disparities* (Toronto: Lorimer, 1978); John Conway, *The West: The History of a Region in Confederation* (Toronto: Lorimer, 1983). Brodie surveys this literature in *The Political Economy of Canadian Regionalism,* chapter 5.

29. V.C. Fowke, "The National Policy – Old and New," *Canadian Journal of Economics and Political Science* (1952); Donald Smiley, "Canada and the Quest for a National Policy," *Canadian Journal of Political Science* (1975).

30. David Smith, *The Regional Decline of a National Party: Liberals on the Prairies* (Toronto: University of Toronto Press, 1981).

31. Roger Gibbins, *Prairie Politics and Society: Regionalism in Decline* (Toronto: Butterworth, 1980); Cairns, "The Governments and Societies of Canadian Federalism."

32. Frederick Jackson Turner preferred the term *sectionalism* (Michael C. Steiner, "The Significance of Turner's Sectional Thesis," *Western Historical Quarterly* 10 [1979]:437-66). Gibbins, *Prairie Politics and Society;* Cairns, "The Governments and Societies of Canadian Federalism."

33. Northrop Frye, *The Bush Garden: Essays on the Canadian Imagination* (Toronto: Anansi, 1971), i-iii.

34. Benedict Anderson, *Imagined Communities: Reflections on the Origin and Spread of Nationalism* (London: Verso, 1983; 1991), 3-7.

35. Ibid., 6.

36. Culture has become a point of convergence in the human disciplines. As social history has matured and displaced politics and economics as the central organizing principle of historical inquiry, it has simultaneously grown so complex and varied that its organizing principles – history from below, the story of an entire society, limited identities of class and ethnic group and gender – have lost the shock of the new. Thus, social history, with its variety of approaches, no longer constitutes an automatic challenge to power.

    This new cultural approach defines culture as "the ways in which people perceive, make intelligible and organize their being" (Maria Tippett, "The Writing of English-Canadian Cultural History, 1970-1985," *Canadian Historical Review* 67, no. 4 [December 1986]:548). To follow Raymond Williams, culture in this sense should be seen as "the signifying system through which necessarily (though among other means) a social order is communicated, reproduced, experienced and explored" (*Culture* [Glasgow: Fontana, 1981], 13). As John Fiske says, culture takes "the meanings we make of our social experience, . . . the sense we have of our 'selves' . . . and situates those meanings within the social system" (*Television Culture* [London: Routledge, 1987], 20). See also: Lynn Hunt, "Introduction: History, Culture, and Text," in *The New Cultural History,* ed. Hunt (Berkeley: University of California Press, 1989), 7; Roger Chartier, "Text, Printing, Readings," in the same volume.

37. Perry Anderson, "Nation-States and National Identity," *London Review of Books* 13, no. 9 (9 May 1991).

38. *Prairie Forum* 15, no. 2 (fall 1990), devoted an entire issue to this subject (*Heritage Conservation*). It contains two articles by Jean Friesen ("Introduction: Heritage Futures"; and "Heritage: The Manitoba Experience") as well as Don Kerr's "In Defence of the Past: A History of Saskatchewan Heritage Preservation, 1922-1983" and Mark Rasmussen's "The Heritage Boom: Evolution of Historical Resource Conservation in Alberta," each of which sustains this emphasis on the rise of provincial consciousness. See also, Gerald Friesen, "The Manitoba Historical Society: A Centennial History," *Manitoba History* 4 (1982), reprinted in this volume.

39. David Smith, "Celebrations and History on the Prairies," *Journal of Canadian Studies* 17, no. 3 (fall 1982):55.

Romantics, Pluralists, Postmodernists: Writing Ethnic History in Prairie Canada

Co-written with Royden Loewen

PRAIRIE CANADIANS are very conscious of ethnicity. Their willingness in social situations to identify themselves with an ethnic group and their interest in the social inheritance (and presumed social networks) of others often astonishes new arrivals to Winnipeg, Saskatoon, or Edmonton. In this essay, we introduce the phenomenon of prairie ethnic identity by the most elementary of research projects – a literature survey. We suggest that historical writing on immigrant groups evolved in three stages – from romanticism and pluralism to postmodernism. The last phase, which is intended to describe today's cultural perspective, may seem far-fetched, but we are trying to say that, today, social identity is perceived as more ephemeral, more ambiguous, more individual than it was in earlier generations. This century-long development, from a fixed or static to a variable identity, is partly the result of social change in the Canadian prairies, but it is also a consequence of trends in the world of academic writing. In this process, the interpretation of ethnic identity has turned away from political and social history to "postmodern" cultural analysis, from describing ethnic identity as "a structure or a closed system" to analyzing "the processes of social and cultural construction of reality."[1]

HISTORICAL WRITING BEFORE THE 1960s

The appropriate dividing line in a survey of early prairie ethnic historical writing is the 1960s. Though the selection of illustrations is arbitrary, the appearance of three works in that decade demonstrates the changing character of Canadian society. One was John Porter's sociological study, *The Vertical Mosaic* (1965); another was the unexpectedly ambitious fourth volume of Canada's Royal Commission on Bilingualism and Biculturalism entitled *The Cultural Contribution of the Other Ethnic Groups,* published in 1969; the third was a short article by one of Canada's senior historians, Professor J.M.S. Careless, which became a byword in historical circles for the next decade and beyond, entitled "'Limited Identities' in Canada."[2] The three works can be taken as representative of a "Great Divide" in Canadian cultural perspectives. They distinguish an earlier phase of writing that might be called "romantic" from the "pluralist" perspective that prevailed in the 1970s and 1980s.

The selective tradition propounded by the nation's educational elite before 1960 suggested that Canada was a distinctly British, as well as a bilingual and bicultural, society, but certainly not a plural or multicultural nation. Historical writing focussed on the survival of the French in North America, the continuity of the British connection, and the accidents of resources and communications systems that created a Laurentian trading empire separate from the United States on the northern half of North America. Ethnic historiography had no place in this scheme. "No one until the 1960s," writes Robert Harney with only slight exaggeration, "thought of Canadian history except in terms of the titanic contest between the British and the French."[3]

When western Canada finally won a little attention in this slowly developing national selective tradition, it was for its nation-building role and its political nonconformity, not for the diversity of its ethnic composition. Western Canada was a segment of a national canvas on which was sketched the National Policy, the Mounties' Great March west, the peace treaties with the Aboriginal peoples, the Canadian Pacific Railway, and the "regional" discontent that sent several dozens of Progressive farmer members of Parliament to Ottawa in 1921, and elected CCF and Social Credit members of Parliament in 1935. True, western historians did acknowledge the immigrant: the "peasant in the sheepskin coat, accompanied by a half dozen children and a stout wife" has made a brief appearance in most texts; and W.L. Morton allowed for a western Canadian identity that was, "because of the diversity of its people, composite." Morton concluded, however, that prairie historians were mostly concerned with ethnic variations on national themes that contributed to local feelings of "subordination" and "sharp sectionalism."[4] Thus, it is reasonable to conclude that immigrants, especially non-British immigrants, received little attention in western Canada's historical writing.[5]

The few histories of immigration that appeared in the first two-thirds of this century saw immigrants chiefly in relation to the romantic theme of nation building. In one version, leaders of the prairie's dominant British-Canadian culture outlined an "inevitable" process of assimilation. Driven by anxiety about the strength of their own status and, ironically, their simultaneous belief that they belonged to the greatest civilization the world had ever known, these writers believed that ethnic differences must be made to disappear. In 1909, J.S. Woodsworth articulated the charter group's public agenda. In this book, J.W. Sparling warned that "either we must educate and elevate the incoming multitudes or they will drag us and our children down. . . . We must see to it that the civilization . . . of Southeastern Europe [is] not transplanted to . . . our virgin soil."[6] Carl Dawson's 1936 discussion of group settlement in western Canada was more sophisticated, but it, too, expressed confidence in the capacity of the prairie community to absorb these strangers. Even the Mennonites, among the most closed and conservative of western settlers, according to Dawson, were happily bound for assimilation. Although the Mennonite migration "was of a distinctly communal type," he wrote, "[in which] entire villages migrated, bringing with them . . . their community leaders and institutions," the norms of prairie Canada would eventually prevail in Mennonite life because of the power of public education, government services, wage labour, railways, and politics.[7] National survival in this view was dependent on cultural uniformity.

A second response to the nation-building theme came from in-group ethnic historians such as B.G. Sack, Vera Lysenko and Heinz Lehman, who wrote histories that have sometimes been described as romantic and "filiopietistic" (*filiopietism* is the praise or worship owed to "the founders" by dutiful sons and daughters). Their writings asserted the virtues of their subjects' Old World roots or ethnic stock, illustrated the newcomers' "physical hardihood, artistry and deep sources of originality," praised the vision of the ethnic community's leaders, and outlined the contributions that these groups had made to their adopted country.[8] Ironically, this view differed little from that of Woodsworth and Dawson. Immigrants were worthy of study insofar as they had made a contribution to the establishment of a Canadian nation. This was particularly apparent in the Manitoba Historical Society's ambitious project to foster ethnic study. The project, launched after the Second World War, included scholarships and research grants on ethnic history, and led to published studies on Icelanders, Mennonites, Poles, Jews, and Ukrainians. The main aim of the series, however, was not to chart a multicultural Canada, but, as described by one of the founders of the series, W.L. Morton, to establish "the degree of participation [of ethnic groups] in the life of the province."[9]

The individual authors in the Manitoba series were supposed to be free to celebrate proudly, to defend, and to explain, as long as they traced how their particular group lent richness to the wider community. Sometimes the authors seemed defensive: Victor Turek argued that Polish Manitobans, who were occasionally described by others as illiterate and socially divisive, nevertheless deserved "respect as the active co-builders of the present well-being of this part of Canada,"[10] and Arthur Chiel insisted in his study that "living as Jews did not detract from the sum total of the Canadian pattern but rather contributed to it more . . . creatively."[11] Paul Yuzyk and E.K. Francis may have drawn different conclusions about the experience of their groups – the Ukrainians and the Mennonites, respectively – but here too was an underlying common theme. Yuzyk's book was unabashedly assimilationist: "The interplay of economic forces, of democratic practice, of the many cultural traits is slowly welding all its component ethnic groups into one dynamic Canadian nation";[12] Francis, however, advanced his international reputation as social scientist by risking the wrath of the Anglo-dominated Manitoba Historical Society with his conclusion that "acculturation among the Manitoba Mennonites [by the 1950s] had by no means led to any significant degree of assimilation."[13] Although drawing different conclusions, both Francis and Yuzyk succeeded in holding up their groups as legitimate and respectable participants in the wider community. Yuzyk's book was an example of the romantic tradition; Francis anticipated the next phase of prairie historical writing with his emphasis on ethnic continuity.

HISTORICAL WRITING FROM THE 1960S TO THE 1980S

John Porter's *Vertical Mosaic,* the Royal Commission on Bilingualism and Biculturalism's volume on ethnic groups, and Careless's "Limited Identities" represented a new perspective that had been emerging in the postwar decades but was clearly articulated only in the 1960s.[14] Canada, in the view of the Royal Commission, was not simply a bicultural community but had become, instead, a plural, multicultural society. The Bi and Bi commissioners recommended that Canadians' tolerance of minority groups be reinforced by new educational and broadcasting policies and that specific support be granted for "the arts and letters of cultural groups other than the British and French."[15] Therein lay the germ of Canada's adoption of a multicultural policy in 1971.

Careless's article, "Limited Identities," became a common point of scholarly reference because it illustrated the ascendancy of pluralism in the professional historians' version of Canada's selective tradition. It suggested that previous historical and cultural interpretations, by engaging in a hopeless quest for Canada's grail, the "Canadian identity," had mistaken the nature of the country's experience. Canadian history was not the story of nation building, he wrote, but the building of limited identities, the identities of class and region and ethnic group. He defined this "national identity" as a paradox. It existed in the *absence* of a uniform, national identity: "The Canadian value system has stressed the social qualities that differentiate people rather than the human qualities that make them the same."[16]

Thereafter, ethnic historiography blossomed. Given the rapid growth of universities in the 1960s and 1970s, the organization of ethnic archives, and the increasing volume of social history publications, it is not surprising that the story of Canada's immigrant and minority groups was rewritten. When Howard Palmer noted in 1982 that the "past decade has witnessed great strides in the field of . . . ethnic history in Canada," he was articulating a widely accepted conclusion.[17]

The expectation that the 1970s and 1980s would establish a new perspective on the history of immigrants and of Canada's minority groups was realized in the form of a widely accepted pluralism. Every type of ethnic identity could be accommodated within the Canadian "mosaic." As an offshoot of this openness, Canadian historians wrote a great deal about immigrants. Indeed, the Generations series commissioned by the Citizenship Branch of the Department of the Secretary of State published many volumes on individual groups. While none of the books dealt specifically with western Canada, several described the experience in the West of such groups as the Chinese, Japanese, Ukrainians, Norwegians, and Dutch. Moreover, several journals, including *Canadian Ethnic Studies* (published at the University of Calgary since 1968) and *Prairie Forum* (published in Regina since 1975), carried historical articles describing the polyethnic cultural landscape of prairie Canada.[18] The development of research institutes, museums, government heritage projects, and especially federally and locally sponsored university chairs of ethnic history illustrated the diverse directions taken by professionals who sought to articulate a vision of a plural society and to educate their communities about its strengths and problems.

It took time for this writing to find its intellectual bearings, however, and, arguably, this historical writing still lacks strong, coherent foundations. The problems begin with filiopietism. While the Generations books provided useful introductions to cultural continuity, some of the volumes were reviewed harshly. One commentator suggested that these works created a "land of make-believe multiculturalism in which the realities of our past must be sugar-coated in 'let's pretend histories.'"[19] This criticism will seem similar to that directed at the romantic pre-1960 ethnic histories and is justified, at least to a degree. Gulbrand Loken's study of Norwegians, for example, may be seen as a sanitized history that celebrated Scandinavian virtues and romanticized the difficult years of pioneering and the harshness of the Depression.[20] Manoly Lupul's 1982 collection of articles about Ukrainians in Canada, *A Heritage in Transition,* may be seen as portraying in uncritical terms the development of Ukrainian churches, political lobby groups, private schools, ethnic presses, and fine arts, and adopting an "essentialist," or monochromatic, approach.[21] To be fair to the authors, a judicious critic would emphasize that the topics – and to a degree the approach – were prescribed by the granting agency that encouraged single-hued celebratory portrayals of these communities.[22] Then, too, many of these authors were pioneers in their fields. As Manoly Lupul put it in *A Heritage in Transition,* an "inadequate state of research is responsible for . . . the emphasis [being] too exclusively on the organized Ukrainian-Canadian community. . . . What is needed are . . . scholars who will probe the changes in family life, patterns of authority, and fundamental values and identity in the typical Ukrainian rural . . . and urban enclaves."[23]

Despite these reminders of an earlier romanticism, many of the new scholarly books focussed on the internal social dynamics of the immigrant community. George Woodcock and Ivan Avakumovic, for example, described the Doukhobor struggle to "halt absorption into Canadian society" by focussing on internal conflicts and on the Doukhobors' debilitating confrontations with the host society.[24] Frank Epp's study of the Mennonites juxtaposed their determination to create a "separate people" with the larger social pressures exerted by an industrializing capitalism and a liberal state.[25] Some authors readily acknowledged group members' failures as well as their successes. Anthony Rasporich's study of Jewish farm settlements in Saskatchewan, for example, distanced itself from B.G. Sack's earlier work by seeking "the harsher daylight of social reality" and acknowledging that internal strife stemming from the diverse Jewish community and from an unhealthy dependence on philanthropic organizations led the communities to founder.[26] Conversely, by emphasizing the internal dynamics of immigrant communities, some writers saw ethnic continuity where none had earlier been recognized; this was especially apparent in studies of "British" migrants, both of workers whose unmistakably "Old World" cloth caps provided a badge of fraternal membership when they sought jobs or social support in the new community, and of British elite public school graduates who transferred preconceptions about "gentlemen," "ladies," and "respectability" to the Canadian prairies.[27]

Another measure of this new-found pluralism in historical writing was the outpouring of volumes on Canadian nativism and racism. By examining Chinese, Japanese, Sikh, and Jewish experiences of immigration and adaptation, as well as government policy toward these groups, many new works of scholarship criticized the dominant culture of an earlier generation.[28] They also challenged the trend in Canada toward Anglo-conformity and assimilation. More important, they contested their predecessors' faith in British and European cultural superiority. The "old" teleologies of assimilation and nation-building, having been found wanting, had been replaced by new definitions of the dominant culture, and by a quite-remarkable pluralism.

Prairie Canada was a community of immigrants, in this view, nearly half of whom were not British or French. Many of the newcomers had found the adjustment to a different society difficult. Many objected to the fact that the new way of life demanded community-wide sacrifices such as loss of a language. In the case of most ethnic groups, however, the creation of a new society in which inherited cultural patterns were replaced by a "pluralistic prairie Canadian" cultural consensus seemed to compensate for the grief and regret associated with the losses. Thus, Alan Anderson discovered that English became the sole public language of a formerly multilingual community; retention of a native tongue, though rates varied among the different ethnic groups, faded with the passing of the third generation.[29] Still, in this historical perspective, a unilateral, unidirectional Anglo-conformity was not the sole prevailing tendency in the prairies. Jews retained Jewishness, Mennonites remained a "separate people," and Ukrainians fought nativist politicians and educators for the redefinition of Canada as a plural society.

Neither the filiopietism, which blindly ignored the changes in prairie ethnic groups, nor the British Canadian triumphalism that assumed the eventual victory of Empire customs, could be sustained in the 1980s. The new orthodoxy was pluralist. The prairies were not, in this interpretation, a melting pot, but rather were a stew in which the varied ingredients of that single dish retained their flavour and identity.[30]

RECENT DEPARTURES IN HISTORIOGRAPHY

Many social and literary scholars have proposed that the late twentieth century constitutes a new phase in cultural history. Clearly, the globalization of economies, along with the communications revolution, the rise of worldwide cultural industries, and the commodification of knowledge, has left old social distinctions in disarray. "Identity" is no longer easily defined. Attempts to write general histories of any group may be branded "metanarratives," a term that reflects a continuing battle over power and "voice." Ethnicity itself is said to be an old-fashioned concept that ignores "the intrinsic dissonance in social life."[31] Postmodernism, described by David Harvey as the cultural response to late-twentieth-century capitalism, takes us away from the very line of enquiry that directed prairie ethnic historiography during its golden age of the 1970s and 1980s.[32]

This contemporary cultural upheaval has illuminated not only the abandonment of old boundaries and the ephemerality of social units, but also the intricate relationship between global industrialization and ethnic groups' strategies of survival. Borrowing from British and European social history of the past thirty years, as well as from peasant, labour, women's, and cultural studies, our picture of industrialization and the farm household, for example, has changed in the last decade.[33]

Several studies of immigrants to Minnesota offer illustrations of how this new rural social history could shape perceptions of ethnic groups. Jon Gjerde's volume on Norwegians and Robert Ostergren's work on Swedes suggest that global economic forces in the nineteenth century shaped the migrations of these groups to the United States.[34] Gjerde demonstrates that immigration constituted a strategy for Norwegian household maintenance within a rapidly changing, increasingly demanding world economy. Thus, one learns in his book that market forces, a rising rate of fertility, land shortages, and increasing demand for exports threatened to uproot old ways in Norway. As a result, a certain number of Norwegian families moved to the United States in order to "retain the essential social fabric of their community." However, once they had crossed the ocean, the Norwegians discovered that the process of adaptation in the United States was simply the continuation of their previous dialectical struggles (in Norway) between old cultural ways rooted in household strategies and new pressures exerted by "modern" economic opportunities. Adaptation, thus, was a complex process in both Norway and Minnesota; freely available land in the United States did not automatically lead to a capitalist mentality and the absorption of immigrants into a one-dimensional American culture. Instead, the free land permitted immigrant families to re-assert the old values of the agrarian household, including generational succession and economic self-sufficiency. However, with the passage of time and the accumulation of property, adaptation to a frontier of free land also strengthened the nuclear family, widened gender roles, and encouraged the *embourgeoisement* of these families. Such changes embodied the very process that the Norwegian settlers had left modernizing Norway to avoid. Here was a dialectic of continuity and change with reference to ethnic household strategies and global economic forces.

Historians of western Canadian rural immigrant groups have just begun to apply this approach that sees immigration and adaptation as a dialectic involving household strategies, ethnic loyalties, and a wider economy.[35] James Urry's study of Mennonites in New Russia and Stella Hryniuk's work on the Ukrainians of Galicia have linked the immigration of these important western Canadian groups to changes in the global economy.[36] The work of John Lehr on small Ukrainian communities in Manitoba re-creates in microcosm the process by which immigrant families sought economic security and group continuity in a rapidly changing world.[37] Francis Swyripa, although focussing to a larger extent on the public image of Ukrainian women and their institutional lives, also links the household economy to evolving ethnic identities.[38]

Another approach to a history of prairie immigrant societies would examine ethnic cultural expression within the context of increasingly global communications and cultural patterns. The body of literature that might sustain this approach can be associated with older schools of thought that utilized such concepts as "primordial attachment" and "basic group identities" in their approach to ethnicity.[39] In these older schools of ethnic study, group identity was an inseparable aspect of human history. Recent approaches move beyond these definitions to re-assess the nature of cultures. They find their subjects in nationalism and national identity, and their challenges in the former Soviet Union and Yugoslavia, and in a globalized, homogeneous "McCulture." This new interest is fuelled, too, by the recent scholarly fascination with literacy, communications, and semiotics. Thus, several contributors to the study of nationalism in the 1980s, including Benedict Anderson and Eric Hobsbawm, emphasize state structure, work organization, and literacy as social forces that evoke the profound sentiments labelled "nationalism" or "ethnicity."[40] These scholars recognize that ethnic mythology originates chiefly in territory or genealogy, but they reject the notion that the ethnic group is a primordial and permanent force in human societies. They also reject the concept of national character – stolid Germans, excitable Italians, bland English – but they find the idea of "national identity" or "ethnic identity" plausible.

Eric Hobsbawm has argued that contemporary nationalistic and ethnic revivals, like fundamentalist religious crusades, are chiefly a response to the changes of the late twentieth century. While nationalism, which involves a political program and encourages ethnic dissenters to seize control of a state, may be slower to develop, ethnicity "can acquire a genuine hold as [a] badge . . . of group identity overnight." This volatility arises in the context of contemporary social crisis: "What we see very generally today is a retreat from [a broader] social [identity] into group identity." When placed under great and continuing stress, members of these limited groups find that "the obvious fall-back positions are ethnicity and religion, singly or in combination . . . [because] they are the frontiers that exist."[41]

If changes in material conditions have inspired new cultural responses, postmodernism itself has raised other questions for ethnic historians. This approach to cultural analysis, now so much in vogue, has challenged the historiography that purported to describe a clearly delineated social unit. The development is best illustrated by the recent work of Fredrik Barth, who, a generation ago, took the study of ethnicity beyond static, descriptive terms to the more dynamic conceptualizations of "social boundaries" and "notions of ascription."[42]

Barth has recently encouraged another turn by accepting the postmodern critique of those older social studies in which logic and social structure and closed systems constitute the chief models of analysis. Instead, he offers three new rules to study by: first, "the image of processes serves us better than that of a structure or closed system;" second, "the sense that is being made, the reality that is being created, in any community or circle must be diverse"; third, "we should focus on how cultural knowledge is produced, the processes of its 'construction' read as a verb, not as a substantive." Barth wishes to concentrate on "the intrinsic dissonance in social life as it actually unfolds . . . the surrealist qualities of the various representations that make up cultural repertoires." This he takes from postmodernism. He does not intend to follow the postmodern fashion "in rejecting every attempt to construct theory." In sum, he calls upon scholars to "focus . . . on process, on the work done by people in the social and cultural construction of their realities."[43]

Ethnic historians have begun to appropriate these methods. In her works on German farm families in the American mid-west, Kathleen Conzen adopts a version of discourse analysis.[44] In this view, individuals and groups create symbols, language, and social constructs by which to interpret and shape their environment. Conzen argues that ethnicity itself is to be understood as a cultural construction accomplished "over historical time"; ethnic groups in modern settings are constantly re-creating themselves, and ethnicity is continuously being reinvented in "response to changing realities" both within the group and the host society.[45] It is important to note that this cultural construction is not unilinear in the way that assimilation or acculturation formerly were perceived: "The concept of invention allows for the appearance, metamorphosis, disappearance, and reappearance of ethnicities."[46]

These two recent approaches to ethnic studies, the one focussing on global forces in economy and communities, the other on postmodern approaches to cultural identity, introduce more flexible ways of thinking about ethnic history in western Canada. They suggest that ethnicity is not a single thing bound for a single destination. Rather, ethnicity is a response to concerns arising in the everyday. These approaches fit well into western Canadian history because they assume that regionalism, chronology, and the broader cultural context matter. In this view, self-identities such as those built on ethnicity are constantly shifting as citizens seek to establish a sense of life's meaning and to secure tenable positions within the wider society.

The historians' agenda in a previous generation may have been to pass judgement on the value of ethnic group contributions, measured either by Britannic superiority or by a defensive, but equally romantic, filiopietism. The agenda of later decades documented persistence, the erection of social boundaries, and the development of social networks that enabled ethnic groups to survive and to re-create Canada as a plural society. In the late twentieth century, historians are focussing on the ephemerality of identity, recognizing that ethnicity may coexist with other identities, may acquire different types of meaning in different contexts, may affect and be affected by the identity of the wider society, and may pass through several stages of relevancy and irrelevancy. The history of ethnicity in prairie Canada is neither a story of unilinear culture change nor one of static transplantation. Rather, it is a narrative based upon perpetual movement and contradictory social processes. In this sense, neither ethnicity nor its study will ever reach a destination. Only in the recognition of this incompleteness does ethnic history "come of age."

NOTES

Earlier versions of this paper were presented to the conference of the Association for Living Historical Farms and Agricultural Museums, Edmonton, June 1991, and the Trier University–University of Manitoba Biennial Colloquium, May 1994.

1. Fredrik Barth, introduction to *Balinese Worlds* (Chicago: University of Chicago Press, 1993), 4.
2. John Porter, *The Vertical Mosaic: An Analysis of Social Class and Power in Canada* (Toronto: University of Toronto Press, 1965); Royal Commission on Bilingualism and Biculturalism, vol. 4, *The Cultural Contribution of the Other Ethnic Groups* (Ottawa: Queen's Printer, 1969); J.M.S. Careless, "'Limited Identities' in Canada," *Canadian Historical Review* 50 (1969):1-10.
3. Robert Harney, "'So Great a Heritage as Ours': Immigration and the Survival of Canadian Polity," *Daedelus* 117 (1988).
4. W.L. Morton, "Clio in Canada: The Interpretation of Canadian History," in *Contexts of Canada's Past: Selected Essays of W.L. Morton,* ed. A.B. McKillop (Toronto: Macmillan, 1976).
5. A 1973 survey of prairie historiography, for example, devoted only three sentences, and a handful of references, to immigration and ethnic topics (T.D. Regehr, "Historiography of the Canadian Plains after 1870," in *A Region of the Mind: Interpreting the Western Canadian Plains,* ed. Richard Allen [Regina: Canadian Plains Research Center, 1973]).
6. J.S. Woodsworth, *Strangers within Our Gates, or Coming Canadians* (Toronto: Missionary Society of the Methodist Church, 1909), 4.
7. C.A. Dawson, *Group Settlement: Ethnic Communities in Western Canada* (Toronto: Macmillan, 1936), 109. The main statement of this perspective was John Murray Gibbon, *Canadian Mosaic: The Making of a Northern Nation* (Toronto: McClelland and Stewart, 1939).
8. Heinz Lehmann, *The German Canadians, 1750-1937: Immigration, Settlement and Culture,* trans. Gerhard Bassler (St. John's: Jesperson Press, 1986); B.G. Sack, *A History of the Jews in Canada: From the Earliest Beginnings to the Present Day* (Montreal: Canadian Jewish Congress, 1945); Vera Lysenko, *Men in Sheepskin Coats: A Study in Assimilation* (Toronto: Ryerson Press, 1947).
9. W.L. Morton, foreword to Arthur A. Chiel, *The Jews in Manitoba: A Social History* (Toronto: University of Toronto Press, 1961), iv. The Mennonite study by E.K. Francis was initiated by the series but not published in it (see footnote 13 below).
10. Wiktor Turek, *Poles in Manitoba* (Toronto: Polish Research Institute in Canada, 1967), 127.
11. Chiel, *The Jews in Manitoba,* 182.
12. Paul Yuzyk, *The Ukrainians in Manitoba: A Social History* (Toronto: University of Toronto Press, 1953), 79.

13. E.K. Francis, *In Search of Utopia: The Mennonites in Manitoba* (Altona, MB: D.W. Friesen, 1955), 275. Indeed, it was this thesis that is said to have led to the collapse of relations between the Manitoba Historical Society, represented by Margaret McWilliams and W.L. Morton, and Professor Francis. The book was published independently by D.W. Friesen Printers of Altona, Manitoba, as a result of the intervention of Ted Friesen, an officer in the firm. Mary Kinnear tells this story in "'An Aboriginal Past and a Multicultural Future': Margaret McWilliams and Manitoba History," *Manitoba History* 24 (autumn 1992).

14. R. Williams, "Base and Superstructure in Marxist Cultural Theory," in his *Problems in Materialism and Culture: Selected Essays* (London: Verso, 1980).

15. Royal Commission on Biculturalism and Bilingualism, *Report Book IV: The Cultural Contribution of the Other Ethnic Groups* (Ottawa: Queen's Printer, 1969), Recommendation #14, 230.

16. Careless, "'Limited Identities' in Canada," 4.

17. Howard Palmer, "Canadian Immigration and Ethnic History in the 1970s and 1980s," *Journal of Canadian Studies* 17 (1982):35, 46.

18. Between 1975 and 1992, *Prairie Forum* featured twenty-six articles on aspects of a multicultural West, while *Canadian Ethnic Studies* dedicated an entire volume in 1977 to the historical geography of several prairie ethnic groups. See Hansgeorg Schlichtman's introduction to the volume entitled *Ethnic Themes in Geographical Research in Western Canada, Canadian Ethnic Studies* 9 (1977):9-41.

19. Edward W. Laine, review of *From Fjord to Frontier: A History of the Norwegians in Canada* by Gulbrand Loken, *Canadian Historical Review* 62 (1981):555. Similarly critical is Roberto Perin, "Writing about Canada," in *Writing about Canada: A Handbook for Modern Canadian History*, ed. John Schultz (Scarborough: Prentice-Hall, 1990), 204.

20. Gulbrand Loken, *From Fjord to Frontier: A History of the Norwegians in Canada* (Toronto: McClelland and Stewart, 1980).

21. Manoly Lupul, ed., *A Heritage in Transition: Essays in the History of Ukrainians in Canada* (Toronto: McClelland and Stewart, 1982).

22. See, for example: Mark Stolarik, review of *A Member of a Distinguished Family: The Polish Group in Canada* by Henry Radecki, *Histoire Sociale / Social History* 10 (1978):487; Perin, "Writing about Canada," 207.

23. Lupul, *A Heritage in Transition,* 5. For a recent charge that little has been written of the internal world views and life worlds of the immigrant community, see, J.W. Berry and J.A. Laponce, *Multiculturalism in Canada: A Review of Research* (Toronto: 1994).

24. George Woodcock and Ivan Avakumovic, *The Doukhobors* (Toronto: Oxford University Press, 1968).

25. Frank H. Epp, *Mennonites in Canada, 1786-1920: The History of a Separate People* (Toronto: Macmillan, 1974); Epp, *Mennonites in Canada, 1920-1940: A People's Struggle for Survival* (Toronto: Macmillan, 1982).

26. Anthony W. Rasporich, "Early Twentieth-Century Jewish Farm Settlements: A Utopian Perspective," *Saskatchewan History* (1982).

27. A. Ross McCormack, "Cloth Caps and Jobs: The Ethnicity of English Immigrants in Canada, 1900-1914," in *Ethnicity, Power and Politics,* ed. J. Dahlie and T. Fernando (Toronto: Methuen, 1981), 38-55; Patrick Dunae, *Gentlemen Emigrants: From the British Public Schools to the Canadian Frontier* (Vancouver: Douglas and McIntyre, 1981).

28. Patricia Roy, *A Whiteman's Province: British Columbia Politicians and the Chinese and Japanese Immigrant, 1858-1914* (Vancouver: University of British Columbia Press, 1989); Ken Adachi, *The Enemy that Never Was: A History of the Japanese Canadians* (Toronto: McClelland and Stewart, 1976); Howard Palmer, *Patterns of Prejudice: A History of Nativism in Alberta* (Toronto: McClelland and Stewart, 1982); Irving Abella and Harold Troper, *None is Too Many: Canada and the Jews of Europe, 1933-1948* (Toronto: Lester and Orpen Dennys, 1982); Peter Ward, *White Canada Forever: Popular Attitudes and Public Policy towards Orientals in British Columbia* (Montreal: McGill-Queen's University Press, 1978); Hugh Johnston, *The Voyage of the Komagata Maru: The Sikh Challenge to Canada's Colour Bar* (Delhi: Oxford University Press, 1979).

29. Alan B. Anderson, "Linguistic Trends among Saskatchewan Ethnic Groups," in *Ethnic Canadians: Culture and Education,* ed. M. Kovacs (Regina: Canadian Plains Research Center, 1978), 83. See also: Alan B. Anderson, "Ethnic Identity in Saskatchewan Bloc Settlements: A Sociological Appraisal," in *The Settlement of the West,* ed. Howard Palmer (Calgary: Comprint, 1977).

30. Gerald Friesen, *The Canadian Prairies: A History* (Toronto: University of Toronto Press, 1984), 273.

31. Barth, *Balinese Worlds,* 7.

32. David Harvey, *The Condition of Postmodernity: An Enquiry into the Origins of Cultural Change* (Oxford: Basil Blackwell, 1990).

33. James Henretta, "Families and Farms: *Mentalité* in Pre-Industrial America," *William and Mary Quarterly* 37 (1978); Steven Hahn and Jonathan Prude, eds., *The Countryside in the Age of Capitalist Transformation: Essays in the Social History of Rural America* (Chapel Hill: University of North Carolina Press, 1985); Robert Swierenga, "The New Rural History: Defining the Parameters," *Great Plains Quarterly* (1981).

34. Jon Gjerde, *From Peasants to Farmers: The Migration from Balestrand, Norway, to the Upper Middle West* (Cambridge: Cambridge University Press, 1985); Robert C. Ostergren, *A Community Transplanted: The Trans-Atlantic Experience of a Swedish Immigrant Settlement in the Upper Middle West, 1835-1915* (Madison: University of Wisconsin Press, 1988).

35. Examples drawn from other regions include: Bruno Ramirez, *On the Move: French-Canadian and Italian Migrants in the North Atlantic Economy, 1860-1914* (Toronto: McClelland and Stewart, 1991); John E. Zucchi, *Italians in Toronto: Development of a National Identity, 1875-1935* (Montreal: McGill-Queen's University Press, 1988); Bruce S. Elliott, *Irish Migrants in the Canadas: A New Approach* (Montreal: McGill-Queen's University Press, 1988); Donald Harman Akenson, *The Irish in Ontario: A Study in Rural History* (Montreal: McGill-Queen's University Press, 1984); Catherine Anne Wilson, *Landlords, Tenants, and Immigrants: The Irish and the Canadian Experience* (Montreal: McGill-Queen's University Press, 1994).

This community-based approach is apparent more often in studies of Anglo-Canadian settlers than of ethnic settlers in the Canadian West. Two works that re-create the shifting identities of western, British-Canadian farmers are: Lyle Dick, *Farmers 'Making Good': The Development of Abernethy District, Saskatchewan, 1880-1920* (Ottawa: Canadian Parks Service, 1989); and, Paul Voisey, *Vulcan: The Making of a Prairie Community* (Toronto: University of Toronto Press, 1988).

36. James Urry, *None but Saints: The Transformation of Mennonite Life in Russia, 1789-1889* (Winnipeg: Hyperion Press, 1989); Stella Hryniuk, *Peasants with Promise: Ukrainians in Southeastern Galicia, 1880-1900* (Edmonton: Canadian Institute of Ukrainian Studies Press, University of Alberta, 1991).

37. John Lehr, "'The Peculiar People': Ukrainian Settlement of Marginal Lands in Southeastern Manitoba," in *Building beyond the Homestead: Rural History on the Prairies,* ed. David C. Jones and Ian MacPherson (Calgary: University of Calgary Press, 1985). This was also a major theme in Royden Loewen, *Family, Church and Market: A Mennonite Community in the Old and the New Worlds* (Toronto: University of Toronto Press, 1993).

38. Francis Swyripa, *Wedded to the Cause: Ukrainian Canadian Women and Ethnic Identity, 1891-1991* (Toronto: University of Toronto Press, 1993).

39. Harold Isaac, "Basic Group Identity," *Ethnicity* 1 (1974); Clifford Geertz, "The Integrative Revolution: Primordial Sentiments and Civil Politics in New States," in *Old Societies and New States: The Quest for Modernity in Asia and Africa,* ed. C. Geertz (New York: Free Press of Glencoe, 1963).

40. Benedict Anderson, *Imagined Communities: Reflections on the Origin and Spread of Nationalism* (London: Verso, 1983; 1991); E.J. Hobsbawm, *Nations and Nationalism since 1780: Programme, Myth, Reality* (Cambridge: Cambridge University Press, 1990).

41. Eric Hobsbawm, "Nationalism: Whose Fault-line is it Anyway?" *New Statesman and Society* (1992):23, 26. An apparently conflicting approach to the study of ethnicization in modern society is developed by authors who have given Geertz's notion of "primordial

attachments" greater credence. Tom Nairn, for example, defends the view that nationalism and ethnicity are inescapable forces in human affairs. He sees the evolution of a post-Maastricht Europe as leading not toward an inexorable homogenization but toward "differential cultural development." His examination of African societies suggests to him that "internal species-diversity through cultural means has always been 'human nature,'" and he concludes that, given this fact, "presumably it will go on being so" (Tom Nairn, "Does Tomorrow Belong to the Bullets or to the Bouquets?" *New Statesman and Society* [19 June 1992], 31).

42. Fredrik Barth, introduction to *Ethnic Groups and Boundaries: The Social Organization of Cultural Difference,* reprinted in *Process and Form in Social Life: Selected Essays of Fredrik Barth,* vol. 1 (London: Routledge and Kegan Paul, 1981).

43. Barth, *Balinese Worlds,* 4, 6-7; for another perspective, see, Marshall Sahlins, "Waiting for Foucault," *Prickly Pear Pamphlets* 2 (1993):5-21.

44. Elements of the approach can be seen in works by American ethnic historians such as Kathleen Conzen, Rudolph Vecoli, Ewa Morawska, and George Pozzetta. See, Kathleen Neils Conzen, "Making Their Own America: Assimilation Theory and the German Peasant Pioneer," *German Historical Institute Annual Lecture Series* 3 (1990):7.

45. Conzen, "Making Their Own America."

46. Kathleen Neils Conzen, David Gerber, Ewa Morawska, George Pozzetta, and Rudolph Vecoli, "The Invention of Ethnicity: A Perspective from the USA," *Journal of American Ethnic History* 29 (1992):3.

Perimeter Vision:
Three Notes on the History of Rural Manitoba

ONE FORTUNATE ASPECT of being a student of the community in which one works is the occasional invitation to lecture on aspects of local history to local groups. To compile this paper I have drawn upon a number of talks I delivered between 1985 and 1995. I offer three approaches to the history of rural Manitoba: first, a comment on economic and demographic history; second, a review of some recent historical writing; and, third, a discussion of prairie cultural history. The audiences ranged from the academic (such as the Assiniboine Historical Society, Brandon) to the political (a rural workshop of the New Democratic Party held in Dauphin) to the popular (the Tiger Hills Arts Association Christmas Gala in Pilot Mound, the Winnipeg Art Gallery, and the Munro Farm Supply Customers' Appreciation Night in Neepawa). I do not claim that this compilation offers a coherent academic analysis of a single topic. Rather, it attempts to say a little about contemporary Manitoba, a little about the university's role in the community, and a little about recent cultural scholarship that might interest an audience of citizens.

An organizer of the 1995 edition of the annual Northern Manitoba Trappers' Festival told a reporter that the event was the "one chance a year that we as a community get to stand together and say to the rest of the world, 'Hey, we're still alive and kicking and The Pas isn't such a bad place to live in and raise a family.'. . . It's the same morale booster that it's always been, in that it picks us up when we're down and helps us cope with the attitude that nothing happens north of the Perimeter Highway."[1]

A hazard of long residence in Winnipeg is an increasing inability to understand the rest of Manitoba. It is as if the Perimeter Highway, the autoroute that encircles the province's capital city, acts as a boundary in one's perceptions of the entire provincial community, like a palisade or moat that separates the city from the country. To be sure, Winnipeggers notice the cottage and campground country, the lakes in summer and the ski trails in winter, but they are accused of ignoring the working and living rural society, the "rural Manitoba" of towns and farms. At least, this is the accusation one hears in the rest of the province.[2]

The charge is apparently threefold: first, that rural citizens do not have adequate opportunity – access to appropriate sources of information or to the media and its specialized arts – to develop their own expression; second, that urban citizens lack knowledge about and interest in rural views; and third, as a corollary of the first two, that the province as a whole is diminished because some important elements of the community have not participated in the discussion of collective choices.

I agree with the criticism. Perimeter vision exists, and I am as guilty as the next Winnipegger in doing too little to resist it. Here, I attempt to respond to the criticism by outlining a few of the many subjects that would be included in a proper history of rural Manitoba.

ECONOMY AND DEMOGRAPHY

After five decades of stories about the population exodus from rural Manitoba, city dwellers might be forgiven for believing that the countryside was empty. They might be forgiven, too, for losing faith in agriculture as a bulwark of the provincial economy, having heard the warnings that world trade is volatile, foreign competitors aggressive, environmental catastrophes imminent, and taxpayer "subsidies" inappropriate. Thus, Winnipeg residents might defend themselves against the charge of perimeter vision by arguing that the rural districts are deservedly ignored because the once-vibrant countryside has ceased to constitute a significant element in provincial life.

"Rural Manitoba," as a place and as a social reality, requires definition. Manitoba historian W.L. Morton, who shared an earlier generation's understanding of this community, worked with an implicit three-unit approach in his writings between the 1930s and 1960s: Winnipeg was the metropolis, both of Manitoba and of the prairie region; northern Manitoba was a resource frontier that must be knitted to a settled "south"; and a rural, agriculture-based Manitoba constituted the strength of the provincial community as it did of his great provincial history. I accept Morton's assumption that the agricultural zone has always been a distinct and important component of provincial society.

If "rural Manitoba" is defined as the agricultural districts, towns as well as farmsteads, extending in an arc from the forty-ninth parallel and the Red River northwesterly to the Saskatchewan border at Swan River (excluding Winnipeg and its densely settled shadow), then this portion of the provincial community has experienced some significant changes during the twentieth century. Its total population, so defined, was about 260,000 in 1911, rose to about 400,000 during the 1930s, and has declined steadily ever since, reaching a total of about 300,000 in the 1980s and early 1990s. Such a symmetrical curve, rising between 1900 and 1940, dropping thereafter to its original level, may seem to imply relative stability. After all, the total rural population now is slightly higher than in 1911, when the rural communities were undeniably central to the province's identity and increasing in power and bursting with confidence.

Several trends of greater meaning are concealed within this story. Two are especially significant: first, there has been a dramatic shift in the balance of population – a change in location – from western to eastern Manitoba. Winnipeg's shadow, the semi-suburban communities within a radius of approximately thirty kilometres (though this is not precise because of the varied reporting districts), has increased rapidly in recent years and now, at 75,000 people, constitutes an important portion of the metropolitan district, raising Winnipeg's total to about 700,000. The western half of the province has experienced relative decline as the centre of gravity of the rural community has shifted eastward.

The second trend of note is that the rural *proportion* of the province's population has also declined steadily, from about fifty-seven percent in the first half of the century to twenty-five percent in 1991. The difference includes a sharp increase in the population of northern Manitoba as well as the steady growth of Winnipeg and district.[3] Naturally, a part that now constitutes one-quarter of the whole, whereas it had once constituted more than half, will exert less influence and will be seen to be declining in force. However, rural Manitoba, as one-quarter of the provincial population, is far from a tiny or negligible fraction.[4]

The farm economy and the export of agricultural products have seemed in recent years to be in a state of perpetual crisis. The most extreme statement of this view was articulated as early as 1986, when Oliver Bertin, agricultural reporter for the Toronto *Globe and Mail*, asked, "Will Farming Comprise Just a Phase in Prairie History?"[5] He suggested that prairie farmers were "a drain on the public purse" and inefficient in comparison with their international competitors. Fears raised by environmentalists, combined with the completion of trade deals both in North America and at the General Agreement on Tariffs and Trade (GATT's Uruguay Round) and the recent drastic revision in Canada's grain transportation policies, now promise to change the world agricultural scene even more.[6] Given the new circumstances, a city dweller might well wonder whether the farm economy has collapsed.

A cursory survey of farm production and trade in recent decades suggests far greater economic viability than one might have expected, though all these calculations will have to be redone under the impact of the 1995 federal budget and the cancellation of the century-old grain transportation policy. It is clear that world production of wheat, rice, and coarse grains has approximately doubled since the 1960s decade. Canadian *wheat* production over this period has increased by roughly fifty percent, and Canada has supplied roughly five percent of world production. In the coarse grains (barley, oats, corn, sorghum, rye, millet, triticale), Canadian production has been roughly three percent of the world total. Canadian production of canola, which has a wider range of competitors, constitutes fifteen to twenty percent of the world canola crop.

The role of Canadian farmers in the international agricultural scene appears even more important – and consistently rewarding – if one switches from global crop *production* to national shares of global *trade*. As an exporter of wheat, canola, and coarse grains to the world, Canada has been second only to the United States and slightly ahead of the European Union throughout most of the 1980s and early 1990s, and has supplied about twenty percent of the wheat traded and about five percent of the coarse grains. These are substantial volumes and represent significant shares of the prairie region's income. A recent study suggests that exports of western Canadian field crops could be valued at nearly four billion dollars annually between 1986 and 1989, or about ten percent of the region's merchandise exports.[7] For Manitoba, the three leading field crops of wheat, flax, and canola constituted about twenty-five percent of the value of the province's commodity exports between 1986 and 1989.[8]

Income from field crops is subject to fluctuation because both yield and market price depend on so many variables. Moreover, Manitoba farms have decreased in number. Nevertheless, the value of production in the farm sector has been remarkably consistent in the last two decades. The total value of Manitoba's crop production has ranged from one billion dollars to $1.7 billion annually (1978 to 1993), and of livestock production from $500 million to $900 million annually (1979 to 1993), for a total agricultural production in the range of $1.5 billion to $2.5 billion. It has constituted between four and five percent (exclusive of government assistance) of the province's Gross Domestic Product (GDP) in recent years, whereas in the decade before 1983 it had represented six to ten percent.[9] If one adds the value of agriculture-related industries, however, the contribution of the sector to the GDP was about ten to twelve percent in recent years (1989 to 1993), down from about twenty percent in the 1960s and 1970s. Moreover, about one job in eight is derived from agricultural production.[10] These levels are lower than in earlier generations, but they demonstrate the continued significance of agriculture in Manitoba's economy.

In sum: rural Manitoba constitutes one-quarter of the provincial population; rural Manitobans, in agricultural production and its directly related activities alone, are responsible for about one-eighth to one-tenth of the provincial economy, and this fraction does not include such indirect spinoffs as education, medical care, or retail/wholesale activity. The power of the agricultural or rural community in provincial life may have declined, but, to the surprise of no one outside "the perimeter," it remains a significant element in contemporary Manitoba.

SOME RECENT HISTORICAL WRITING

An historical tour of rural Manitoba will define more precisely the territory under consideration and introduce some of the recent historical writings that have attempted to understand its character. The tour might begin in what is known as the southeast, a term that illustrates Winnipeg's role as the fulcrum of social discussion in Manitoba. The farming district around Stuartburn, where immigrants from Ukraine settled after the turn of the century, is marshy, wooded, and difficult to cultivate. However, these immigrants chopped farms out of the bush and, despite enormous material obstacles, maintained themselves for several generations. The key factor in their selection of this difficult terrain was the availability of land for their entire group. As John Lehr has demonstrated, they ignored negative evaluations of the land and timber because they wanted to settle with people from their original villages in eastern Europe.[11]

From Stuartburn, our tour can move west across the Red River and onto the flat lands of the Red River Valley, through Mennonite villages, and pause near the Pembina Hills and the villages of Crystal City and Pilot Mound, where Ontario settlers founded a bastion of British Manitoba in the late 1870s and 1880s. In a doctoral dissertation on one rural municipality in this district, Donald Loveridge argues that the first fifteen years of agricultural settlement on these rich plains were remarkably unstable. An important problem was the get-rich-quick ambitions of the men. It took a number of reverses, and a slow adjustment to prairie conditions and possibilities – a process led, interestingly, by the women – before this community could be seen as a thriving part of a new rural Manitoba.[12]

Another kind of reflection on this rural society was offered by Jeffery Taylor, who asked why rural Manitobans think the way they do about the economy, social relations, and gender.[13] He focusses on the development of academic disciplines in North America, especially economics, home economics, and rural sociology, and the communication of these ways of thinking from university lecture halls to the farm groups that met in country elevator offices and churches and living rooms across southern Manitoba. He suggests that an intellectual and political consensus developed around what are essentially American disciplinary constructions. Though one might prefer to add British and Ontario community assumptions to the mix that Taylor has described, one can still appreciate his view that this disciplinary understanding of economy and community structure has shaped rural Manitoba. The market came to dominate daily reality for these people, and farm as capitalist business – not farm family as working family or some other metaphor – became the dominant structure of thought in Manitoba rural conversation. Farms were viewed as just one type of enterprise in a world of competing enterprises, and farm men and women perceived themselves as competitive, middle-class professionals. Though this explanation did not dominate to the same degree in Saskatchewan or in some parts of the American mid-west, it did become common language in much of southern Manitoba, as it did in much of rural Alberta.

Leaving this district of south-central Manitoba, the tour might travel west through some of the most beautiful landscape of the prairies, from the Pembina Hills and along Gabrielle Roy's *Road Past Altamont,*[14] through some of the Belgian and French settlements – Bruxelles, Mariapolis, St. Alphonse, St. Leon – to another thriving agricultural district centred on Killarney, Cartwright, and Boissevain. The Turtle Mountains, which form part of the southern margin of this district, offer travellers an opportunity to reflect on another rediscovered theme in prairie rural history, that of Aboriginal agriculture.

Four scholars – Douglas Elias, Laura Peers, Sarah Carter, and Katherine Pettipas – have contributed to the delineation of this theme in recent years and, in doing so, have identified how the federal government placed obstacles in the way of Aboriginal enterprise in the decades between the 1880s and the 1930s. Peers describes the westward migration of the Ojibwa from the Lake Superior–Rainy Lake region to the prairies.[15] Elias traces the Dakota exodus from Minnesota in the 1860s and their subsequent economic activity in western Manitoba.[16] Carter outlines how Aboriginal people willingly accepted the challenge of export agriculture, only to be prevented from building cash-crop, export-oriented farms by government interference.[17] Pettipas demonstrates that Ottawa actively suppressed not just economic innovation but also the very festivals and ceremonies that had hitherto sustained the individuals' sense of self and group.[18] These four works demonstrate how independent peoples adapted to changing territories over a period of several centuries, took advantage of different resources in their quest for food and shelter, and then, in the late nineteenth century, ran into an economic disaster. At this moment of crisis, with the buffalo gone forever, the Aboriginal people of the plains found little support from the state. Instead, they ran into a bureaucracy determined to undermine adult decision making and to erase adult worship.

These events took place in the southwest of Manitoba, involved Dakota and Ojibwa people in particular, and can be traced in the history of Birtle and Sioux Valley and other reserves along the route that we have been following through rural Manitoba. By this point in the trip, having reached what Winnipeggers would label the "southwest corner" of the province, the historical tour might turn northward to follow the Assiniboine River. Skirting the wide, deep valley and observing the mixed plain and parkland on either side, the travellers will eventually reach a point where uplands, or "mountains" in the Manitoba vocabulary, stand out on the horizon.

Somewhere in this district, perhaps around the Asessippi Provincial Park, or near the Riding Mountain National Park, or crossing the Gilbert Plains, or gazing at the starkly defined Duck Mountains, one might reflect on the environmental circumstances of the province. Where better to inquire about land use? Floods in this area raise questions about water management. A proposed ski hill and associated development have provoked a debate between advocates of two apparently irreconcilable interests – bird habitat and tourism – concerning which is the wiser use of the land. The tree resources of the region offer the prospect of "value added" forest management, but the arrival of a paper company also raises concerns about pollution and excessive cutting. In these debates, not for the first time, one hears echoes of accusations that "city conservationists" and rural "developers" are scheming to get their way, each trying to subvert the far-sighted, district-serving designs of the other.

Though geographers have dedicated much attention to these questions, historians have accepted environmental history as an appropriate subdiscipline only recently. It is now very fashionable, however, and one can anticipate histories that relate the history of the land itself to the history of the peoples who have lived on and shaped it, that focus as much on animal and fish and bird resources as on the human activities – hunting, farming, forestry, tourism, manufacturing – that derive from them.[19]

We have travelled 700 kilometres by this time, 400 on the westward part of the journey and 300 northward, and we have reached the rich soil of the Swan River Valley that A.J. Cotton made famous at the turn of the twentieth century.[20] The hypotenuse on this right-angled triangle must be 500 kilometres, a rough gauge of the distance from Swan River to Steinbach, the last leg of our trip. It is a considerable distance but hardly a challenge, given today's cars and planes and televisions and internet-linked computers.

The question of distance becomes interesting, however, if one pauses during this journey at Grandview or Benito or their larger neighbour, Dauphin, to view the women's rest rooms and to reflect on the meaning of distance in an earlier era of transportation.[21] When public amenities in towns were few, and women with children might have no place to wait during the transaction of "business" by the men in the families, and when the distance from farm to town might be measured in hours behind a horse rather than minutes in a car, the rest room was a political cause. At one time or another between 1910 and 1950, more than sixty villages had rooms set aside "for rest purposes for ladies and children from out of town," many of them established in the face of opposition. The story of this amenity – an institution in danger of being forgotten – underlines the question of what is significant in the historical record and who does the remembering. Distance has acquired new dimensions and so, too, in the recording of such a story, has the place of women in the community's history.

A women's history of Manitoba has not yet been written, but more has been published on this theme in the last decade than in the previous century. These works mark the changing political balance in our community. Increasing numbers of historians are finding important themes in, for example, the application of new technology to household work, the washing and cleaning and food preparation that had previously been ignored because giant threshing machines and tractors had dominated pioneer celebrations and male studies of material culture.[22]

In the last stage of this historical tour from Swan River through the Interlake to Steinbach, one discovers anew that rural Manitoba is a mosaic of ethnic groups – Ukrainian, Swedish, German, Polish, French Métis, French, Belgian, Icelandic, Hutterite, Jewish, English, Ontario Irish, Ontario Scottish, Orkney Métis, for example. One important historical work underlines some common threads in the stories of all these peoples. Royden Loewen, in his *Family, Church and Market: A Mennonite Community in the Old World and the New,* considers how one group of Mennonites was affected by international economic change.[23] These members of the small Kleine Gemeinde congregation, who were dwelling in southern Russia in the early 1870s, chose to migrate to North America and ended up in two settlements, one in Nebraska and the other around Blumenort, Manitoba. Naturally, they wished to adapt to the inevitable changes in the world economy while retaining the elements of individual, family, and community culture that they believed to be indispensable. Loewen discovered that the economic strategies in the Canadian and American branches of this apparently identical sample of immigrants differed substantially. So, too, did the role of the church as the collective voice of the community, especially as differences emerged concerning the pace and direction of social change. He concluded that the family unit was the pivotal institution in absorbing the forces of change and ensuring a sense of stability and continuity for each person, and that women's networks – mothers and daughters, sisters, friends – established and maintained the most enduring links and provided the strongest sense of consolation.

What has this imagined historical tour revealed? Besides circumnavigating the area under discussion, it has demonstrated that historical research is continuing to address issues of importance to rural Manitoba. A short trip across the agricultural districts of this province can be illuminated by a remarkable outpouring of scholarly writing, of which this is a small sample drawn from one discipline. Most of these substantial works have been written by scholars who themselves grew up in rural Manitoba. Moreover, these works address contemporary rural Manitoba concerns – gender, Aboriginal economy and culture, ethnic settlement and identity, adaptation to rural capitalism – competently and with due regard to the language and standards of international scholarship.

PRAIRIE CULTURAL HISTORY: A PERIODIZATION

Perimeter vision in the 1990s originates not in the arts and sciences but in the sphere of public expression that is called "culture." Admittedly, the distinction between the two categories, art and culture, is not obvious in ordinary conversation. Morley Walker, the entertainment editor of the *Winnipeg Free Press*, illustrated this problem of definition in a column on government grants to artists:

The arts have little to do with Canadian culture.

What defines Canadian culture? A variety of things, from hanging out at shopping malls to watching hockey on Saturday night. From endlessly debating what it means to be Canadian to expecting government to bail us out of tough spots.

The culture the arts lobbyists talk about – serious music, literature, theatre, gallery and museum offerings – is far removed from what it means to be Canadian.

The arts, of course, are an integral part of a civilized life, and many Canadians have an interest in being civilized. But these are attitudes shared with civilized people all over the world. They are not aspects of Canadian culture.

Walker then argued for the economic worth of cultural production as well as its entertainment value and its contribution to "the life of the mind." However, his main concern was to deliver an admonition: artists must forego their claim to be the creators of an irreplaceable "Canadian culture."[24]

While accepting Walker's general approach to culture, one need not agree that the distinction between culture and the arts should be drawn in quite this way. My concern is that Walker would not include, for example, the universities, the museums, the archives, and the art galleries of the province in his definition of *culture*. I prefer that we see the arts and scholarly work as components – among several other components, including hockey games and mall visits – of the broader phenomenon that we call *culture*. As a recent government policy document in another country suggested, "Culture arises from the community; . . . it encompasses our entire way of life, . . . not only interpreting our world but shaping it."[25]

The Royal Winnipeg Ballet company, the Jets hockey team, a novel, a song, and a painting in a gallery all carry collective importance. They figure in our conversations, they represent us and are acknowledged to do so even if we never see them, and they express community meanings unrelated to the works or performances themselves. This way of thinking subsumes both the arts and popular entertainment within a broader definition of culture.[26] It also enables us to draw a distinction between works of art, on the one hand, and the heritage and identity of groups of people, on the other. *Culture* can then be utilized as a term that recognizes both. It comprises both a "common heritage," shared ideas and values and traditions and experiences that define and distinguish a group, and individual creative works that represent innovation, a drive for new insights, and synthesis.

By adopting this distinction between art and culture, we can then see culture, in particular, as "the *signifying system* through which (though among other means) a social order is communicated, reproduced, experienced and explored."[27] Culture can be pictured as a community's system of sign making in which it discovers and discusses its community-ness, its sense of the meaning of life and the relations between individual and group identity. While acknowledging the special role of art as innovator and synthesizer in the larger culture, this approach also enables us to acknowledge Raymond Williams's dictum that "culture is ordinary."[28]

Has the rural community participated effectively within Manitoba's "signifying system"? This question can be addressed in terms of three historical phases of communication: first, that of print, newspapers, and the railway; second, radio, film, and the automobile; and third, the contemporary phase dominated by television, a phase that is far from over but is itself now undergoing rapid change.

In the era dominated by print communications, the daily newspapers based in Winnipeg offered quite remarkable coverage of the entire province. Despite the obvious isolation of a newly settled, horse-drawn society, especially for those people living in non-English-language communities, the foundations of a province-wide conversation had been established in the press. Moreover, individual Manitobans participated in a wide range of exchanges because the transportation and communications system sustained local travel, not national or international intercourse. This was also the railway age, an era before mass communications had taken a complete hold over Canadians. Thus, the chautauqua, the drama and music festivals, the sports leagues and bonspiels were events in which rural and metropolitan talents met and mingled more or less on an equal footing. This exchange found its most important expression in the official place of public conversation, the Legislature. This is not to suggest that the government made all, or even the most important, decisions, but, rather, that party and public debate represented the community's focal point. Debates about language and school law, the tariff and labour-management relations, child-welfare provisions and economic development represented rallying points for the Manitoba community (urban and rural), and in them was established the vocabulary of a provincial identity.

Radio and film, which constituted important new forms of mass communications between the early 1930s and the late 1950s, have not been written into our historical consciousness with sufficient clarity. They represent, it might be argued, another distinct phase in prairie cultural history. This phase was marked not just by weekly cinema attendance for many Manitobans but also by National Film Board rural film circuits and by remarkable experiments in adult education, including rural drama groups, handicraft leagues, and agencies dedicated to community activism, such as The Pas Adult Education movement.

Hollywood film represented a foreign intrusion into Manitoba life. The story of film censorship in the province in the 1930s, 1940s, and 1950s illustrates how suspect, and yet delightful and important, this particular version of cinema was: not only sexual scenes but politically inappropriate messages, undue emphasis on illegal activity, and detailed attention to the physical process of childbirth all fell afoul the Manitoba Board of Film Censors between 1930 and 1950.[29] Despite this community-sponsored caution, the screen itself seemed to constitute another world, one utterly removed from the daily realities of a Manitoba audience. This celluloid world was prettier, slicker, and funnier than daily reality, but it was also very foreign, to a degree that one cannot recover today, simply because it was "American" in a way that Manitoba was not. As the emphasis on politics and Legislature attests, and as entry into the Second World War confirmed, Manitoba's public conversation remained stubbornly and unshakably British.[30]

If the gulf between Manitoba and American mass culture was beginning to narrow in the 1930s, the rapprochement was less because of film than of radio. Manitoba's experience with the new vehicle of mass communication commenced with several unusual experiments, including a transmitter in Kelvin High School and an oral newspaper transmitted from the offices of the *Free Press* and *Tribune*. In 1923, the Manitoba Telephone System established a monopoly over broadcasting through its CKY station.[31]

Thus, Manitoba has the unusual distinction of being Canada's foremost experiment in state ownership of a monopoly radio system. Undertaken to protect the government's investment in telephones (and out of fear of the loss of grain company long-distance business), the product received little attention and very little financial support from Premier John Bracken's cautious administration. The CKY station produced farm extension programs, musical concerts, and religious material on five evenings, a total of forty hours a week, and it left two "silent nights." Its content ratio was about fifty-five percent music, fifteen percent news, fifteen percent lectures, and six percent church services. It also offered strictly equal time to the political parties. Because it served western Manitoba poorly, this CKY service was supplemented by CKX in Brandon in 1928, which was mainly a re-broadcast of Winnipeg's material. It was a parochial system, driven by economy rather than by aspirations of service or of excellence in programming. It did not provoke creative discussions on the possibilities of this new technology and has been judged an indifferent venture in early radio.[32] However, since only eighteen percent of Manitoba farm households had radio receivers in 1930, one could conclude that radio itself was a phenomenon that interested urban and wealthy citizens more than the rest of the province and, thus, would not soon be a priority for an economizing, rural-oriented government.[33]

Radio consolidated its hold on Canada during the 1930s, became the centre of attention during World War Two, and did not release its grip on the prairies until the late 1950s. Thus, for over twenty-five years, from the early 1930s to the late 1950s, radio provided an extremely important cultural medium through which prairie residents came to understand the world and their place in it. The proportion of homes with radios rose from about thirty percent in 1931 to about seventy percent in 1941, one sign that it had come of age. Just as television programs later provided subjects for daily conversation, so radio shows became a topic of daily discussion. Not surprisingly, radio also raised new versions of issues that had long been fundamental to Canadian life.[34]

The national origin of radio programs constituted one kind of challenge to Canadian communities, but another problem, perhaps far greater in significance, lay in the cultural message embedded in the listening and broadcasting processes themselves. That message concerned the proportion of one's daily life that could be measured by and conducted within the "market." Henceforth, prairie Canadians, like those in other prosperous countries, would be purchasing more goods and services in order to maintain their households and their sense of self. It was a change as important in its way as the arrival of industrial capitalism in the North Atlantic world around the turn of the nineteenth century, or the agricultural revolution in pre-Christian times. Moreover, it arrived at different times in different places, exacerbating social and political tensions between communities.

How can the differences in the adaptation of different parts of the prairie community to this important cultural change be measured? A social survey conducted between 1929 and 1931 noted the rise of differentials between villages and farms based on access to radios. Residents of towns and villages adjusted more quickly to changing fashions in clothing, hair style, house decoration, and cars than did those who dwelt in more isolated rural areas, the authors suggested. Members of ethnic minorities, especially those wherein the daily language was not English, were especially handicapped by the double barrier of language and radio.[35] Jean Burnet conducted a similar survey of rural society in Alberta in the 1940s and concluded that the town-country divide was, indeed, significant and long lasting, though she attributed the differences to factors other than the radio.[36]

Radio ceased to be an exclusively metropolitan institution when, during the 1950s and 1960s, broadcasting stations opened in smaller Manitoba centres. At that point, one could argue, the accompanying conversation in Manitoba ceased to run *from* metropolis *to* rural residents and, instead, was reconstructed *within* the countryside. These stations in Portage la Prairie, St. Boniface, Altona, Dauphin, and several other centres established rallying points for each community because they provided a means of maintaining contact with a larger, more scattered population. What was – and still is – talked about in this community conversation? Festivals, store openings, deaths, hockey games, and, yes, politics. The medium had been domesticated and democratized, though its links with the wider world – through the music industry and standard news packages – demonstrate that the rhythms of radio are stubbornly global as well as distinctively local.

Manitobans' experience with television has differed from their adaptation to radio. Like other citizens of the developed world, we have changed our living habits substantially to fit the television set into our lives. We pay court to the machine to the tune of twenty to twenty-five hours per week, on the average, and for most of this time are quite happy – indeed prefer – to consume products created in the United States, just as we enjoyed the American radio programs of the 1930s.[37] Partly as a consequence of this preference, we have been integrated into a wider consumer market, have become accustomed to commodification of many more parts of our lives than ever before, have acquiesced in the absorption of our spectator sports into a continental and international television-driven business, and have accepted that commercial advertising should be a major communication form in our culture. We accept too, that the rhythms of the economy should follow the same path, and therefore look with tranquillity upon the globalizing rhythms of finance, goods production, and communications, even though these trends entail the undermining not just of the former power of the nation state but also the very dimensions of space and time to which we were once accustomed.

If the foregoing smacks of technological determinism – an assumption that what can be produced and sold will inevitably take over the community – its tenor should be carefully reviewed. This is not the intent. What is striking in the case of radio, and perhaps will be true of television, is the change in production costs and distribution patterns over a period of several decades. Given the rapid changes, one could not possibly predict the course of today's cultural technologies with any degree of certainty. At the moment, there are television stations in Portage la Prairie and Brandon, there is a provincial French-language station, and there are local facilities for broadcast or cable re-transmission in Dauphin and Swan River as well as in the northern cities of The Pas, Flin Flon, and Thompson. There are also some local production facilities on several Aboriginal reserves.

Television has not yet been as susceptible to local production as has radio. The pattern in television has been to centralize production and content in the largest metropolis, and to leave very little to what has become known as the "local market." The idea that there might be room for intermediate communities of cultural production – the town, the province, increasingly even the nation state – seems inevitably to have been defeated by the market calculations of the global players.

Does either radio or television offer a bridge between rural and metropolitan Manitoba today? There are attempts, of course, including a noon-hour show on CBC radio dedicated to local subjects, especially those of rural interest, and the shows that have culminated with a thirty-minute weekly offering on CBC television. Clearly, the most important links have been established by news programs. Though any connection between city and country is valuable, and one should not underestimate the contribution to community understanding that the suppertime "news hour" represents, it is a far cry from a full range of cultural expression in the dramatic arts.[38] Radio and television do not, at present, constitute vehicles of rural-urban exchange that make a vital contribution to a province-wide signifying system.

SOME QUESTIONS

Rural Manitoba continues to occupy an important place in the provincial economy and its citizens continue to represent a significant fraction of the total provincial population. Neither its economic role nor its demographic proportions justify urban ignorance of rural concerns and priorities. Can perimeteritis be cured?

The cultural neglect of rural Manitoba by the metropolis has not been evident in Manitoba's recent historical writing. Jeff Taylor's interest in the specific qualities of rural capitalism, the volumes that examine Aboriginal adaptation to the newcomers' civilization, the contested nature of gender studies and the emergence of women's history as a newly prominent theme in our society, and Roy Loewen's synthesis of market, church, and family history demonstrate that not only are rural Manitobans writing their own story, but they are doing so while taking into account contemporary pre-occupations with economic and cultural change.

The continuing inadequacies of the Manitoba conversation are most apparent in radio and television. These technologies, which are very powerful in cultural terms, have been domesticated by some rural districts. Citizens within these sub-provincial communities have found a medium through which to speak to each other, despite being restricted by the range of a transmitter and by the relevance of such messages to a "market." However, neither radio nor television has solved the problem of communication between rural Manitoba and Winnipeg. The Perimeter Highway constitutes a boundary both for those who live outside it and those who dwell within it.

An ideal social order that possessed an ideal signifying system would find a way to eliminate this sense of disparity in cultural power. Rural Manitobans' grievances represent a failure of the market, of course, but also a failure of the government. They constitute a decisive challenge to this once-coherent provincial community.

How might the challenge be met? Prairie history offers part of the answer. In the face of the vast economic changes of recent centuries, and despite the sweeping nature of the communications revolution, individuals and groups have been able in previous generations to re-establish community-wide conversations. The labour of scholars has been presented in the technology of the book without difficulty. Today's problem is to adapt as effectively to modern technologies as we have to the old form of print.

The Perimeter Highway need not be a barrier if the market is not the sacred centre of our civilization. Do Manitobans subscribe to the principle of a society sustained by its economy, or to the practice of a society determined by a market?[39] How will we establish a compromise between these two impossible poles? A vital democracy is the answer, of course, but that will seem to be a cliché if it is not coupled with practical suggestions to make a society function in the changed conditions of the "modern age." It can be achieved in daily life only through the operation of an effective signifying system – in other words, a vital Manitoba and Canadian "culture." As The Pas needs the Trappers' Festival, so Manitoba must repatriate a corner of its television system – and perhaps soon a part of the internet as well – in order that its signifying system actually reflects all parts of the community to each other.

NOTES

1. Sonny Lavallee was quoted in William Hilliard, "They're 'Still Alive' and Jigging at Spirited Town's Winter Fest," *Winnipeg Free Press*, 19 February 1995; he added that "the province doesn't recognize us as a cultural event. The [fact that we utilize 600 volunteers] shows our community spirit and how important this festival is." In the same issue, see, Bob Lowery, "Games Highlight for Northern Students."

2. As Fred McGuinness and Ken Coates wrote in their provincial history, some Winnipeggers have "needed regular reminders that there were urban environments outside Winnipeg" (*Manitoba: The Province and the People* [Edmonton: Hurtig Publishers, 1987], 180).

3. One might visualize the rural community as embracing two distinct spheres. In eastern Manitoba, four small cities averaging 10,000 residents (Portage la Prairie, Selkirk, Steinbach, Winkler-Morden) and eight larger towns averaging 2,000 residents (Teulon, Arborg, Lac du Bonnet, Pinawa, Beausejour, Morris, Altona, Carman) ring the metropolis and dominate an area of mixed, fairly intensive agriculture and small manufacturing. In western Manitoba, two cities (Dauphin and Brandon) and eleven larger towns (of 1,000 to 4,000 residents) anchor the network of agricultural and service activities distributed across the southwestern quadrant of the province. Winnipeg has doubled in population since 1941 and seems to continue to grow at a rate of about one percent per year. The population of northern Manitoba nearly tripled between 1950 and 1980. I would like to thank John Grover for the preparation of this statistical material.

4. Saskatchewan discussions of this trend are illuminating. See: Jack C. Stabler, M.R. Olfert, and Murray Fulton, *The Changing Role of Rural Communities in an Urbanizing World: Saskatchewan, 1961-1990* (Regina: Canadian Plains Research Center, 1992); and, Jack C. Stabler and M.R. Olfert, *Restructuring Rural Saskatchewan: The Challenge of the 1990s* (Regina: Canadian Plains Research Center, 1992).

5. Oliver Bertin, Toronto *Globe and Mail,* "Will Farming Comprise Just a Phase in Prairie History?," 19 September 1986, 6.

6. *Winnipeg Free Press,* 26 January, 18-19 February, 9-10 May 1995, offers some coverage of the new agricultural situation.

7. Edward J. Chambers and Michael B. Percy, *Western Canada in the International Economy* (Edmonton: University of Alberta Press, 1992), 10-18. Other major exports were petroleum and natural gas, lumber and wood pulp/newsprint, coal, potash, minerals, and fish.

8. Wheat – 17.4 percent, flax – 3.8 percent, canola – 3.3 percent, according to Chambers and Percy, *Western Canada in the International Economy,* 17.

9. The GDP of Manitoba ranged from twenty to twenty-five billion dollars between 1987 and 1991, as opposed to ten to fifteen billion dollars between 1979 and 1984. I would like to thank John Grover for his assistance with these statistics. I also owe a debt of gratitude to Brian Oleson of the Canadian Wheat Board for his assistance.

10. Manitoba Department of Agriculture, *Manitoba Agricultural Review,* 1985 to present (annual).

11. John Lehr, "'The Peculiar People': Ukrainian Settlement of Marginal Lands in Southeastern Manitoba," in *Building beyond the Homestead: Rural History on the Prairies,* ed. Ian MacPherson and David Jones (Calgary: University of Calgary Press, 1985), 29-46.

12. Donald M. Loveridge, "The Rural Municipality of Louise," Ph.D. dissertation, University of Toronto, 1986.

13. Taylor's book on rural education and knowledge is one of the most challenging, in theoretical terms, of the recent works in Canadian history. It introduces, as he says, "poststructuralist, feminist and regulationist critiques of historical materialism" into the analysis of the University of Manitoba's Schools of Agriculture and Home Economics as well as of men's and women's farm organizations (Jeffery Taylor, *Fashioning Farmers: Ideology, Agricultural Knowledge and the Manitoba Farm Movement, 1890-1925* (Regina: Canadian Plains Research Center, 1994], 2).

14. Gabrielle Roy, *La Route d'Altamont* (Montreal: HMH, 1966).
15. Laura Peers, *The Ojibwa of Western Canada* (Winnipeg: University of Manitoba Press, 1994).
16. Peter Douglas Elias, *The Dakota of the Canadian Northwest: Lessons in Survival* (Winnipeg: University of Manitoba Press, 1986).
17. Sarah Carter, *Lost Harvests: Prairie Indian Reserve Farmers and Government Policy* (Montreal: McGill Queen's University Press, 1990).
18. Katherine Pettipas, *Severing the Ties that Bind: Government Repression of Indigenous Religious Ceremonies on the Prairies* (Winnipeg: University of Manitoba Press, 1994).
19. Parks Canada has sponsored a series of research reports on the area of Riding Mountain National Park. One such manuscript is Teresa Tabulenas, "A Narrative Human History of Riding Mountain National Park and Area: Prehistory to 1980," 1983.
20. Wendy Owen, ed., *The Wheat King: Selected Letters and Papers of A.J. Cotton, 1888-1913* (Winnipeg: Manitoba Record Society, 1985).
21. Donna Norell, "'The Most Humane Institution in All the Village': The Women's Rest Room in Rural Manitoba," *Manitoba History* 11 (spring 1986).
22. Angela Davis, "'Valiant Servants': Women and Technology on the Canadian Prairies, 1910-1940," *Manitoba History* 25 (spring 1993):33-42.
23. Royden K. Loewen, *Family, Church and Market: A Mennonite Community in the Old World and the New* (Toronto and Urbana: University of Toronto Press and University of Illinois Press, 1994).
24. Morley Walker, "Arts Lobby Group Goes Too Far in Culture Claim," *Winnipeg Free Press*, 24 February 1995. It is noteworthy that Walker's name appeared with the title "entertainment editor." A second column on the same topic appeared on the same page of this newspaper. Written by Kevin Prokosh, this column was designated "The Arts."
25. Australia, Government of the Commonwealth of Australia, "Preamble," *Creative Nation: Commonwealth Cultural Policy* (October 1994).
26. Art focusses on and draws its definition from the art object, the work that goes into creating it, and the persons who undertake that process. In this view, art is "a cultural practice that involves the creation of a specific and definable object; . . . the function of that object is as a self-conscious, personal, or collective expression of something" (Justin Lewis, *Art, Culture, and Enterprise: The Politics of Art and the Cultural Industries* [London, New York: Routledge, 1990], 5).
27. Raymond Williams, *Culture* (Glasgow: Fontana Paperbacks, William Collins Sons and Co., 1981), 13.
28. Raymond Williams, "Culture is Ordinary," in *Border Country: Raymond Williams in Adult Education,* ed. John McIlroy and Sallie Westwood (Leicester: National Institute of Adult Continuing Education, 1993). This essay was first published in 1958 and has been re-published several times.
29. James M. Skinner, "Clean and Decent Movies: Selected Cases and Responses of the Manitoba Film Censor Board, 1930 to 1950," *Manitoba History* 14 (autumn 1987).
30. This atmosphere is conveyed by Margaret McWilliams's sections on Manitoba in H.F. Angus et.al., *Canada and Her Great Neighbour: Sociological Surveys of Opinions and Attitudes in Canada Concerning the United States* (Toronto: Ryerson, 1938).
31. Mary Vipond, "CKY Winnipeg in the 1920s: Canada's Only Experiment in Government Monopoly Broadcasting," *Manitoba History* 12 (autumn 1986).
32. Vipond, "CKY Winnipeg in the 1920s," 11, quotes a *Free Press* editorial of 15 January 1931 that criticized the government's link to the utility, not public ownership itself, and said CKY should be "what so far it has only pretended to be – that is, a publicly-owned station, not an adjunct to another utility, nor primarily an advertising vehicle. . . . [It] should be a station, in fact, which would arouse envy, not pity, in the sister provinces."
33. Carl A. Dawson and Eva R. Younge, *Pioneering in the Prairie Provinces: The Social Side of the Settlement Process* (Toronto: Macmillan, 1940), 194, citing the 1931 census.

34. Canada's place on the continent, inevitably, was challenged by the boundary-hopping radio waves. The United States refused for two decades to accommodate Canadian broadcasters and thus occupied ninety of the ninety-six available channels through the 1920s and early 1930s. Only in 1937 was this proportion reduced to sixty-six of ninety-six, with twelve reserved exclusively for Canada and twenty-four to be shared. This was confirmed in the Havana agreement in 1941 (see, Donald Wetherell and Irene Kmet, *Useful Pleasures: The Shaping of Leisure in Alberta, 1896-1945* [Regina: Canadian Plains Research Center, 1990], 288-308). American radio shows were free and they were better. Or, so it was said. A survey of 800 Manitoba students (grades seven to eleven) in the mid-1930s found that nearly two-thirds placed an American show as their favourite, usually music (dance and jazz), though a number also expressed enthusiasm for a CKY program of barn-dance music, Round-up Rangers. On any list of radio favourites from the 1930s, American shows such as Amos 'n' Andy, Lux Radio Theatre, Charlie McCarthy, Eddie Cantor, and the hours sponsored by Firestone, Eveready, and Colliers would have been near the top along with such sports events as the Dempsey-Tunney fights and the baseball World Series (Angus, *Canada and Her Great Neighbour*, 379).

What were Canadians to do about the "air bombardment of this country," as the *Free Press* put it? Americans were producing programs for thirteen-year-olds, an editorial said, and were making Canada into a "merchandising annex" of the United States. It was nothing more than a "racket," probably run by private interests of which "the electrical trust [is] foremost" (Angus, *Canada and Her Great Neighbour*, 138, 148-9). It is true that the giant transmitters in Salt Lake City, Denver, and Chicago, not to mention a legion of smaller stations, attracted a good deal of attention on the Canadian prairies. However, the inundation was not quite as complete as the alarmists feared. A survey of listeners in Moose Jaw in 1938 discovered that, from 7:00 to 10:00 in the evening, sixty-seven percent were tuned to the CBC outlet in Saskatchewan, seventeen percent to another Canadian station, and eighteen percent to American transmissions (Wayne Schmalz, *On Air: Radio in Saskatchewan* [Regina: Coteau Books, 1990], 68). On the other hand, as a perceptive critic in the Prince Albert *Herald* argued during 1934, radio was becoming an important cultural medium and its direction deserved greater attention from all citizens (Schmalz, *On Air*, 74).

35. Dawson and Younge, *Pioneering in the Prairie Provinces*, 62, 71-2, 194.

36. Jean Burnet, *Next-Year Country: A Study of Rural Social Organization in Alberta* (Toronto: University of Toronto Press, 1951; 1978), 75-95.

37. Jeffrey Frank and Michel Durand, "Canadian Content in the Cultural Marketplace," *Canadian Social Trends* (autumn 1993) (Statistics Canada 11-008E); and, Mary Sue Devereaux, "Time Use of Canadians in 1992," *Canadian Social Trends* (autumn 1993).

38. It is noteworthy that most of these examples emanate from state-supported outlets and, as of recent months, are in jeopardy or defunct. The explanation of this state role in urban-rural conversation lies in the contemporary pattern of politics as well as culture. One of the great divides in modern society lies in the conflict between market and state, or the private and public sector. The tendency of the former is toward the universal, of the latter toward the local. The late Graham Spry argued during the campaign that led to the founding of the CBC that one could choose only between "the state and the United States." This tendency would apply to communications in any small country that existed on the periphery of a great imperial centre. Today, Spry's aphorism might be rewritten to say that the choice for Manitobans, and Canadians, lies between the state and the global market, though for this small province the market's regulations and restrictions will always be expressed by the American version of capitalism.

39. This question reflects the approach taken by Raymond Williams, in *Towards 2000* (Harmondsworth, England: Penguin 1985; first published 1983).

Hockey and Prairie Cultural History

MANY CANADIANS, and surely all Manitobans, have heard of the departure of the Winnipeg Jets hockey team for an American destination and of the public attempt in the spring of 1995 to forestall the city's loss. After so many expressions of popular support, including the commitment of twelve million dollars by ordinary citizens in one dramatic week (the United Way annual campaign raises between eight and nine million dollars), any student of society would have to conclude that hockey, and this professional league, occupied an important place in prairie culture.

I present here a series of speculations about hockey in prairie Canada. Though there are many ways to inquire into such an issue, the following comments address only one type: that is, I examine the game itself and the movement, drama, and conversation that originate in the action on the ice. I do not address the political economy of professional sport, the distinctive character of property and industrial relations within the National Hockey League (NHL), the place of advertising and sport in modern society, or male athletes as creators of gender identities and of spectacle. Nor do I ask the obvious questions related to the departure of the Jets: how large is the appropriate hockey "market" in North America? how much community investment in infrastructure (such as an arena) is appropriate? how much marketing advantage is won and lost when franchises arrive in or depart from a metropolis? Each of these approaches, and many others, are worthy of investigation. However, for the purpose of this essay, I will take the Winnipeg fans at their word by addressing simply their love of *the game*. How might we understand this affection?

I begin by declaring an interest in the story. My involvement with the Jets begins with their arrival in Winnipeg. Memorable moments in our family history are associated with visits to the Winnipeg Arena when Bobby Hull and his Swedish teammates created such wonderful entertainment. This link was consolidated by the admission of the team to the world's premier hockey competition, the NHL, in 1979. In November of that year, a colleague, Morris Mott, and I wrote an essay for the *Winnipeg Tribune* on the "historic" qualities of the first regular-season contest between the Jets and the former standardbearer of English Canadian hockey fans, the Toronto Maple Leafs. I did not participate in the campaign to save the Jets in 1995, nor did I oppose it. And I share with many Winnipeg residents both the belief that the city will survive the team's departure and the recognition that its cultural life will be different.

From the outset, one should acknowledge that many reasonable and perceptive citizens criticize the popular interest in competitive sports, especially professional sports. The generally harmless and laudatory platitudes in which the games are bundled offend these citizens' sensibilities. The attention lavished on athletes and the money dedicated to such activity seems to them misguided, if not outrageous. They would like to see a change in our society's priorities and sense of proportion. Each year, some among them condemn the Canadian Broadcasting Corporation's preemption of its spring schedule to show NHL playoff games. In Winnipeg, a voluntary pressure group called Thin Ice, which opposed public subsidies for the Jets and for the construction of a new arena, represented this perspective. The Thin Ice advocates consistently condemned the Jets rescue campaign as an attempt by a few wealthy investors to secure private gains at public expense. Among the citizens who endorsed their analysis, however, one could discern a number of additional criticisms: too much money expended, too much time absorbed, too little added to the store of community resources.

A slightly different critique of spectator sports focusses on the effect of such cultural activities on society itself. Some scholars have argued that popular faith in the community is undermined by the individualism, the competitive ethic, and the profit seeking embedded in these high-profile activities. They believe that the widespread popular faith in peace, order, and good government necessary in today's communities – the citizen's faith that a community can possess coherence and intelligence, that reason can prevail and that democracy can work – is being undermined by a devotion, nay, an addiction, to "spectacle." This term signifies the endless sequence of publicity-driven events (from sports competition to royal divorce to murder trial) that prevail in the media and are presumed to pre-occupy ordinary citizens. The rapid succession of headlines in our daily news seems to defy proper analysis. Discussion of cause and effect, and of broader social context, seem to become impossible. Moreover, as Guy Debord argues, "When the spectacle stops talking about something for three days, it is as if it did not exist." His concern is that we are losing our sense of history and, thus, our perspective on what is possible.[1]

I respond to these critics of public priorities and the society of specta-cle by asserting that hockey matters to many people of the Canadian prai-ries – hardly a revolutionary insight – and that it has good reason to be considered in any survey of prairie cultural history. I suggest that expla-nations for its importance lie in the very nature of spectator sports in gen-eral, and this game on ice in particular. The explanations include the child-hood experiences of many citizens, the relations between spectator sports and art forms, and the particular Canadian conversation generated by a bi-national hockey league that remains stubbornly Canadian in popular understanding. If it takes seriously the popular support for spectator sports and professional hockey, however, the essay does not dismiss the fears of hockey's critics.

Several parts of my response to hockey rely on the work of Trinidad-born historian C.L.R. James, who wrote *Beyond a Boundary*, a series of essays on the history of cricket. In its dedication, James expressed the hope that his book would "extend our too limited conceptions of history and of the fine arts." Later, he noted the extraordinary public celebration that occurred in England in 1895 when the greatest player in the history of the game, W.G. Grace, at the age of forty-six, established yet another batting record, this on the thirty-first anniversary of his first season in the highest competitive level (county) of cricket.

James says that the batsman, now burly and slow,

> was sustained and lifted higher than ever before by what has been and always will be the most potent of all forces in our universe – the spontaneous, unqualified, disinterested enthusiasm and goodwill of a whole community. . . . On what other occasion, sporting or non-sporting, was there ever such enthusiasm, such an unforced sense of community, of the universal merged in an individual? At the end of a war? A victorious election? With its fears, its hatreds, its violent passions? Scrutinize the list of popular celebrations, the unofficial ones; that is to say, those not organized from above. I have heard of no other that approached this celebra-tion of W.G.'s hundredth century.[2]

I agree with James that spectacle can be good as well as corrosive. It can sweep us up in a moment of self-forgetting, unite us in a moment of solidarity with others, illuminate the potential goodness in humankind.

That each of these sentiments has a dark side, however, and that each such experience of collective emotion implies risk, should also be evident.

Eric Nesterenko expressed the joyful side of hockey as spectacle in a remarkable interview with American journalist Studs Terkel. Speaking in the early 1970s, near the end of a very successful career in the NHL, Nesterenko turned first to the excitement generated by the public contest:

The pro game is a kind of stage. People can see who we are. Our personalities come through in our bodies. It's exciting. . . . I remember one game: it was in the semifinals, the year we won the Stanley Cup. I was with Chicago. It was the sixth game against Montreal. They were the big club and we were the Cinderella team. It was three to nothing, for us, with five minutes left to go. As a spontaneous gesture twenty thousand people stood up. I was on the ice. I remember seeing that whole stadium, just solid, row on row, from the balcony to the boxes, standing up. These people were turned on by us [sighs]. We came off, three feet off the ice . . . [softly] spring of '61.[3]

No one would want to challenge the authenticity of such an experience. Each of us may have one or two moments in our lives that involve a crowd, intense excitement, and a moment of transcendence. We would respond to Nesterenko that we knew exactly what he meant. Some moments in some competitive games create such sensations.

The same could be said about prairie Canadians' relations with particular moments in hockey. Most of these moments are felt keenly and then forgotten. I am sure that not more than a few dozen people recall a moment in the history of the Prince Albert Minto hockey team when a home-town boy saved the home team with a goal that secured a championship. The goal and the intensity of the crowd response were engraved in my mind (I was then about six) and on the minds of a few others in my childhood community. My certainty about the survival of the incident in the memory of others is central to my sense of belonging in that community. The same sensation was evoked during the second sudden-death period of a playoff game between the Winnipeg Jets and the Edmonton Oilers nearly forty years later. Many Winnipeggers would recall that goal and share the identification that comes with it. To choose a more-famous illustration, a few million Canadians recall the moment in 1972 when a Canadian hockey player shot the puck past Vladislav Tretiak, goalie for the Soviet Union team, to win the eighth game of the first – in Canadians' minds – genuine world ice-hockey competition of the modern era. Paul Henderson's goal is magical for most Canadians over a certain age because it is something they hold in common as Canadians, in the way that citizens of other countries "possess" a national victory in soccer's World Cup. The fact of shared sensation and shared memory creates a community, establishes who are the participants in this meaningful conversation, and sets out the first topic on which they can build a more extensive relationship. It may start with parent and child. It may be conducted among neighbours at that ubiquitous prairie institution – the "community club." However, the memory need never be discussed, the topic need not even be broached, but the tacit awareness of that moment contributes to the foundation on which an edifice can be built.

Given the centrality of such moments of celebration in the life of a community, it may be surprising to citizens of Canada to discover that very little serious historical writing has touched upon their national game.[4] The reason, it is said, is that historians have been too concerned with the activities of the political and economic elites or, more recently, with the themes of class and gender, to reflect on this popular pastime. Yet James said of cricket and the W.G. Grace celebration: "If this is not social history, what is? It finds no place in the history of the people because historians do not begin from what people seem to want but from what they think the people ought to want."[5] What is it that moves Canadian audiences? Is the apparent mourning in Winnipeg for the death of the Jets hockey team – a widespread sentiment that informs this essay – of no consequence?[6] Games do matter to people. They inspire a pure, unalloyed joy in those who are open to such moments of physical and emotional expression. And they shape one's awareness of community by distinguishing insider from outsider: the very lines of competition help communities to define themselves.

HOCKEY AND CHILDHOOD

One explanation of hockey's influence must lie in its association with the early years of most Canadians who have grown up in the ice-bound parts of the country. In this aspect, hockey belongs with the autonomous world of children's play, where rules are shaped by children's movement and children's bargaining, and where the only legislation that matters is the decree of the group.

This approach to the game accepts the assertion that "Culture" is ordinary.[7] Though culture is often seen to refer only to the "high arts," such as theatre and opera and painting, many scholars today follow Welsh scholar of cultural studies Raymond Williams in asserting that this is an unfortunate mistake. Everyone has a culture and participates in cultural expression, in this view. Our task is to understand the differences in the patterns of such expressions. I begin from the assertion that one of the most ordinary prairie activities in an ordinary winter in any year of the twentieth century, especially for children, is to skate.

Eric Nesterenko understood the centrality of skating in his early life.

He grew up in the northern mining town of Flin Flon, Manitoba:

In the middle of nowhere, four hundred miles north of Winnipeg. It was a good
life, beautiful winters. I remember the Northern Lights. Dark would come around
three o'clock. Thirty below zero, but dry and clean. I lived across the street from
the rink.
    That's how I got started, when I was four or five. We never had any gear. I
used to wrap *Life* magazines around my legs. We didn't have organized hockey
like they have now. All our games were pickup, a never-ending game. . . . It was
pure kind of play. . . .
    My father bought me a pair of skates, but that was it. He never took part. I
played the game for my own sake, not for him. He wasn't even really around to
watch. I was playing for the joy of it, with my own peers. Very few adults around.
We organized everything. . . .
    I was a skinny, ratty kid with a terrible case of acne. I could move pretty well,
but I never really looked like much [laughs]. Nobody ever really noticed me. But
I could play the game. In Canada it is part of the culture. If you can play the
game, you are recognized. I was good almost from the beginning. The game
became a passion with me. I was looking to be somebody and the game was my
way. It was my life.[8]

There it is: hockey is associated with the equality and autonomy and agency
– as historians would say – that originated in children's experience on the
ice. It also has overtones of class mobility, opportunity, escape from the
ordinary, and challenging winters.
    There is something compelling about such an explanation of hockey's
reach, and yet it is difficult to locate precisely. Another angle from which
to approach the thesis is to consider memory itself. Any older person can
attest to the phenomenon of aging memory: one's first ten years remain
crystal clear in one's recollection – parents, siblings, playmates, games,
and, of course, places; the second decade offers memories almost as vivid,
almost as distinct; and the intervening thirty or fifty or seventy years, by
comparison, seem to have passed in a blur. Saskatchewan poet Eli Mandel
suggested that this phenomenon is crucial to the novels and stories and
poems that make childhood the vital constituent of "regional" literature:
"the *first* place, the *first* vision of things, the *first* clarity of things. Not
realism, then, but rather what in painting is called magic realism."[9]
    If Eric Nesterenko offers a particular vision of childhood and hockey,
another prairie story – the encounter known as "Gordie Howe's skates" –
offers another. The story begins in the depth of the drought and depression of the Dirty Thirties, perhaps in 1937 when Saskatchewan's crop failed
miserably, the worst disaster in an eight-year string of crises. A poor woman
presented herself at the Howe household in the railway hamlet of Floral,
just outside Saskatoon, with a sack of odds and ends that she wanted to
exchange for a little cash in order to feed her children. It was a cold winter

day, and, though she had no need of the items, Mrs. Howe recognized the situation and offered the woman whatever change could be scrounged in exchange for the goods. When the sack was dumped out on the floor, a battered pair of skates clattered into view. Gordie and his sister each grabbed one, donned it, and went out to try sliding and gliding with the new toy. Before the week was out, Gordie had inveigled the other skate from his sister and committed himself utterly to mastering the game of hockey on the ice-covered sloughs and eventually the rinks of his district. A shy and awkward child had found his place in the world and, as the story goes, lived happily ever after.[10]

The key to the attractions of this story, I suggest, is the juxtaposition of several relatively timeless elements in narrative. These include a community mired in hardship, a reticent child who succeeds, a generous-hearted mother, and a proud recipient of charity who has something miraculous to offer. Equally important, for a prairie Canadian, are the *specific* places and dates and persons. After all, the precise details that establish the story's authenticity include the child's recreations in a rural prairie community, the limited material possessions of most prairie residents during the Depression years, and the enveloping context of a prairie winter. Not to mention the name itself, Gordie Howe, and the place, Floral, Saskatchewan.

This strong connection between childhood and a specific place is easily ignored, or lost, in today's world. Yet it is a fundamental source of a human's sense of identity or belonging, second in importance only to parent and family. This identification of self with place is described in many works of literature and philosophy. When asked specifically about his perception of class identity as opposed to his obvious affection for the valley communities of his native Wales, Raymond Williams replied:

I've always been very aware of the complicated relationships between class and place. I've been enormously conscious of place, and still get an extraordinary amount of emotional confirmation from the sense of place and its people. Now the key argument in Marxism was always whether the proletariat would be a universal class – whether the bonds it forged from a common exploitation would be perceived as primary, and eventually supersede the more local bond of region or nation or religion. On the one hand the recognition of exploitation continually reproduces class consciousness and organization on a universal basis. On the other hand, I don't know of any prolonged struggle of that kind in which these other issues haven't been vital, and in some cases decisive. So I'm on both sides of the argument, yes: I recognize the universal forms which spring from this fundamental exploitation – the system, for all its local variety, is everywhere recognizable. But the practice of fighting against it has always been entered into, or sometimes deflected, by these other kinds of more particular bonds.[11]

From Nesterenko and Howe one gathers a sense of the place and the game; from them, but also from Mandel, one links literary pattern and childhood. Add to this mix the suggestion from Williams that place sustains being. The sum – children and games – constitutes a narrative of cultural importance. In the connection between place, childhood, winter, and hockey lies an explanation of the depths of the game's meaning in the prairie community.

HOCKEY AND ART

The tie between childhood and place can be supplemented by another crucial connection in hockey's cultural web: that between human perception and physical movement. My comments are, again, purely speculative. And, again, I begin with an illustration provided by Eric Nesterenko, who concluded his interview with a brilliant flourish:

> I still like to skate. One day last year on a cold, clear, crisp afternoon, I saw this huge sheet of ice in the street. Goddamn, if I didn't drive out there and put on my skates. I took off my camel-hair coat. I was just in a suit jacket, on my skates. And I flew. Nobody was there. I was free as a bird. I was really happy. That goes back to when I was a kid. I'll do that until I die, I hope. Oh, I was free!
>
> The wind was blowing from the north. With the wind behind you, you're in motion, you can wheel and dive and turn, you can lay yourself into impossible angles that you never could walking or running. You lay yourself at a forty-five degree angle, your elbows virtually touching the ice as you're in a turn. Incredible! It's beautiful. You're breaking the bounds of gravity. I have a feeling this is the innate desire of man.
>
> [His eyes are glowing] I haven't kept many photographs of myself, but I found one where I'm in full flight. I'm leaning into a turn. You pick up the centrifugal forces and you lay in it. For a few seconds, like a gyroscope, they support you. I'm in full flight and my head is turned. I'm concentrating on something and I'm grinning. That's the way I like to picture myself. . . . I'm on another level of existence, just being in pure motion. Going wherever I want to go, whenever I want to go. That's nice, you know [laughs softly].[12]

This is a statement about the ordinary daily practice – the cultural expression – that rests in the minds of many Canadian children. Most of them learn to skate by following the same pattern: first, to keep the ankles firm and the blades vertical, as they attempt to walk erect through the "shack" or dressing room, and then to step unwaveringly onto the ice; having acquired the ability to stand up, to stride purposefully, and to move in straight lines across the ice, they tackle the next skill – the turn; as Eric Nesterenko says, to lean and swoop, or, as it often is at the town rink or city community club, to evade the tag, recover the toque, or just to sweep around a corner – a skill that might take a year or two to possess properly; then, children move on to the powerful crossover step, learning to accelerate in full strides in a longer curve, movements that are taught very early in today's "power skating" classes but that require another winter or two of practice for the neophyte; at some point, too, preferably sooner than later, they learn to stop – most desirable is the dashing punctuation point that generates a shower of ice and snow. These are the movements of an ordinary activity so embedded in our lives as to be archetypal – a Canadian art, the dance on ice from which both hockey and figure-skating competitions are descended, and to which so many citizens devote so much time in a winter childhood.

In their valuable book, *Home Game*, Ken Dryden and Roy MacGregor write that "sport is not an art."[13] They mean, I think, that the contests are too chaotic, too unpredictable, too subject to accidental twists and turns, to have the effect that a scripted play or carefully designed painting might create. This is precisely the point that I would like to contest. I think sports *are* arts, both as expressions of line, colour, and movement, and as a dramatic version of theatre in which audiences participate in script writing by "willing" a team's success or failure.

The significance of movement itself in the visual arts is probably the most difficult concept to express, and yet the most fundamental. Drawing on aesthetics, art, and philosophy, students of this unlikely analysis are attempting to put into words what does not belong in the wooden, awkward shapes of written language. C.L.R. James tried to reach this plane in his discussion of cricket by writing about excellence in painting. This excellence was "a quality that existed in its own right, irrespective of the object represented. It was the line, the curve, its movement, the drama it embodied as painting, the linear design, the painterly tones and values taken as a whole."[14] James was seeking to isolate what he called a "tactile consciousness" or "specially artistic sense" that enables the viewer to grasp what is "life-giving, life-enhancing" in works of art.[15] Having attempted to sketch the theory of movement in painting, James returned to familiar ground – the cricket pitch – and wrote of the line, the curve, the carriage, the physique, the glide, the "poetry of motion," and the "quality of style" that memorable batters and bowlers and fielders displayed while playing cricket. These images, he contended, are engraved in the minds of the audience, to be recalled, compared, criticized, and appreciated as one would assess and reassess paintings in a gallery.

James believed that the spectator's attention to specific athletic movements should be likened to the peculiar genius that resides in the visual arts – sculpture, painting, drawing, perhaps photography and film – because the interest in the line itself belonged to both types of appreciation: "The eye for the line which is today one of the marks of ultimate aesthetic refinement is not new. It is old. The artists of the caves of Altamira had it. . . . The use of sculpture and design among primitive

peoples indicates that the significance of the form is a common possession. Children have it."[16]

My untutored response is to agree that attention to line and a keen
appreciation of movement, and a recogntion of dignity in performance
are learned in our early years and remain with us. These are elements of
art that spectator sports share with dance and the visual media.

HOCKEY AND COMMUNITY

One further element in hockey that attracts my attention is a quality that
it shares with theatre, television, and the performing arts, on the one hand,
and with politics, on the other. This dual characteristic, at once individual
and social, has served to make hockey one of the "networks" through
which a national conversation is conducted. As a result, the fate of individual teams such as the Winnipeg Jets takes on more-than-ordinary
significance.

It requires no great leap of the imagination to understand that hockey
is also a theatrical art. As such, it belongs in the same category (for some
purposes) as drama, opera, and mime. If this list seems eclectic, it nonetheless is consistent in certain respects: all of these events begin with an
audience, one or more performers, a standard exhibition venue that distinguishes observer from actor, and some rules of procedure, perhaps including audience silence at certain moments and restrictions upon audience participation, for example. Most of all, like its more "respectable"
partners, hockey expresses universal and timeless cultural meanings. These
are, in part, the "elemental" qualities and emotions of life. When a goal
scorer races in upon the goaltender, a tableau of individual courage and
skill is instantly sketched for the onlooker; when a comedic movement
prompts involuntary laughter, or an unexpected, brilliant action evokes
awe, we are moved outside ourselves; the versions of such tableaux are as
infinite as life itself. As Dryden and MacGregor suggested, "Hockey is
Canada's game. It may also be Canada's national theatre. On its frozen
stage, each night the stuff of life is played out: ambition, hope, pride and
fear, love and friendship, the fight for honour for city, team, each other,
themselves. . . . It is a place where the monumental themes of Canadian
life are played out – English and French, East and West, Canada and the
U.S., Canada and the world, the timeless tensions of commerce and culture, our struggle to survive and civilize winter."[17]

Through the repetition of patterns, notably the succession of games
and seasons and playoffs, NHL hockey has established a predictable
rhythm. It has become a staple of Canadian existence, like the weather
and politics. Of course, it is some distance removed from children learning to skate. The movements are the same, roughly, but the competition

and the glitter and the game's very centrality in popular consciousness place it on a different level. This elevated status is partly the result of marketing; indeed, to those who see only the sales of beer and cars that are riding on the game's popularity, its celebrity seems a hollow thing.[18] But, like all highly organized, much publicized sports, such as baseball and soccer and cricket, it has a recorded past. By this I mean that it possesses recognizable rhythms, noteworthy turning points, and outstanding heroes *because* it has occupied a central place in the culture for so many years.

Hockey's historic rhythms begin with the local contests of the late nineteenth century. They proceed to the national contests that developed during the first thirty years of country-wide Stanley Cup competition (1893 to 1926) and that depended, more prosaically, on the emergence of the telegraph and daily newspaper as central forces in the consolidation of a "nation." Hockey acquired another injection of cultural consequence with the expansion to a Canada-wide audience of Foster Hewitt's Saturday-night radio broadcasts of NHL games from Maple Leaf Gardens in the 1930s, and Roland Beaudry's Montreal Forum broadcasts in French. (Radio's "imagined communities" constituted an important means of consolidating the country between the early 1930s and the late 1950s.) The transition to television as dominant communications vehicle in the 1950s and 1960s was accompanied, not surprisingly, by the ascendancy of Hockey Night in Canada, a Saturday-night telecast, as the most popular program in the Canadian viewing week and year. Like the events in the larger organization of the game, the generations of superstars, as they came to be called, folded into one another: Joliat and Shore, Richard and Howe, Orr and Hull, Lafleur and Dryden, Gretzky and Lemieux, and – but the list is endless. Memorable hockey moments were similarly imprinted upon Canadians from coast to coast: the Morenz funeral in 1937; the Richard riot in Montreal in 1955; the Henderson goal in Moscow in 1972; the death of the Quebec Nordiques and Winnipeg Jets in 1995 and 1996. This is a history on which countries are built and from which countries are maintained.

If this seems rather too great a claim, one might turn to dozens of authorities in other countries and other sports for support. In Australia, the "bodyline" cricket series sustained a national outcry. In the United States, the vast literature on baseball is replete with declarations about the game's relations to the national psyche. James made similar statements about cricket's role in creating national sentiment in the West Indies. In Canada, Peter Gzowski declared that "Hockey was us," and Dryden and MacGregor concluded their *Home Game* with the categorical statement, "Hockey is Canada's game. Nothing else is. Nothing else will be."[19]

A game can build a nation. It may also provide one of the vehicles by which a country's temper is maintained, whether the conversation be grumpy or affectionate, from day to day and year to year.

WINNIPEG, THE JETS, AND CULTURAL HISTORY

My visit to several professional hockey games at the Winnipeg Arena in February 1996 prompted this rethinking of hockey and prairie culture. I had been struck, once again, by how intense the hockey experience could be when the game is played at the highest levels of skill. The skating, the rhythms of the game, the national conversation about the teams and the league, had always had an attraction. But I had been unable, during these months of public debate, to explain to critics of the game, and opponents of the campaign to build a new arena, why one should have patience with the struggle to keep the Jets in Winnipeg. I had not found the words to explain that this was a people's art.

These games in February reminded me that, for many spectators, hockey possessed authenticity because it was an expression of movement and line, because it was theatre, and because it exhibited remembered skill. The link between team and community, of course, was inescapable in the winter that Winnipeg lost its NHL hockey representatives. Finally, there was the role of such connected competitions (represented in league schedules and playoffs and championships) in broader conversations among provinces, regions, and even countries.

One must appreciate the degree to which hockey became an expression of Canada as country in the twentieth century. This high-flown generalization is not overstated: it implies that there is a need for effective means of communication among vast numbers of people in a huge democracy. It implies, too, that the ostensible subject of communication – in this case, a hockey game – may be the least important matter transmitted by the participants in the exchange.

Common subjects of conversation must be cultivated in a large and diverse community. Inevitably, the weather and taxes provide two topics for such exchanges but, not surprisingly, matters that move us because of their art and drama must be included on such a list. Canadians are not especially equipped to find subjects of conversation in the formal arts of earlier centuries such as painting, sculpture, opera, and theatre. Television and the newspaper provide many of our daily points of contact, and so does the professional sport that is conveyed by these media. Like politics, then, hockey is "a great point of contact." Using the example of their observations in Saskatchewan, Dryden and MacGregor argue that hockey offers "a way of extending the web of community outward to regions, to the province, to the country itself, even if the web often burned with rivalry. Through Gordie Howe, the Bentley brothers, and countless more, perhaps more than any other, through Foster Hewitt, hockey was a connection to the rest of Canada more vivid and far more acceptable than banks and federal bureaucrats."[20]

A small flaw in this thinking, a point of irritation, remains to be considered. The Winnipeg Jets moved to Phoenix because the economics of television, sport, and global culture dictated this business decision. Does this mean that Canada's national conversation, as conducted through this sport and this league, must give way to continental rhythms? Is a separate Canadian conversation possible in the modern age? No one would suggest that the child's knowledge of skating and ice will be soon effaced. But what of the broader question, the country-wide nature of the people's hockey conversation? Time will tell, of course, but I wonder why the *Canadian* portion of this communication process cannot remain distinguishable from the networks that circulate in other societies.

Is this simply a succession of tautologies? The child skates, learns about the arts embedded in hockey, enjoys the conversation based on the game, finds others in the community who are similarly disposed to talk about it, and identifies insiders and outsiders on that basis. Perhaps I have merely suggested that a Canadian boundary reinforces a Canadian conversation about a particular pastime. Or perhaps my logic constitutes another kind of truism: the great athletic effort produces a striking game and, thus, evokes an attentive response from a rapt audience. Why is this not true for any other activity in Canada, or for hockey in any other society?

In reply, I return to the Winnipeg Jets, and to the two hockey games of February 1996 that will illustrate my point. Unremarked, after season-long crowds of 9,000 or 10,000, the Winnipeg Arena was filled with nearly 14,000 spectators on Monday and Wednesday, 26 and 28 February 1996. Monday was Wayne Gretzky's last visit to the Arena. Not, as the publicity put it, Gretzky's final appearance as a member of one team rather than another (next day he was traded, as expected, from Los Angeles to St. Louis, and, after the season ended, he negotiated a new contract in New York), but, rather, the final appearance in this city of the greatest NHL player of his generation. Similarly, barring end-of-season playoff miracles, Wednesday was the final visit of the Toronto Maple Leafs to face the NHL team in Manitoba. These games marked the end of an era. The fans had turned out to say goodbye, or to acknowledge that this was a farewell. In a few weeks, the Jets relinquished their name and location in favour of a new corporate entity, the Phoenix Coyotes. The regular visits to Winnipeg of the world's best hockey players ceased. A pendulum that had been swinging for 100 years continued its stately progress: from "first hockey clubs" in the West (1890), to Stanley Cup winners (Winnipeg Victorias, 1896, 1901, and Kenora Thistles, 1907), to minor league status (1913 to 1973) and second-class professional league (World Hockey Association, 1973 to 1979), to NHL (1979 to 1996), and now the minor leagues once again.[21] But the popular affection for the game has not been extinguished. Rather, it will have to find new outlets. Winnipeggers, too, will have to find new ways to participate in the national conversation. This is not an unprecedented circumstance. Hockey is ordinary movement and exceptional movement. It is accustomed pattern and high drama. It is, in prairie Canada, a people's art, and one among many vehicles of a national conversation. It is, finally, a means among others by which human societies have sought to express – to celebrate – truth and beauty.[22]

NOTES

I would like to thank Morris Mott for his many generous contributions to discussions about sport and society, and David Williams, Tom Nesmith, and Jean Friesen for their comments on this paper.

1. Guy Debord, *Comments on the Society of the Spectacle* (London: Verso, 1990); Bryan D. Palmer, *Working-Class Experience: Rethinking the History of Canadian Labour, 1800-1991*, 2nd ed. (Toronto: McClelland and Stewart, 1992), 386-92.
2. C.L.R. James, *Beyond a Boundary* (New York: Pantheon Books 1983), 182-83 (first published London: Stanley Paul and Co., 1963).
3. Studs Terkel, "Hockey Player: Eric Nesterenko," in *Working: People Talk about What They Do All Day and How They Feel about What They Do* (New York: Pantheon Books, 1971; 1974), 382.
4. In addition to the works cited elsewhere, I would like to mention several other sources, including: Ken Dryden, *The Game: A Thoughtful and Provocative Look at a Life in Hockey* (Toronto: Macmillan, 1983); Richard Gruneau and David Whitson, *Hockey Night in Canada: Sport, Identity, and Cultural Politics* (Toronto: Garamond, 1993); David Cruise and Alison Griffiths, *Net Worth: Exploding the Myths of Pro Hockey* (Toronto: Penguin, 1991); Garry Whannel, *Fields in Vision: Television Sport and Cultural Transformation* (London: Routledge, 1992); Bernard Suits, *The Grasshopper: Games, Life and Utopia* (Toronto: University of Toronto Press, 1978); Grant McCracken, *Culture and Consumption: New Approaches to the Symbolic Character of Consumer Goods and Activities* (Bloomington: Indiana University Press, 1988; 1990); Benedict Anderson, *Imagined Communities: Reflections on the Origin and Spread of Nationalism* (London: Verso, 1983; 1991).
5. James, *Beyond a Boundary*, 183.
6. The Winnipeg Jets' story is surveyed critically in Doug Smith, "Score! How the Millionaire Owners of the Winnipeg Jets Got the Public to Pay for Their Hockey Team," *This Magazine* 29, no. 2 (August 1995).
7. Raymond Williams, "Culture is Ordinary," in *Resources of Hope: Culture, Democracy, Socialism*, ed. Robin Gable (London: Verso, 1989).
8. Terkel, *Working*, 381; the relevance of such novels of childhood as William Golding's *Lord of the Flies* will be apparent.
9. Eli Mandel, "Images of Prairie Man," in *A Region of the Mind: Interpreting the Western Canadian Plains*, ed. Richard Allen (Regina: Canadian Plains Studies Center, 1973), 206.
10. Roy MacSkimming, "A Hockey Legend," in *The Middle of Nowhere: Rediscovering Saskatchewan*, ed. Dennis Gruending (Saskatoon: Fifth House, 1996) (first published in MacSkimming, *Gordie: A Hockey Legend* [Vancouver: Greystone Books, 1994]).
11. Raymond Williams and Terry Eagleton, "The Politics of Hope: An Interview," in *Raymond Williams: Critical Perspectives*, ed. Eagleton (Cambridge: Polity Press, 1989), 180.
12. Terkel, *Working*, 386.
13. *Home Game: Hockey and Life in Canada* (Toronto: McClelland and Stewart, 1989), 231.
14. James, *Beyond a Boundary*, 196.

15. Other words he employed include "style," "elegance," and "beauty."

16. James, *Beyond a Boundary*, 204.

17. Dryden and MacGregor, *The Game*, 101.

18. If the globe warmed sufficiently to eliminate ice from the parts of Canada that are now populated by child skaters, then beer and cars and the entire marketing business associated with hockey would presumably move on to new games that better expressed the rhythms and movements of childhood. Perhaps soccer, perhaps basketball, perhaps even cricket might then be embedded in Canadians' consciousness. In the meantime, the investment of marketing dollars demands a return, so the endless cycle of hype is renewed annually, and we citizens are inundated not simply by the art of skating but by another kind of cultural message – consume, consume – conveyed by the players, the teams, and the competition itself. The very etymology of "hype," which includes the Greek prefix for "over, above, excessive," defines the character of the activity.

19. Peter Gzowski, *The Game of Our Lives* (Toronto: McClelland and Stewart, 1981), 84; Dryden and MacGregor, *Home Game*, 267; Stuart Macintyre, *The Oxford History of Australia*, vol. 4, *1901-1942: The Succeeding Age* (Melbourne: Oxford University Press, 1986), 304; A. Bartlett Giamatti, "Baseball and the American Character," in *The Baseball Chronicles*, ed. David Gallen (New York: Carroll and Graf, 1991).

20. Dryden and MacGregor, *Home Game*, 21.

21. Morris K. Mott, "Manly Sports and Manitobans: Settlement Days to World War One," Ph.D. dissertation, Queen's University, 1980; and, Mott, "'Tough to Make It': The History of Professional Team Sports in Manitoba," in *The Geography of Manitoba: Its Land and Its People*, ed. John Welsted, John Everitt, and Christoph Stadel (Winnipeg: University of Manitoba Press, 1996).

22. To give C.L.R. James the last word: "It is an unspeakable impertinence to arrogate the term 'fine art' to one small section of this quest and declare it to be culture. Luckily, the people refuse to be bothered" (*Beyond a Boundary*, 205).

Afterword:
Still Teaching the Same Stuff?

I HAVE NOW TAUGHT Canadian history to university students for over twenty-five years. Several times recently, when I have met graduates of increasingly distant classes, I have been asked politely whether I'm "still teaching the same stuff." It is true that I am still teaching Canadian and prairie history, but the real answer to the question is no. Since the early 1970s, Canadian history has been swept by waves of intellectual change, and the discipline of history itself has faced several serious challenges. While I still teach the same courses, and while the purposes of each new class are no different, the subjects and the underlying purpose of many of the lectures – and perhaps even aspects of the spirit of the enterprise called *history* – have changed.

As an undergraduate in Dr. Roger Graham's course on Canadian history at the University of Saskatchewan in 1962-63, I had a choice of four or five Canadian history textbooks (by Creighton, Careless, Brebner, Lower, and McInnis) and received a thoroughly political education grounded in the economic history of northern North America. As a graduate student at the University of Toronto in the late 1960s, I was a member of the largest classes ever in graduate studies in Canadian history (Donald Creighton's class alone, which was split into two seminars, must have numbered close to thirty). There, I learned the techniques of positivist research and was taught to appreciate the intellectual boundaries staked out by the first professional generations of Canadian specialists who wrote between the 1920s and 1960s. Whatever our backgrounds, we students must have assumed that we could respond to the intellectual agendas of our professors simply by supplementing the Canadian historical narrative they had created. As a novice teacher at the University of Manitoba in the early 1970s, I constructed my first series of lectures for the "Canadian survey" on more or less the same foundations, and even the same text-books, as had been available ten (and twenty-five) years earlier.

Then historical fashion began to change. The 1970s brought social his-tory. Scholars pursued a vast range of stories with the fervour of converts. Aboriginal people, labouring people, the regions, cities, women, ethnic groups became the focus of sub-groups in the discipline.[1] As the number of books and articles multiplied, the sharp narrative line of national his-tory, which had been unmistakable in the story of staple exports (fish, fur, timber, wheat) and in politics (colony to nation and, perhaps, to colony once again), became blurred.

New textbooks published in the 1990s synthesized this generation's outpouring of social history. These texts, each in two-volume sets and approximately triple the length of their counterparts of the 1940s, con-tained vast amounts of information. Indeed, the student of 1945, or of 1970, would not recognize the course content today. The Aboriginal his-tory is sympathetic, detailed, and evocative. The same can be said for the picture of Atlantic Canada, of habitant life, of Métis adaptation, of north-ern mining towns, of urban working-class families, of a wide and repre-sentative sample of ethnic groups, and of the differing experience of women. The Canada presented in today's classrooms is more compli-cated and more diverse than ever before. Today's Canadian history text-books offer many more models for a life.

Does the new Canadian social history "add up" to the story of a coun-try? The historian's answer will depend on his or her approach to the discipline. Michael Bliss, among others, believes that part of the explana-tion for today's fragmented politics lies in the fact that Canada's history – the narratives that should explain why we live together – is fragmented.[2] Other historians who share some of Bliss's views, and emphasize the cen-trality of "national political" themes, have blamed the fragmentation on social historians' alleged interest in irrelevant esoterica such as "house-maid's knee in Belleville." By concentrating on ordinary people's "limited identities," this criticism suggests, the social historians have left untold the great stories of nation building that would sustain the country today.

The essays in my collection would presumably be part of the problem, in the view of national political historians. These papers are regional in subject and social in approach. Moreover, they celebrate nation-building leaders less than they inquire into the alternative traditions of labour leaders, French-speaking Canadians, and Aboriginal people, for example. However, I believe that the selection by these "political" critics of "national" heroes and "national" ideas is as tendentious as any other. As Bliss noted in his essay, Canada has room for a wide variety of "national policies" and "national heroes." And to turn to the question of why we have yet to create new and satisfying syntheses, I prefer to share the blame with all Canada's historians. As long as the country exists, an integrated narrative that explains its transcontinental presence, global relevance, and social complexity (not to mention shortcomings) *must* be discernible. If historians haven't got it right yet, they must keep on trying. After all, we're not alone: the "great Canadian novel" is still around the corner, and so is the "great Canadian film." The task may be unending, like the labour of Sisyphus, but it must be performed.

If one critique of this essay collection could be made by national political historians, another could come from the scholars who have taken the "linguistic turn," including those influenced by cultural studies, semiotics, poststructuralism, and postmodernism. Their challenge to history has been expressed in a series of theoretical departures concerning language itself, the act of narration, and the place of the reader in the text. Often, these scholars stand conventional narrative history on its head, denying that objective reality can be grasped and insisting that signifying practices and cultural modes are all we can really expect to sketch. Even these verbal patterns, according to Roland Barthes, are duplicities. History, in his view, offers a series of narrative conventions and rhetorical strategies that encourage the reader to suspend disbelief but do not constitute an adequate translation of the real world into meaningful impressions. Thus, scholars such as Michel Foucault have shifted the focus of historical study from economy and politics to values and mentalities. Foucault explained that he wished to clarify the structure of knowledge itself, to write the "history of systems of thought," as the approach was encapsulated in the title of the late Professor Foucault's chair at the Collège de France. Politics, in this new order, becomes not the warring of class and race and economic interest but "the power of rhetorics." In the words of Louis Althusser, who travelled a different but parallel path, these scholars take as their subject "the imaginary relationship of individuals to their real conditions of existence."[3]

It is possible to dismiss the poststructuralists and grammatologists and flagbearers of postmodern ways of knowing as simply fads and to carry on as if they said nothing of importance to one's Canadian scholarship. However, professional obligations require scholars to keep in touch with the latest currents of thought. Consider a judgement offered by the distinguished Canadian economist Clarence Barber, formerly of the University of Manitoba, who attributed the failure of the Canadian government's economic policy during the Great Depression to professional economists. He may or may not have been correct in this assertion (as a conclusion about an historical matter, it is subject to research and verification), but, in passing, he added this striking observation:

Among economists in Canadian universities there appears to have been no-one who was abreast of Keynes' thinking in the twenties and early thirties and certainly there were no Canadian economists whose contributions in this area of economics were at all comparable to those of the Swedish economists in this period. When I graduated from the University of Saskatchewan in 1940 with an honours degree in economics, I had never been asked to read Keynes' *General Theory*, a book which was published in December, 1935, and was in the process of revolutionizing economic thinking.[4]

Barber's admonition represents a warning that scholars ignore at their peril.

Historians of the prairies, like Canadian historians in general, have been slow to adapt to the postmodern shift. One explanation must lie with the circumstances of academic life. The story of the prairie past was rewritten in one short generation by university and public historians during the social history renaissance. Their strengths included Aboriginal history, the National Policy era, urban and labour and ethnic history, and even the well-researched subjects of politics and economic change. The many books and articles of this era constituted the scholarly equivalent of the baby boom.[5] The field awaits another similar burst of energy.

I've put together this volume during the transitional phase of Canadian scholarly writing, when national political, social, and postmodern approaches are vying for influence. All but one of the essays were written after 1983. They illustrate, collectively, some of the pressures that have developed in the discipline as well as in our society during the 1980s and 1990s. The volume does not embrace postmodernist or linguistic approaches, but it does, especially in the recent essays, accommodate them. Thus, the battles over French and English in Canada illustrate that questions about sign systems (language) and the production of meaning play a more significant role in contemporary political debates, and in cultural study, than in earlier phases of world history. Class as a phenomenon in society and politics has not gone away and still requires reflection. The centrality of Aboriginal people in prairie society must be acknowledged. The issue of culture and of community-wide conversations differs from the role played by such topics in earlier societies.

None of the essays in this volume would be described as poststructural, but those written in the 1990s could be said to have taken a "linguistic turn." By this I mean that the *categories* of historical analysis, which once seemed so solid and unshakable, now seem to be merely words. Class and nation and region and ethnic group, for example, are not treated as eternal and fixed entities in the later essays but, rather, as social and historical constructs. These postmodern influences have ensured that the categories of our thought are being exposed to the same analysis that scholars once reserved for the "characters" and the "events" themselves.

The issue of language has become a central theme in social studies because we live in a world driven by the economics of communications and information. Today's technological developments in computers, satellites, and fibre optic cable may well permit a renewed defence of minority languages in the longer term (Frisian in Friesland, Basque in northern Spain), but, for the moment, the global sweep of American English in television, movies, and the internet seems inescapable. Inevitably, the continued survival of local languages in prairie Canada – whether low German, Ukrainian, Cree, Ojibwa, or Canada's other "official language," French – is far from certain. The extraordinary experiments with French-English immersion and other types of bilingual education during the past generation, however, testify to the interest of many prairie Canadians in the continued existence of a Canadian society that conducts its affairs in at least two languages. The willingness of prairie Canadians to contemplate constitutional revisions, as they did during the Manitoba Legislature's committee hearings in 1989 and 1991, also expresses this loyalty to a transcontinental community on the northern half of North America. That prairie Canadians have participated in an important country-wide experiment in cultural and linguistic resistance is worthy of historical note as we move on to the next phase of language and communications history.

The rapidly changing patterns of global trade also present challenges to prairie Canadians. In retrospect, one can see that Canada developed its own version of the welfare state in the decades after 1945. This process reached its apogee with the Royal Commission on the Status of Women, the country-wide medicare system and pension plan, and federal government interventions in "cultural trade," including legislation on magazines, music, radio, and television during the 1960s and 1970s. Canada then reversed this social process in the 1980s and 1990s, as a wide range of economic activities from grain transportation to airport management to home-nursing care were taken out of government control and thrust into the marketplace. Such policy choices present questions about wealth distribution, work discipline, and the relative roles of government and market in our lives. For most of the twentieth century, prairie Canadians have participated in the debate about how to control the unpleasant face – as opposed to the creative potential – of capitalism. This latest formulation of the debate, which employs such keywords as *deficit, market, privatization,* and *government intervention,* will not be the last. Whether we will continue to employ the concept of "class" in our analyses of such debates is less certain. For the moment, class offers one time-honoured and relatively well-defined approach to the problem, and to the issue of power that underlies it, but, because it implies fixed and stable loyalties, it is being challenged by such organizing concepts as "industrial relations" and "identity politics."

Aboriginal relations with other Canadians present difficult policy choices today. The history of these relations helps to explain how deeply interrelated were Aboriginal and European people in the eighteenth and nineteenth centuries, and how fateful were the federal government's policy decisions in the 1870s. That these policies are only now being dismantled is testimony to the difficulty of the task. However, the changes can also be described as necessary and urgent.

One might say that all these trends – language, organization of the economy, and Aboriginal history – are simply versions of a fourth theme represented in this collection, cultural history. The study of culture has become a point of conjuncture in the "human sciences." It represents the site where the boundaries of "community" are challenged and where the relations among citizens and between the state and the market are debated. A recent book on historical writing suggests that all stories about the past "start with the end. It is *a conclusion* that arouses our curiosity and prompts us to ask a question." Histories, then, represent our wish to understand the present and future as well as the past. As the authors of this useful book suggest: "Successive generations of scholars do not so much revise historical knowledge as they reinvest it with contemporary interest."[6]

Each of the subjects in this volume had some sort of contemporary relevance when I decided to write about it. Moreover, each had attracted the attention of scholars in other places and disciplines. It is my hope that these two motivations, local relevance and a broader context, are still apparent now that they are part of this collection of articles. I want to place the discussion of this place and society in the contemporary international conversation. I also want to assert the importance of locally centred, locally generated, historical writing. And I hope that such study helps citizens of this community to maintain their acquaintance with the currents of discussion in the contemporary scholarly world by placing familiar stories into the language employed there.

Such challenges confront every community, and one cannot claim that Canadians, or prairie Canadians, have been distinctively successful at meeting them in the 1980s and 1990s. Nevertheless, when one lists the great public discussions in our society during the last few years, one must acknowledge that the debates have been conducted with expertise and seriousness. The list would include the Constitution (Meech Lake,

Charlottetown), free trade, the status of women, immigration and multiculturalism, Aboriginal self-government, official language policy, the Wheat Board, management of the economy (deficits, and the relative role of governments and markets), cultural and communications policy, rail and road transport, the environment (including development and resource policy), and industrial relations policy, for example.

Has there been a Canadian, a Manitoba, a prairie, debate, as opposed to the general international struggle over these great questions? In the introduction to this volume, I implied that the O.J. Simpson trial absorbed more energy than did issues of public policy and community priority. Now, I would like to take back those words. I think there have been useful, informed, clarifying discussions of these matters over coffee and tea and beer in every part of the prairies. I agree, too, that in an age of television and spectacle, new vehicles have helped us to maintain a community-wide conversation. But I would add that some old vehicles can also provide us with help. History – stories about our common past – the same old stuff expressed in new ways – is an essential part of our being and, thus, must be part of our reflections on today and tomorrow.

NOTES

Versions of this discussion were presented to meetings of the Friends of Dafoe Library Association (University of Manitoba), February 1993, and to the University of Manitoba Graduate History Association's Riding Mountain Conference, 1993.

1. A Canadian example rests in the seventy-odd titles of the National Museums of Canada / National Film Board joint production for history classrooms, the slide series *Canada's Visual History / L'Histoire du Canada en Images*. An American observation is, Lynn Hunt, "Introduction: History, Culture, and Text," in *The New Cultural History,* ed. Hunt (Berkeley: University of California Press, 1989).
2. Michael Bliss, "Privatizing the Mind: The Sundering of Canadian History, the Sundering of Canada," *Journal of Canadian Studies* 26, no. 4 (winter 1991-92):5-17; three responses (one by Gregory S. Kealey; a second by Linda Kealy, Ruth Pierson, Joan Sangster, and Veronica Strong-Boag; and a third by R.B. Fleming) appeared in the *Journal of Canadian Studies* 27, no. 2 (summer 1992):123-35.
3. See: Raphael Samuel, "Reading the Signs," *History Workshop: A Journal of Socialist and Feminist Historians* (autumn 1991):106; also, "Reading the Signs 2: Fact-Grubbers and Mind-Readers," in *History Workshop: A Journal of Socialist and Feminist Historians* 33 (spring 1992).
4. Clarence L. Barber, "Canada and the Great Depression: An Economist's Retrospective Review" (paper presented to University of Manitoba seminar, February 1974), 5.
5. The context was surveyed in Jeffery Taylor, "The Canadian Prairies: A History and a Historiography" (paper presented to Great Plains Historical Conference, Brandon University, September 1995). The bibliography is discussed in Gerald Friesen, "Recent Historical Writing on the Prairie West," in *The Prairie West: Historical Readings,* 2nd ed., ed. Howard Palmer and Douglas Francis (Edmonton: University of Alberta Press, 1992).
6. Joyce Appleby, Lynn Hunt, and Margaret Jacob, *Telling the Truth about History* (New York: W.W. Norton, 1994), 265 (emphasis added).

Index